W9-BOC-410

FLOWER
POWER!

✤ ✤

OTHER TITLES BY JERRY BAKER

Jerry Baker's Lawn Book
The Impatient Gardener
Jerry Baker's Happy, Healthy House Plants
Jerry Baker's Fast, Easy Vegetable Garden
Plants Are Still Like People

The New Garden Line Series
Jerry Baker's Problem Solver Series
"On The Garden Line®"— America's Gardening Newsletter™

For more information on Jerry Baker's *amazing*
lawn and garden tips, tricks, and tonics, please write to:

The YardenCare Company, P.O. Box 1001, Wixom, MI 48393

or visit Jerry Baker online at

http://www.jerrybaker.com

FLOWER POWER!

Jerry Baker

Mechanicals by Graphic Arts & Production, Inc.

Illustrations by Heidi Sigrid Sorensen and
Susan Johnston Carlson

Ballantine Books • New York

Sale of this book without a front cover may be unauthorized.
If this book is coverless, it may have been reported to the publisher as
"unsold or destroyed" and neither the author nor the publisher
may have received payment for it.

A Ballantine Book
Published by The Ballantine Publishing Group

Copyright © 1998 by Jerry Baker and The YardenCare Company

All rights reserved under International and Pan-American Copyright
Conventions. Published in the United States by The Ballantine Publishing Group,
a division of Random House, Inc., New York, and simultaneously in Canada by
Random House of Canada Limited, Toronto. Originally published by Jerry
Baker's YardenCare Company in 1998.

All efforts have been made to ensure accuracy. The author and publisher
assume no responsibility or liability for any injuries, damages, or losses incurred
during the use of or as a result of following this information. **IMPORTANT**:
Study all directions carefully before taking any action based on the information
and advice presented in this book. When using any commercial product, always
read and follow label directions. When reference is made to trade or brand
names, no endorsement by the author or publisher is implied, nor is any
discrimination intended.

www.randomhouse.com/BB/

Library of Congress Catalog Card Number: 98-96696

ISBN: 0-345-43415-3

Cover photo courtesy of *Country Folk Art Magazine*
Cover design by Kim Adam Gasior

Manufactured in the United States of America

First Ballantine Books Edition: February 1999

10 9 8 7 6 5 4 3 2 1

To my family,
whose love, support, and dedication
has kept me going, and *growing*,
all these years

Contents

❧2❧
PERENNIALS
YEAR-AFTER-YEAR FAVORITES

❧3❧
BULBS
DARLING DUTCH DANDIES

❦4❧
ROSES
EVERYTHING IS COMING UP ROSES!

❦5❧
FLOWERING TREES
A SPLASH OF COLOR

❦6❧
FLOWERING SHRUBS
BLOOMING WALLS

PREFACE

This book is all about two of my favorite subjects—flowers and flower gardening. Most homeowners limit their use of flowers to the most popular annuals, like petunias, zinnias, marigolds, and impatiens, while their choice of perennials only includes chrysanthemums. What I hope to do with this book is inspire you to venture further into the beautiful and exciting world of flower gardening, so that you too can discover the challenge, beauty, and reward of a well-planned and well-planted flowering landscape.

If you and I have been gardening together for very long, then you already know that my tips, tricks, and tonics may seem rather "nontraditional" to say the least. But the fact of the matter is that they really do work! So, if you're new to the Jerry Baker way of gardening, then please, just have faith, and you'll be handsomely rewarded many times over later this year. As silly as my suggestions may sometimes seem, believe me, your flowering garden will love them. How do I know? Because I've used them for many, many years, and never had one complaint!

You may not know it, but a home yard can be planted to provide a different face for each season, even when the grass withers and the flowers fade. There are evergreens that change color in the winter, and trees and shrubs with interesting and colorful bark to show off after their leaves have dropped, not to mention the broad-leaved evergreens, like rhododendrons and mountain laurel, that retain foliage and berries throughout the year. Even in the short-season areas, where you are lucky to get ninety frost-free days a year, you can plan and plant combinations of flowers that will fill your days with beauty.

In this book, I'm going to give you all of the information I can to help you create a flowerscape that will be the envy of the neighborhood. We're going to wander down the garden path, discussing the various families of flowers in the order of their importance to the average American homeowner, taking in account their longevity, return on time and money invested, ease of maintenance, and, of course, beauty. We'll talk about amazing annuals, perky perennials, beautiful bulbs and robust roses. Unlike most books on flowers, I've also included separate chapters on flowering trees and shrubs, since they are a very important part of any flowering garden.

Above all else, I want you to remember that you don't have to be rich or have a large piece of property to have a big, bold, beautiful bunch of blooms. A few simple seeds, properly placed and lovingly cared for, will soon burst forth into a dazzling display of flowers. And you, who have planted and cared for them, will become a gardener, and my friend forever.

Jerry Baker

JERRY BAKER'S FLOWER POWER!

❧1❧

ANNUALS
The Annual Parade

Annuals are without a doubt the hardest-working, most productive, attractive, and undemanding flower group in the whole garden. Once annuals are planted, a gardener seldom need spend much attention to them. (To tell the truth, they seldom get any attention from most home gardeners, and yet continue to bloom day after day throughout most of the summer, and in some cases, far into the fall.) To top it all off, an annual lives its full life span in one year!

These amazing flowers have only one purpose in life, and that is to give beauty and enjoyment to the world around them. These beauties are the elves of the flowering nation. Happy-go-lucky, carefree ramblers, they complement and help accent all of the other plants in your garden.

Annuals keep the rest of your garden in stitches most of the summer with their antics. They crawl under the pines and tickle their limbs, they snore beneath the maple, and dance with the birch. They are truly the lovable jesters of the queen's court, and will seemingly try anything once. For instance, they'll try growing in the shade just because you want them to.

Anyone can grow annuals if you will just relax, and plan to have fun. There are only a few things that you need to know to have a beautiful and successful annual garden. So pay close attention, and follow me down the garden path.

DESIGN WITH A PURPOSE

Sketch It Out

When it comes to adding annuals to your garden, you must stick with a pre-planned sketch. As simple as it may seem, planning a garden without a garden plan is like taking a trip without a map. A well-thought-out plan allows you to get the best possible results from the flowers you select.

You must make certain that you have a place for everyone. It's embarrassing to invite a flower over to spend the summer, only to find that you don't have a spare bed for her, and then you have to rush around and find a makeshift spot where she will be uncomfortable all season long. Her discomfort will be reflected in her performance, and you will have no one to blame but yourself! All it takes to have a successful annual garden is a little foresight, which will only take a few minutes of your time.

GREEN THUMB TIPS

1. Before buying annuals, plan your beds on paper, close to scale, so that you eliminate waste.

2. Don't plant annuals that crowd and grow wildly in the same bed with perennials because they will crowd out the perennials.

3. You don't have to wait until frost-free weather to start your flower garden. Lots of bedding plants, such as sweet alyssum and calendulas, actually enjoy cool weather.

Give Your Flowers A Home

Do you have a new home and want flowers right <u>now</u>? Or maybe you are renting, and want to create a lovely effect without spending a lot of money. If so, then annuals are for you.

If the property already has shrubs, plant annuals between the shrubs or in front of those that are well established.

Do you love the bulb blossoms that are such a delight in the early spring, and then vanish for another year? Plant annuals among them, either in the fall or early spring, and they will do much to hide the fading bulb foliage. You might try centaurea, larkspur, or phlox.

SIZE IT UP

Plan your design, and keep it simple. Before running out and buying bedding plants, first measure the size of your flower bed(s). Then decide what types of annuals you want to plant based upon their appearance and care requirements. In addition, it will be easier to maintain the beds if a limited number of different annuals are transplanted into each flower bed.

To calculate the number of plants needed in each bed, *multiply* the recommended spacing of each type of plant (see the "Annual Planning Guide" on pages 8–12) by the area in which it is to be planted.

Recommended spacing	Plants per sq. ft.	x (Sq. feet in garden) = (# Plants needed)
4"	(9.0)	x (sq. feet in garden) = (# plants needed)
6"	(4.0)	x (sq. feet in garden) = (# plants needed)
8"	(2.3)	x (sq. feet in garden) = (# plants needed)
10"	(1.4)	x (sq. feet in garden) = (# plants needed)
12"	(1.0)	x (sq. feet in garden) = (# plants needed)
15"	(.65)	x (sq. feet in garden) = (# plants needed)
18"	(.45)	x (sq. feet in garden) = (# plants needed)
24"	(.25)	x (sq. feet in garden) = (# plants needed)

Example: For petunias, the recommended spacing is 10 to 12 inches apart. So, if you had a 2' x 5' bed (10 sq. ft.), you'd need between 10 and 14 plants to fill in the area at the recommended spacing.

Annuals are very obliging. Use them to fill gaps in your perennial beds where they will supply lovely color all summer long while the perennials are resting. Most perennials are either spring or fall-blooming, and without annuals in these beds, you aren't going to have very much color during the summer months.

Of course, you can also use annuals by themselves to provide a quick and inexpensive wealth of blooms in beds and borders. If you have the space, consider making a cutting garden. Actually, most annuals will bloom far longer and more abundantly than perennials. Many, such as pansies, even benefit from constant cutting.

And today, with the diversity of form, color, size, and height available, you can plan for just about any effect you feel will best express "you."

PLANNING

You Make The Bed,
But They've Got To Sleep In It

The two most important things to consider when planning an annual garden bed are **exposure** and **size**.

Here Comes The Sun!

Most annuals are sun-loving plants (though some will obligingly grow in shade and half-shade), so you can logically expect them to flower most vigorously and abundantly in a sunny location. Dig your bed in an area that can offer them five or six hours of full sun each day, and then stand back and watch them grow!

Don't make your beds less than 3 feet wide; anything narrower won't give you much of a showing of color. Generally speaking, 5 to 6 feet wide is plenty of space for a well-planned bed; if you make it any larger, the effect of individual flowers may be lost.

The length of the bed will, quite likely, be determined by the layout of your property. And right here, in the middle of all this excitement, I will inject a sobering thought: remember, we want this flower-growing business to be a fun thing—don't bite off more than you can chew. You'll enjoy your flowers much more if you tailor the beds to what you can take care of handily in the time you have available. Gardening is fun, but it does take time to do it well. Weeds are always with us and constant vigilance is the price of liberty—liberty from a frustrating and back-breaking accumulation which can seemingly grow up overnight if you don't keep a watchful eye.

When you plant too much in a frenzied burst of spring enthusiasm, gardening can become a burden, and defeat its own purpose, which is to give you pleasure. If you are a first-year gardener, plan beds of manageable size so you can always keep them looking good, and enjoy them at the same time. Don't try to grow too many different plants. Confine yourself to a few, choosing them after considering color, variety, and growth habit.

The mail-order catalogs are beguiling, the descriptions glowing, and the profusion from which to choose bewildering. But after awhile, you can begin to get your bearings and sort things out.

OUCH—NO PINCHING ALLOWED!

Most shady annuals do not require pinching, pruning, or "deadheading" (removing spent blooms by hand). However, seed alyssum, candytuft, and lobelia may sprawl outside their planting area, and can be sheared back with hedge clippers. This will also encourage heavy blooming.

ANNUAL PLANNING GUIDE

FULL SUN

NAME	IDEAL SPACING (INCHES)	POTENTIAL HEIGHT (INCHES)	COLORS	* HARDINESS	SUGGESTED USES
Ageratum	8	8-12	Lavender, blue, white, pink	Tender	Edges, borders
Alyssum	8	3-6	Lavender, purple, white	Very hardy	Edges, rock gardens
Amaranthus	24	24-36	Colored foliage	Half hardy	Colorful background plants
Antirrhinum (Snapdragon)	6-10	6-36	White, yellow, pink, red, orange	Hardy	Borders and backgrounds
Browallia	10	10-18	Blue, white	Half hardy	Vines, hanging containers
Calendula	8-10	12-20	Yellow, orange, apricot, white	Hardy	Cut flowers; sometimes used as an herb
Celosia:					
Crested	24	10-18	Yellow, orange, dark red, red, lavender	Tender	Can be dried; also colorful with evergreens
Feathered	24	12-36	Yellow, orange, dark red, red	Tender	Same as Crested Celosia
Cleome	15	36-48	Pink, lavender, yellow	Tender	Set along a wall or fence
Cosmos	24	36-60	Light red, pink, white	Hardy	Nice for cutting
Dahlia	16	12-24	White, pink, light red, yellow	Tender	Blossoms profusely; good cut flowers
Dianthus (Garden pinks)	12	15-18	Pink, red, white, yellow, dark red	Hardy	For fragrance
Gaillardia (Blanket flower)	15	15-24	Yellow, orange, dark red	Hardy	Window boxes, planters
Geranium	12-24	18-30	Red, pink, white	Tender	Ideal for container plantings and window boxes

ANNUAL PLANNING GUIDE

FULL SUN

NAME	IDEAL SPACING (INCHES)	POTENTIAL HEIGHT (INCHES)	COLORS	* HARDINESS	SUGGESTED USES
Gomphrena	12	18-24	White, pink, dark red	Hardy	For dried arrangements
Helichrysum bracteatum (Strawflower)	30	30	White, pink, yellow, orange, dark red, light red	Hardy	For dried arrangements
Ipomoea (Morning glory)	6	Vine	Pink, light red, blue	Half hardy	Great climbing plant
Lathyrus odoratus (Sweet pea)	6	Vine	White, pink, light red, blue, lavender, purple, red	Very hardy	For fragrance; excellent climber
Matthiola (Stock)	15	15-30	White, pink, lavender, dark red, purple	Hardy	Excellent cut flower, fragrant
Phlox	18	10-20	White, yellow, dark red, lavender, pink	Hardy	Rock gardens, window boxes, and beds
Portulaca grandiflora (Moss rose)	10	4-6	Pink, red, white, yellow, orange	Tender	Good for rock gardens
Salvia	14-21	24	Red	Tender	Excellent for beds
Tagetes (Marigold):					
African (tall)	20	24-36	Yellow, orange	Half hardy	
French (dwarf)	15	8-15	Yellow, orange, dark red	Half hardy	Great for beds
Tropaeolum (Nasturtium)	15	12	Red, orange, yellow	Tender	Some can be trained to climb
Vinca (Periwinkle)	10-12	12-15	White, pink, light red, red, blue	Tender	Can stand hot or dry conditions, low maintenance
Zinnia	18	12-36	White, yellow, orange, light red, red	Tender	Superior cut flower

ANNUAL PLANNING GUIDE

SUN TO PART SHADE

NAME	IDEAL SPACING (INCHES)	POTENTIAL HEIGHT (INCHES)	COLORS	* HARDINESS	SUGGESTED USES
Aster	15-24	15-36	Lavender, pink, purple, white, light red	Half hardy	Great cut flower
Begonia (fibrous or wax)	12	6-10	White, red, pink, light red	Tender	Hanging baskets, container plantings
Centaurea cyanus (Cornflower)	24	24-30	White, blue, lavender, red, pink	Very hardy	Good cut flower
Clarkia	18	24	White, purple, light red, red, lavender	Hardy	Good cut flower
Coleus	12	8-16	Colored foliage	Tender	Edging in shady garden
Cynoglossum amabile (Chinese forget-me-not)	12	30	Blue, white	Hardy	Good background for beds
Iberis (Candytuft)	12	12-18	White, pink, lavender, red	Hardy	Nice for bouquets, edging
Lobelia	8	4-10	Red, white, blue	Hardy	Edging, hanging baskets
Nicotiana	24	15-30	White, pink, dark red	Tender	For fragrance
Petunia	12	10-18	All colors and color combinations	Half hardy	Borders, beds, hanging baskets
Salpiglossis	18	30	Yellow, lavender, dark red, white	Tender	Unusual flower, good for cut flowers
Verbena	18	8-18	White, pink, light red, red	Tender	Excellent for beds
Viola x wittrockiana (Pansy)	10	4-8	White, yellow, orange, blue, multicolor	Very hardy	Edging, rock gardens

ANNUAL PLANNING GUIDE
PART SHADE

NAME	IDEAL SPACING (INCHES)	POTENTIAL HEIGHT (INCHES)	COLORS	* HARDINESS	SUGGESTED USES
Ageratum	5-7	4-6	Lavender, blue, purple, white	Half hardy	Edges, borders
Alyssum	10-12	3-5	Lavender, purple, white,	Very hardy	Edges, rock gardens
Aster	6-18	6-30	blue, white lavender, purple, yellow, red, pink	Half hardy	Cut flowers
Balsam	10-15	12-36	pink, red, white, lavender, yellow	Tender	Background for beds
Begonia (Fiberous)	7-9	6-8	white, yellow, orange, red, pink	Half hardy	Pots, hanging containers
Begonia (tuberous)	8-10	8-10	white, yellow, orange, red, pink	Tender	Window boxes, hanging containers
Browallia	8-10	10-15	blue, white	Half hardy	Vines, hanging containers
Coleus	8-10	10-24	foliage color	Tender	Edging in shady gardens
Dahlia	8-10	8-15	white, pink, red, yellow, orange, purple, lavender	Tender	Cut flowers
Dianthus	7-9	6-10	white, pink, red	Hardy	Beds, borders
Dusty Miller	6-8	8-10	silver foliage	Tender	Borders, color contrast
Forget-me-not	8-12	6-12	blue, white, pink	Hardy	Background for beds
Fuchsia	8-10	12-48	pink, red, white, lavender, blue, orange, yellow	Tender	Hanging containers
Impatiens	8-10	6-18	pink, white, red, lavender, orange, purple	Tender	Edges, massed planting
Lobelia	8-10	3-5	blue, purple, white	Half hardy	Edges, hanging containers

ANNUAL PLANNING GUIDE
PART SHADE**

NAME	IDEAL SPACING (INCHES)	POTENTIAL HEIGHT (INCHES)	COLORS	* HARDINESS	SUGGESTED USES
Mimulus	5-7	6-8	yellow, red	Half hardy	Edges, borders
Nicotiana	8-10	12-15	white, pink, red, lavender	Half hardy	Fragrant, background
Pansy	6-8	4-8	blue, lavender, purple, yellow, white, red, pink	Very hardy	Edges, rock gardens
Salvia	6-8	12-24	red, white, blue, purple	Half hardy	Beds, borders
Torenia	608	8-12	blue, lavender, purple	Half hardy	Hanging containers
Vinca	6-8	12-14	white, pink	Tender	Window boxes, beds

* HARDINESS:

    Very hardy—will survive heavy frosts

    Hardy—will survive light frosts with little change

    Half hardy—stands cold weather, but no frost

    Tender—Does poorly in cold weather; susceptible to frost

** PART SHADE:

    Partially shaded areas are those that receive 4 hours or less of direct sunlight per day.

TO SEED OR NOT TO SEED...
THAT IS THE QUESTION

When it comes to annuals, you have a choice of starting with seeds or waiting until the professionally-grown bedding plants appear in your favorite garden shop. If you choose to grow from seed, you can either start the seeds indoors, or sow them directly into your garden.

An Inside Job

Let's concentrate on starting seed indoors, which is fine, as long as you don't do it too early; seedlings grown too long indoors become tall and spindly. The result is a tendency to fall over. And don't start too many—you may run out of sunny windows!

Keep 'Em Healthy

You must also address the problem of damping-off up front. Damping-off is a fast-spreading fungus which attacks young plants, and can cause a whole flat of your pretty baby plants to topple over and die overnight—just like that!

There are a number of ways to avoid this problem. You can buy a sterilized commercial soil mix, or you can sterilize the soil you use by baking it in your oven at 250°F. until a potato bakes through. Various seed disinfectants, such as Semesan, also can help prevent this flower tragedy.

You can also use vermiculite instead of soil. Vermiculite is weed-free, holds moisture extremely well, and is so light that the delicate seedling roots can penetrate it easily. When transplanting time comes, the roots will slip out easily. Vermiculite is inexpensive and obtainable at most garden supply stores.

In addition, don't overwater your seedlings, and give them plenty of sunlight and ventilation—these cultural practices will help prevent damping-off.

A TREAT FOR THE BIRDS

I'm sure that most of you know that many kinds of birds love to eat sunflower seeds. That's one of the primary reasons for buying them at the store or growing sunflowers in your garden. When you grow your own sunflowers, however, you don't have to harvest and clean the seeds. Simply leave the seeds in place, and the birds will find them and eat them up.

You can also have fun by cutting off a sunflower head and hanging it upside down somewhere near the house where you can see it from a nearby window. Birds that are not adverse to feeding upside down, like nuthatches, will come to the sunflower head, and perform their antics for you.

Plant With Tender Loving Care

Wooden seed flats now have been replaced almost entirely by plastic ones. These trays average about 2" x 4" x 12".

Cover up the holes in the bottom of your flats with some coarse stones, bits of brick, or broken flower pots. This must be done carefully, or your seeding medium will sift out of the flats.

Fill your container to within a half-inch of the top, working the soil or vermiculite down into the corners with your fingers. Make sure the surface is level and smooth. Soak the soil thoroughly, then let it drain. Make shallow furrows 2 to 3 inches apart; the depth of furrows will depend on the size of the seed. Very small seeds need no soil covering at all; larger seeds should be sown 2 or 3 times as deep as their diameter. To sow small seeds, tear a corner off the package and tap it gently with your finger to shake the seeds out. Pour larger seeds into your palm, and sow them individually.

After planting, water lightly. Don't let the soil become soggy. Cover the flat with a pane of glass or a sheet of plastic film. Pots or small flats can be enclosed in plastic bags. Place the seeded flat or tray in a warm (65° - 75°F), partially shaded place.

Watch Your Babies Grow

When the seeds have germinated, remove the glass or plastic cover, and put the container in the sun. But what if there is no sun, or you are in for a spell of cloudy skies? What then?

Well, if there's a will, there's a way! Actually, seedlings need a much higher intensity of light than full-grown plants; they will grow even faster and into sturdier plants under fluorescent light than they will in a greenhouse. Indoor light units, especially those designed for growing plants (such as Gro-Lux fluorescent tubes), are excellent, but not essential. The fluorescent lights sold in your supermarket will work too—buy the ones labeled "daylight" or "white."

MILK IT FOR ALL IT'S WORTH!

Just suppose you don't want to buy flats or pots or fluorescent lights. Here's a really good, inexpensive way to start seedlings. Take a half-gallon milk carton, wash it carefully with warm soapsuds, rinse it out, and dry it in the sun. Staple the open end back together. Using a sharp knife or scissors, slice off one side. You now have a starting tray. Use a knitting needle to make several small drainage holes in the bottom. Fill with vermiculite, and moisten it well. Plant the seeds. Then, take a large polyethylene bag and slip it over the tray. Secure the open end with a twist 'em. You've got a handy little tray that costs nothing, and is light enough to move from one window to another to catch the sun.

If your seedlings come up too thickly, as they almost certainly will, they will soon begin to crowd each other. If you do not correct this situation quickly, they will grow leggy and spindly as they compete for light and room. The answer, of course, is to thin and transplant them. As soon as the seedlings develop their first pair of true leaves, they are ready to be transplanted. Moisten the soil, and remove the seedlings with a small spoon. Be gentle, and keep as much soil around the roots as possible.

You can transplant seedlings to larger flats, but it's best to move them to individual containers—pots, peat pellets, or planting blocks—so their roots won't become intertwined. The pots may be clay, plastic, or peat, and should be 2 or 3 inches in diameter. Peat pots are convenient and inexpensive, and they can be put into the ground right along with the plants. Clay and plastic pots, of course, are reusable.

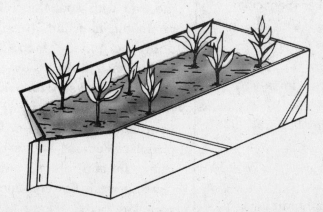

The Great Outdoors

Prepare For Guests

I said earlier that you can sow seed directly into the garden. If you do, you must prepare your guest beds ahead of time. No matter how fresh the seed you've purchased, their success depends in large measure upon how well you prepare the soil in their future bed. First, I want you to break up the soil with a spading fork, and remove all stones, sticks, cans, and other rubbish.

Then, to each 100 sq. ft. area, add 10 pounds of peat moss, 5 pounds of garden food, and 5 pounds of gypsum, along with 5 bushels of compost, if available. Mix these into the soil, then rake the surface smooth. Moisten the soil, and after the water has soaked in, rake again. You are now ready to sow your seed or set out your plants.

Don't Forget To Cover Them Up!

Once you soak the seedbed thoroughly and plant your seeds, cover the bed with something like burlap to retain the moisture. Keep covered just until the plants peep through. The instant their little heads are above the ground (and be sure to look each day, for they may surprise you), remove the covering. I would suggest that you plant portulaca, annual baby's breath, candytuft, annual phlox, zinnias, sweet alyssum, strawflowers, and marigolds in your late beds. These flowers love the sun, and are dependable bloomers.

JERRY'S TOP 20 LOW-MAINTENANCE PLANTS

For you lazy gardeners:

African Daisy (Arctotis)
Ageratum
Sweet Alyssum (Lobularia)
Begonia (fibrous)
Begonia (tuberous)
Celosia (Cockscomb)
Spider Flower (Cleome)
Coleus
Cosmos
Dusty Miller (Senecio)
Flowering Kale/Cabbage
Impatiens
Lobelia
New Guinea Impatiens
Nicotiana
Petunia (multi-flora)
Phlox
Portulaca
Salvia
Vinca (Catharanthus)

16

Put 'Em To Bed

When sowing seed in a timely manner, place the seed on the soil's surface, being careful to sow it evenly. Cover it very lightly with soil or, if the seeds are very fine, not at all. In fact, no annual seed should have a soil covering more than $1/4$ inch thick, for the delicate seedlings find it difficult to break through too much soil cover. Remember, it's better to plant your seeds too shallow than too deep!

Firm the soil around the seeds, using your foot or the flat part of your hoe. This will ensure your seeds make good contact with the moisture in the soil. If the soil is quite dry at the time of planting, make a shallow trench, and soak the soil in it. Plant your seed in the moist soil, cover lightly with dry soil, and tamp the seeds down. This will give them enough moisture to start growing.

GREEN THUMB TIP

Beware of Jack Frost!

Before you plant outdoors, you had better be sure that ol' Jack Frost isn't going to take one more swipe on his way to bed.

Generally speaking, you can sow hardy annuals about two weeks before the date of the last killing frost in the spring. Half-hardy annuals can be sown a week or two later, but delay the sowing (or transplanting) of the tender annuals until the weather has settled, and you are reasonably sure that it has warmed up for good.

Thinning Is A Must!

You will, at first, feel like a serial killer, so brace yourself. If you do not give each plant the space it needs, it will be thin and spindly instead of straight and sturdy, and you will have far fewer flowers than you would have had if you had thinned out the plants properly. If you have sown your seeds quite thickly, you will undoubtedly have far too many seedlings. Decide which plants you want to keep, and remove the rest.

If it will help you feel less guilty, thin them with great care. Carry a little flat with you, lay the uprooted seedlings in it, and cover their roots with a bit of soil to keep them from drying out.

17

Many of these plants can be used somewhere else in your garden, or maybe a neighbor would like to have them. You might even arrange to trade with a friend who has something you want. Lots of times, these little extras can be put in some out-of-the-way spot and used later on to fill in bare spaces where other plants have outlived their usefulness or died. If you plan ahead a bit, you won't have to throw any of your little friends away!

SUPER GROWING SECRET

To ensure a uniform and attractive display of annuals all season long, sprinkle some seeds of the same variety in among the rooted seedlings when you plant them. That way, the seeds will just be reaching the bloom stage as the older ones are fading. Using "back-up blooms" ensure color all season long.

Some annuals, usually those with a long taproot, should not be transplanted at all. The taproot is easily broken when you dig up the plant, and its survival then becomes very uncertain. However, most annuals stand transplanting very well when they are small.

PRE-GROWN TIMESAVERS

If you are short on time (yours or the growing season), and don't care to start your plants indoors, I suggest that you purchase pre-grown bedding plants, but I want you to remember, BUYER BEWARE! Here are some buying and planting tips for bedding plants:

Buying Plants: Get The Most For Your Money

Good-quality plants can be distinguished quite easily from those that will struggle the entire growing season. A short, compact plant with good green leaves of moderate to large size has the greatest potential for producing an abundance of blooms. Inexperienced buyers often focus on the size and number of flowers, which are no indications of how a plant will continue to grow. A well-grown plant, with lots of branches emerging near the soil surface, will produce flowers not only in May and June, but throughout the summer and fall.

The plants you buy should look crisp and fresh—this reflects adequate watering, good light, and protection from adverse weather and strong winds. Remember, when buying annuals, they should not necessarily be in bloom; in fact, some grow better if planted when they are all green.

And also remember, the price you pay for plants most often reflects plant quality, newness of cultivars, and services available from the garden center operator. New, improved selections, often designated as All-American Winners, may carry a premium price tag. It's no bargain to purchase an inexpensive plant that has little potential for growing or producing flowers.

New Introductions

Hybridizers from around the world continue to bring forth many superior flower selections each year. The new introductions often differ greatly from older selections in terms of color, size, and shape of bloom, resistance to pests, and vigor. We now have a wide range of plant heights for snapdragons, salvia, marigolds, zinnias, and geraniums. Pay particular attention to posters at retail outlets and labels accompanying plants for information on growth characteristics and planting recommendations. Look for the All-American selections which signal some of the new, superior introductions for our gardens.

Color: A Touch Of Beauty

Gardeners frequently are drawn to bright colors, such as the many shades of red. If used extensively, this color can overpower the garden so that one really doesn't see pinks, yellows, or blues that are also present.

RECYCLING ROUND-UP

You can make plant markers from old hangers. Simply cut a long piece of hanger, wrap it around a 2" piece of pipe twice, slide it off, and then press together. Now insert plastic cards or seed packs into the slot.

White, often overlooked, fulfills an important role in helping to separate bold, clashing colors, and highlighting blue and lavender blooms. A warm feeling can be achieved by planting red, yellow, and orange flowers. Blue and green tend to create a cool setting in the border.

Planting And Tending: Keys To Success

Get Tough

If you've followed my directions for preparing your bed, then your garden is now ready to receive your seedlings or bedding plants. Bedding plants from a greenhouse need to be "hardened off," or toughened up, before they are planted. Set them outside in a warm, protected area for about a week, and bring them back indoors at night if frost or chilly air is expected.

TIMELY TONIC

Feed all of your flowers with the following tonic every two weeks for fantastic foliage and beautiful blooms:

1 cup of beer,
1 oz. of Fish Fertilizer,
1 oz. of liquid dish soap,
1 oz. of ammonia,
1 oz. of whiskey,
1 tbsp. of clear corn syrup,
1 tbsp. of gelatin, and
4 tsp. of instant tea
dissolved in 2 gallons of
warm water.

Their New Home

Before planting, water both the ground and the plants. Dig a planting hole deeper and wider than the root ball and, after carefully removing the plant from the pack, fill in around the roots with soil while holding the plant at the same depth it had grown before. If the roots are tight at the bottom of the pot or pack, gently loosen them with your fingers. Firm the soil and water thoroughly. It's best to plant late in the afternoon or on a cloudy day to prevent transplant shock, and to shade the new plants from sun and wind for a few days.

Water deeply so the soil is moist to a depth of about 3 inches about once a week if it doesn't rain. Frequent light waterings will encourage shallow roots and poor growth.

Well-prepared soil should need no further feeding. If it does, however, use 5-10-5 fertilizer like my liquid Rose and Flower Food, every three weeks, and make sure they get a dose of the Timely Tonic on the previous page every other week.

PROTECTING YOUR BEAUTIES

A Gentle Pinch Does Wonders

Your little annual friends are climbers, creepers, and crawlers, and it becomes necessary from time to time to pinch them back to keep them alert and in their own backyard. I let them bloom the first time, and then I cut some of them back with grass shears to encourage more blooms. I do this again just before I go on vacation, since I won't be around to miss the flowers.

To keep your beauties blooming and vigorously healthy, also remove spent flowers and seedpods. This is known as **deadheading**. This is particularly necessary with annuals like ageratums, pot marigolds, cosmos, marigolds, pansies, gloriosa daisies, pincushion flowers, zinnias, and petunias.

Stop The Weeds In Their Tracks

Don't kid yourself—your garden is not going to take care of itself. Those sneaky invaders, the weed seeds, are always lurking about, ready to rush in and crowd out your darlings if you give them a chance!

Weeds will be a problem only if you let them get the upper hand. Remember, that innocent-looking little sprig of green can quickly tower over your flowers, and take away the food and water you have so lovingly prepared for them.

When you first start gardening, you may not be able to tell flower seedlings from weeds, which often sprout at the same time. Until you become more experienced, you can overcome this situation by planting your flower seeds in rows and labeling them. When a number of identical seedlings sprout, you will just naturally know these are your flowers. After awhile, you will learn to recognize your flower seedlings as soon as they pop out of the ground.

Outwitting The Weeds

1. Cultivation—The best way to outwit the weeds is to never let them get the best of you. Go over your garden conscientiously at least once a week with a cultivator—or by hand if your garden is small. Cultivation should not be more than an inch deep. Remember, annuals are shallow-rooted.

2. Mulching—If you dislike the work of cultivating, there is a way out—one that will, in all probability, be better for your plants as well as save you a lot of work. And you do want to enjoy your flower garden—remember? The answer, of course, is mulching.

You are going to have to cut the lawn anyway, so why not save the clippings for your flower beds? It's better not to leave clippings on the lawn because they prevent air from getting to the roots of your grass. So, do yourself,

SUPER GROWING SECRET

You can protect roots, eliminate weeds, and prevent soil from splashing up on your flowers by mulching your flower beds! Start with 1" of grass clippings, and add 1" every week until you've got a uniform 4" to 6" depth.

Also, keep grass, tree, and shrub roots where they belong by installing metal or rigid plastic edging 6" to 10" into the ground around the flower bed's perimeter.

your lawn, and your flowers a favor! Bag up those clippings and use them in your flower beds.

But don't, I beg of you, put them on too thickly. They are green and they will heat up as they decompose. Put on a light layer each time you mow, and distribute it evenly so it will dry quickly. If you have more clippings than flower beds, put them into a compost heap somewhere and let them go to work for you there. Six months later, you'll be glad you did.

3. Peat Moss—If you don't like the looks of clippings, hay, or straw, try buckwheat hulls or peat moss. Peat, which has a high water-holding capacity, is especially good.

4. Plant 'Em Close—You don't like any of these ideas? Well, if you like, you can avoid both mulching and weeding (or almost, anyway) by placing your annuals close together so that they will shade the ground when they are grown up. Then only a few really daring weeds are likely to appear. You will quickly notice them, and can get rid of them with one quick pull.

5. By Hand—Hand-weeding is slow, but effective work. And, in most plantings, such as rock gardens, it is the most practical means of dealing with weeds. The best time to pull weeds by hand is when the soil is moderately moist. Naturally, it is easier to take out fairly small plants than big ones. When dealing with perennial weeds, it is essential to remove their roots as well as their tops.

6. Workless Weeders—Workless weeders, also known as the kneeless weeders, are something else. Science has come up with a real winner in the form of a pre-emerge weed killer for gardens. It eliminates the job of weeding on bended knee, which has never been one of my favorite pastimes. All the major garden product manufacturers have a pre-emerge garden weeder. They all contain a chemical that will not interfere with any plant that is above the ground, but will prevent any other new growth from coming through—namely weeds.

Apply one of these kneeless weeders as soon as you plant your seedlings, or as soon as your new seeds have sprouted. After you have removed any existing weeds, you will not be plagued the rest of the summer (provided you do not disturb the surface of the soil). This scientific breakthrough has saved me many hours of work that I now spend on more enjoyable projects.

Annuals Aren't For The Birds

Newly planted seeds in your flower garden are definitely not "for the birds," as much as we may love our fine-feathered friends and appreciate their songs and friendly presence.

Annuals, which are planted right on or very near the surface of the soil, are especially subject to their depredations. Seed-planting time is really the only time when you have to think about birds very seriously, for, other than picking off an occasional insect or two, they seldom bother mature flowers.

DON'T LEAVE ME!

Leaves can be used in a number of different ways in your garden.

1. Add them to your compost heap along with kitchen and other yard waste. Avoid putting on too many at one time as they may clump together and inhibit good air circulation. Put some leaves aside to add to the compost heap gradually over the following months.

2. To compost leaves using a slightly different approach, try the following: shred the leaves with a lawn mower (smaller pieces decompose faster), place them in garbage bags, moisten, close the bags, and leave them until spring. Anaerobic decomposition (i.e., without oxygen) will give you leaf mold which can be dug into your garden in the spring.

3. Use leaves as a mulch on your flower beds. Use some now, and save some for next spring. As mulch, leaves conserve soil moisture, insulate the soil, control erosion, and reduce weed growth. Also, as the leaves decompose, they add organic matter and nutrients to the soil.

And if you act wisely, you can prevent the birds from upsetting your flower cart without harming them.

1. Netting—is one of the best safeguards. It admits light and keeps out the birds—and often insects as well.

2. Homemade Portable Screen—can protect newly planted seeds. Old window or door screens can be used for this. Cut it into 18-inch strips, and nail it to an old lath to make a framework. If you think this is a bit unsightly, remember, it is a temporary measure to be used only until the plants are up and established.

3. Hot Caps—paper covers that fit over young plants, may also be used to protect small areas.

4. Noise and Motion—Sometimes gardeners use it to frighten away birds and small animals. You can make all sorts of devices from inexpensive materials. For instance, the discarded tops and bottoms of empty tin cans may be strung together to wave in the breeze, creating noise, shine, and movement. Crumple thin sheets of aluminum foil into balls and suspend them here and there above your beds. Sometimes fluttering strips of cloth will scare birds away from newly planted seeds. Small mirrors are sometimes left on the ground to discourage crows. Birds will usually become accustomed to any device if it is used constantly, so you need to try different approaches on alternate days.

Critters Don't Belong

1. Commercial Traps—There are all sorts of traps on the market now for rats, rabbits, skunks, minks, raccoons, and other midnight marauders. I prefer the ones that capture the animals without injuring them. Once caught, the animals should be taken far enough away from the site of capture to make sure they do not return.

ROTATE

SCARE ITEMS

FOR

MAXIMUM

EFFECTIVENESS

2. Plant Repellents—You might also consider using plants to repel certain animals. Moles and shrews can be discouraged by plantings of daffodils, spurge (or annual poinsettia), and castor bean plants. The castor bean plant is an annual which will grow quite large in one season. It is rather coarse, but has an interesting tropical look about it. Its large root system takes so much water from the soil that this, in turn, will decrease the insect population upon which the moles depend for food. The beans, placed in their burrows, also act as a repellent.

CASTOR OIL

IS AN

EFFECTIVE

MOLE

REPELLENT

3. Noise—The family dog often acts as a defender of your garden, chasing away small unwelcome creatures such as rabbits and mice. Sound will often discourage animals from entering. Moles especially do not like noise. If you are overrun by them, set several toy pinwheels into their runs. I've also had good luck setting empty bottles in the runs. As air passes over the mouths of the bottles, it creates a vibration that moles find very irritating.

Bugs Are Pests!

Annuals are prone to attack from the wiggling and winged warriors, so it is important that they get the soap-and-water treatment, and that you keep your eyes open for insects. At the first sign of an invasion, use **Dursban, Malathion,** or **Sevin** at the recommended rates.

If it's something nibbling at their feet, use **diazinon**. From time to time, a little rash or mildew will appear on the foliage, especially on zinnias. A soapy shower and an after-bath powdering with rose dust will help.

But no matter how carefully you plan and try to carry out good cultural practices, there are times when things simply get out of control. Sometimes,

THUG BUSTERS

Cigarette filters can save plant lives by killing bugs. Break the smoked filter from the cigarette, remove the paper, place 6 to 8 of them on the soil surface and water throughly. The nicotine will make the bugs wish they had shacked up in someone else's pot.

you find your garden suffering from a sudden insect invasion. An explosion of army worms may seem to materialize out of nowhere, and march pitilessly on your defenseless flowers, devouring everything in their path. Sometimes a horde of grasshoppers suddenly appears. Of course, on such occasions, you must do whatever is necessary to control them. Such incidents are infrequent, so you must learn to distinguish between a moderate amount of insect activity, and the build-up of insect populations as they get ready to launch a full-fledged, all-out attck.

For a few insects, there are probably enough natural controls at work in your garden, such as birds or ladybugs, to keep things in balance. For other pests, there are many home, organic, or chemical remedies which may give relief. Here are a few of my favorites:

1. Home Remedies—Some people use **empty beer cans** to trap snails and slugs. **Halved cantaloupe hulls** can be used to trap sow bugs, which will eat plants' roots. Another way to control these bugs, sometimes called pill bugs, is to save **used corncobs**. Put them under pans or flowerpots, and tap the bugs off into another container. They can then be destroyed.

Newly set-out plants can be protected from cutworms by putting little **cardboard collars** around them. The thin cardboard that the laundry puts in your shirts is fine for this. Cut strips about 3 inches wide, press one inch into the ground, and leave 2 inches extending above ground.

One of the best ways I know to keep plants healthy is to plant **garlic cloves** among them. The small flower

TOBACCO JUICE

Chewing tobacco juice is one of the best bug killers around. To make it, buy a package of chewing tobacco, draw three fingers of tobacco from the package, place it in the toe of a nylon stocking, and place the stocking in a quart of boiling water. Let it marinate until the mixture is dark brown.

Add a teaspoon of the juice per pint of water once a month when spraying your beds to ward off any possibility of anything bugging your plants. The bugs will be so busy throwing up in the bug bathroom that they won't bother your plants!

27

heads that develop from them (which in turn contain many more tiny bulblets) are not unsightly. And since garlic multiplies quite rapidly, you can quickly increase your stock, and plant some around your fruit trees to repel borers.

If you also have a vegetable garden, grow some **hot peppers**. Ground, dried hot pepper makes a very effective spray against ants, spiders, caterpillars, fleas, and many other small insects. You might even try grinding some onions and garlic with your hot pepper; cover the mash with water, and let it stand overnight. The next morning, drain off the vegetables. Add this liquid to enough water to make a gallon of spray. You can use it as an all-purpose spray on roses, azaleas, chrysanthemums, and other flowers. If you have a heavy rain, you must, of course, repeat your spraying.

2. Organic Remedies—Use **ground rock phosphate** against flea beetles and striped cucumber beetles. You may prevent attack by insects, mites, and fungi by using **granite meal** or **dust**. Even such dry, powdery materials as **lime**, **tobacco**, and **road dust** have been used to advantage against striped cucumber beetles. Dust these substances on the leaves as well as the tops.

An effective control for red spiders (often seen on columbines) is **wood ashes**, dusted on the foliage.

And one of your best and safest bets is simply **water**! Turn a forceful spray on the infested plants—you may succeed in dislodging so many aphids that you won't have to use anything more toxic. Aphids so rudely dislodged generally will not return.

3. Chemicals—When it's necessary to use a chemical control, I mix 6 teaspoons of Tomato and Vegetable Dust into a paste, and add it to a gallon of water with one ounce of liquid dish soap. Spray it on your flowers after 6:00 p.m. If problems continue, take the insect to your local garden center for identification and for recommendations on how to combat it.

OTHER WAYS TO GROW ANNUALS

There are a lot of folks who don't have a lot of room to grow annuals in beds—so why not try potting, hanging, or letting them climb?

Hanging Baskets

Hanging basket gardens allow you to grow attractive plants in the most unlikely places. A basket or suspended planter can add a flowering annual to your porch or balcony without really taking up any space. Hanging baskets display colorful blooms at eye level, and can disguise a plain or unsightly view.

Hold It!

Numerous types of containers are available for hanging gardens. Any container, whether it be plastic, wood, or a wire basket lined with peat moss, will work fine. The most important things are that the containers should be lightweight and have good drainage.

DRYING FLOWERS

The best time to preserve flowers is right when they are at their peak performance. Cut them on a sunny morning, never after a rain.

To dry them, I mix 3 cups of Borax® and 1 cup of cornmeal together in a container that can be sealed. Then I place the freshly-picked flowers in the container, cover them with the mixture, seal, and let it stand for four to five days.

Choose Wisely

Special varieties of plants have been developed specifically for use in hanging baskets. Most bedding plant annuals make attractive instant baskets. Purchase the plants and design your own baskets, or buy them pre-planted. If you decide to plant your own basket, choose one color and one type of flower for a bright, showy splash of color, or design a mixed planting.

29

Keep Design In Mind

When mixing different plants in one basket, start with more upright plants at the center, such as marigolds, ageratum, or coleus; then add trailing plants around the edges of the pot. Some suggestions for vining plants are fuchsia, vinca, alyssum, or black-eyed Susan vine. You might also want to add some variegated foliage, such as English ivy. Be sure the plants in combination baskets have similar sun requirements. For example, in a shady location, a good combination might include fibrous begonias with English Ivy, coleus, or impatiens. In a semi-shady to sunny spot, try browallia, alyssum, fuchsia, tuberous begonia, lobelia, or pansy. Good sun-loving companions include ivy geraniums, petunias, spider plants, alyssum, dusty miller, lantana, nasturtium, and black-eyed Susan vine. Fibrous begonias can be used in shade, semi-shade, or sunny locations.

DECORATING TIP

To keep a basket with several different plants from looking too weighted down or "heavy," mix broadleaf plants with light, airy ones such as asparagus or maidenhead fern.

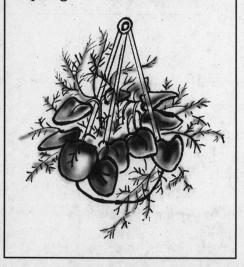

Plant With A Purpose

Set your basket plants in a porous planting mix rather than garden soil. Commercial potting soil is sufficiently porous to allow good drainage, while garden soil may be too heavy to drain properly and may contain insects, weed seeds, and disease. Plant the plants as soon as possible after buying them, and keep them well watered and out of direct sunlight for a couple of days. For a spectacular full basket, plant the annuals rather close together, allowing only a little extra space for continued root growth.

Watering Wisdom

Under average outdoor conditions, medium-sized flowering plants in 10" (diameter) hanging baskets will need up to 1 quart of water a day.

A thoroughly watered 10" hanging basket should weigh between 6 and 8 lbs. Under average conditions, a thoroughly watered 10" basket should not require water for 2 to 4 days. But, I said average conditions. Don't be fooled; to be on the safe side, check your baskets daily.

Fertilizing Facts

Watch out for the signs of insufficient fertilizer: a reduction of blooms and/or leaves turning yellow. Note: yellowing leaves can also be due to wilting.

My recommended dosage for outdoor hanging baskets: apply 1 to 2 tsps. per gallon of water of 20-20-20 or 15-30-15 water soluble fertilizer every 2 weeks, depending on the appearance of the plants. If the plants show signs of insufficient fertilizing, go with 2 tsps. of fertilizer per gallon. Or sprinkle 1 or 2 tbsps. of slow release, coated fertilizer on a 10" hanging basket; one application may suffice for the entire summer.

COLORFUL CLIMBERS

Need to cover an unattractive fence? Want privacy at one end of your porch—or perhaps some shade? Consider the colorful climbers—annual vines—that will provide cover, shade, flowers, or fragrance almost instantly.

❀ For color and fragrance, it's hard to beat a trellis or fence covered with **sweet peas**. Plant them early because as they are a cool-climate crop. Also, the blooming period and geographic range of sweet peas have been extended by new hybrids, so if the old types didn't do well in your area, the newest ones may.

❀ If **morning glories** charm you, rig up an invisible zigzag support of nylon fishing line from floor to ceiling at the sunny end of your porch. Put 8- to 10-inch pots containing several morning glory seedlings at the base of each line, and watch them grow! The vines will reach the ceiling in a few weeks, providing both privacy and color. Remember that this type of pot culture is intensive, so you must water and feed frequently.

❀ If your preferred color scheme is orange and yellow, try a patch of climbing **nasturtiums**. In addition to enjoying the beauty of the flowers, you can eat the young leaves in salads, and pickle the green seeds to use like capers.

COLORFUL CONTAINER GARDENS

Sunny Locations:
   *Geraniums ringed with petunias
   *Parsley or pepper plants with an edge of low-growing dwarf marigolds,
      dwarf zinnias, or alyssum
   *Medium-sized marigolds edged with dwarf marigolds
   *Medium-sized zinnias edged with dwarf zinnias
   *Salvia fringed with cascade petunias

Shady Locations:
   *Begonias centered with a few impatiens
   *Wax begonias circled with alyssum
   *Coleus center ringed with begonias
   *Begonias ringed with lobelia and alyssum

      Specimen Pots

For Shady Areas:
   *Impatiens in solid and striped colors
   *Wax begonias, solid red, green, and variegated foliage varieties

For Sunny Areas:
   *Geraniums
   *Petunias, mixed or single color
   *Chrysanthemums

❉ The **black-eyed Susan** vine is another yellow or orange beauty. More fragile in appearance than the other annual vines, it is particularly suitable for sunny hanging baskets or window boxes.

So, whatever your need, there's a vining annual that fits the bill. Try one or more in your garden this year, and you'll be glad you did!

GOING TO POT IN THE GARDEN

If the gardener can't get to the garden, then the garden can come to her through the versatile world of containers. More and more people are trying their hand at growing flowers, vegetables, and herbs in containers, as they realize that this method of gardening allows for the best of all possible worlds. Just think of all the places that bright, bold, plant-filled containers can add a special touch to balconies, patios, decks, poolsides, or steps.

Creative Container Ideas

Anything that will hold planting mix can be used as a container, from plastic, stone, or clay pots to improvised containers made from bird cages, wheelbarrows, tires, fruit crates, or wooden barrels. All that is required is a container with adequate drainage and a soilless mix of one half peat moss mixed with one half perlite or vermiculite.

Picking Your Flowers

Buying bedding plants at your local garden center is the instant way to have a container garden. Choose plants for shade or sun as your conditions dictate. Flowering annuals may be of any size or shape—erect, mounded, or trailing—but should be in proportion to

DECORATING TIP

You can turn a simple clay pot into a hanging basket by making a cradle for it. Simply link 3 metal chains together, thread them through a hook, and then hang the pot by the hook. That's all there is to it!

the size and shape of the container. Your container planting can be as simple as a pot filled with glorious geraniums, petunias, or marigolds for the sun, or impatiens or begonias for the shade, or as complex as a mixed bouquet of a half-dozen different annuals in different textures and colors.

Handle With Care

Whatever you choose, space the plants more closely than you would in the ground. Most important in caring for containers is to check the moisture at least daily during hot weather because containers can dry out rapidly. Increased watering will also increase fertilizer needs; so give your plants a dose of their Timely Feeding Tonic every weekend instead of every other week.

CUT

FLOWER

GARDENS

SHOULD BE

PRACTICAL,

NOT

FORMAL

OTHER WAYS TO USE ANNUALS

Don't just gaze at them longingly in their beds; bring them in to admire a little longer.

Annuals For Arranging

Behind the fence or in a sunny spot beyond the vegetables, plant a cutting garden this year. It doesn't have to be formal; after all, it's for your own enjoyment.

No need to pay lots of attention to the design or other aesthetics—simply grow neat rows of annuals in the colors and forms that please you best.

Little Beds

If you have space for only a tiny cutting bed, try tall zinnias and snapdragons. Their white, yellow, orange, red, and pink colors blend well and their forms contrast nicely. Zinnias provide rounds and the snaps, vertical lines. Both are long-lasting as cut flowers and the plants will continue to bloom and provide color until frost.

Big Beds

More space? If your color scheme calls for pinks and blues, plant larkspur, canterbury bells, asters, bachelor buttons, felicia daisies, or stock. In this cutting garden, be sure to add some dusty miller for its gray foliage—it's most compatible with pink tones.

For vivid reds, yellows, and oranges, grow marigolds, plumed celosia, geraniums, gloriosa daisies, and gazanias. The taller varieties are best, so read the labels to be sure you're buying tall plants. Coleus makes a fine foliage filler with these flowers.

Poppies—both the Shirley and the Iceland types—are great additions to mixed bouquets. They are long-lasting if you sear the stem ends after you cut them. Taking a lighted candle or disposable lighter with you into the garden in full sunlight may look ridiculous, but any flower arranger will understand.

And for airy fillers, grow some annual baby's breath or dill. The latter plant is dual-purpose, useful both in flower arrangements and cooking.

DRY ANNUALS FOR LONG LASTING BEAUTY

Your beautiful garden won't last forever, even in the warmer climates. How sad it is to watch the advancing cold weather, and the end of the gardening

CHEAP FLOWER FROG

Use those plastic mesh strawberry baskets—upside down in a bowl or a vase—to hold your cut flower arrangement in place. Leave a little extra lower foliage on the flowers to hide the "frog."

season. Vegetables and fruit are easily preserved for the future by freezing and canning, but what about your lovely garden flowers? Must their lives be limited to a few days? Not if you take a little time and use a little of my grow-how to preserve them.

Hang Them By Their Toes

The easiest way to dry flowers is by air-drying. The first step is to choose a place that is dry and dark, with good air circulation. An attic is usually good; a basement is usually too damp. Harvest the flowers before they are fully open, and strip the foliage from the stems. Tie small flowers in bunches so that their flower heads do not touch, then hang them upside down. Most will dry in two to three weeks.

The Popular Crowd

The most popular annual for drying is probably the **strawflower**. It grows up to 2 feet tall with flowers in all shades of red, pink, and gold. The showy, stiff bracts surround and conceal the tiny flowers inside.

If you like vivid purple or fuchsia-colored flowers, try drying **globe amaranth** or **statice**. The $3/4$ inch round flower heads of globe amaranth dry quickly, and are long-lasting. Purple statice and sea lavender, like the florists use, are easy to dry at home. Rat-tailed statice has 18-inch-long, pencil-thin spires of tiny lilac-colored blossoms, and should be cut when the flowers are fully open.

CUT FLOWER EXTENDERS

There are several things you can do to extend the life of cut flowers:

1. Add 2 tbsp. of clear corn syrup per quart of very warm water; add this to the vase.

2. A cube of sugar per pint of water and a copper penny in the vase are said to extend their life.

3. Any one of the cut flower preservatives or Christmas tree extenders sold in flower shops are great.

4. To hold blossoms longer, spray the cut flowers with hairspray after they've been cut for a day or so.

For warm colors—yellows, golds, and reds—grow **calendula** (also known as pot marigold), **marigolds, yarrow,** and **cockscomb**. All retain their colors when dried; but the bright, clear colors of cockscomb *(Celosia cristata)* are unsurpassed. Its distinctively shaped flowers come in brilliant shades of yellow, orange, red, and purple. Other types of celosia are plumed or feathered.

Bells of Ireland *(Molucella laevis)* are delicate green spikes which enhance any arrangement. Pick off most of the leaves so that the bells will be more conspicuous. **Dusty miller** dries to a delicate silver-white and complements soft pink and purple flowers.

For a light, airy touch, add dried grasses. Just about any ornamental grass will do, especially **animated oats,** **quaking grass** *(Briza maxima)*, **squirrel-tail grass,** and **rabbit-tail grass**.

FLOWERS TO DRY

Baby's breath	Larkspur (annual)
Bee balm	Lavender
Bells of Ireland	Lemon verbena
Blanket flower	Marigold
Butterfly weed	Okra
Calendula	Onion
Castor bean	Plumed celosia
Chinese lantern	Plume poppy
Chives	Sage
Cockscomb	Salvia
Dusty miller	Statice
Globe amaranth	Strawflower
Grasses	Yarrow
Honesty	

Year-Round Beauty

Air-drying is quick and easy; when the flowers are dry, use them generously in flower arrangements, bud vases, door swags, or wreaths. Viewing these flowers through the winter will remind you how beautiful your garden will be next spring. Consider adding even more flowering annuals to your garden just for drying. Annuals which can be dried by hanging them upside down are listed on page 37.

A SEED SAVED
IS A DOLLAR EARNED

Protect Your Young Ones

You can save seeds from your own plants if you want to and know what you're doing. When saving seeds, remember that many hybrids are developed by intercrossing one kind with another, and they do not breed true to type from seed. Most of the original species or wild types of plants do breed true, provided the flowers have not cross-pollinated.

To prevent cross-pollination, enclose the flowers in muslin bags, and artificially pollinate them with pollen from flowers of the same plant or from the same species of plants. Unless protected in this manner, the flowers may be cross-fertilized by the wind or insects.

Gather Them,
And Put Them To Bed

As soon as the seeds are ripe, they should be gathered and spread out to dry in a well-ventilated room.

BEE KIND!

Bees are among gardeners' best friends. Searching for nectar and pollen, they carry pollen from flower to flower, fertilizing the plants in the process. To attract them to your garden, plant colorful, fragrant flowers that are rich in nectar, particularly those that have contrasting colors, or are yellow and/or violet.

When completely dry, the seeds may be packaged and stored in a cool, dry place.

I have done some pretty exhaustive research on the best method of storing seeds and I have not, as yet, come up with a completely satisfactory answer. This applies both to seeds saved from my own plants and those purchased from a nursery. The life span or viability of different flower seeds varies so much that there simply cannot be any hard and fast rule to cover all varieties.

However, if you do get carried away with your purchasing, and find yourself in possession of partial or full packets of perfectly good seed when the spring planting season is over, give some thought to storing these seeds properly. You may lengthen their life span.

I seal my leftovers in their original packets, put them in small, dry, airtight jars, and place them in my refrigerator. Small baby-food jars are perfect for this, or if you have several packets, put them in a pint jar with a tight lid.

The best temperature is between 36 and 45°F. Check your refrigerator with a thermometer, and adjust the setting accordingly.

To Keep Or Not To Keep

Larkspur and dwarf hybrid marigold seeds do not keep well. Buy these fresh annually from a reliable seed person.

Generally speaking, oily seeds quickly lose their vitality, whereas those with hard seed coats are the longest lived. Morning Glory is an example of this.

TESTING SEED

To tell the good from the bad from the ugly, test your seed by dumping them in a bowl of water. The duds float, while the "studs" sink to the bottom.

THE BIG

THREE—

MARIGOLDS,

PETUNIAS,

AND

ZINNIAS

The seeds of ageratum, alyssum, summer forget-me-nots, snapdragons, asters, begonias, coleus, coreopsis, cyclamen, blanket flowers, flowering tobacco, schizanthus, sweet Williams, violas, and wallflowers will remain viable about two years.

Chrysanthemums, clarkia, nasturtiums, and papaver are viable for three years; sunflowers for four years; and sweet peas for up to ten years.

GET TO KNOW YOUR ANNUALS

Getting to know your plant can mean the difference between success and failure. The more you know, the less chance there is for surprises that could result in disappointment for both you and your annuals. So let me begin with the top three contenders for annual popularity and then continue with the introductions.

THE MOST POPULAR ANNUALS IN THE CLASS

Let's just suppose that this first year, you're going to plant only three different kinds of flowers—marigolds, petunias, and zinnias. These are three of the most popular and they remain so, year after year. There are sound reasons for this. They come into flower quickly, they have an immense and evergrowing color range, and perhaps most importantly, they flower gloriously even during hot, dry summers when other blossoms go limp and droop. These girls can take a licking, and keep on ticking!

MARIGOLD POWER

Marigolds are one of the best double-duty flowers out there. Besides providing a splash of showy color, plant them in and around your outdoor living areas (and vegetable garden) to keep mosquitos and other bugs away.

Mighty Marigolds

It's hard to get into trouble with marigolds; since their color range is largely confined to yellow, orange, and blending shades of copper red, there are no clashing colors. Of course, Burpee, who has done such marvelous things with marigolds, is still searching for that elusive white marigold which has not yet been found. The 'Whitemost Marigold' is, so far, the nearest to white.

What we are really concerned about is a glorious bed of golden color, and there is ample range to choose from. Let's consider the Burpee Lady Marigolds, an ideal bed or border plant 18 inches tall. These are carnation-flowered semi-dwarfs, fully double with some blooms measuring 3- $1/2$ inches across. They spread about 20 inches wide, making almost round, bushy, compact plants that retain their neatness all season long. Wouldn't these look lovely bordering a walk?

You can also choose from 'First Lady,' a clear light yellow; 'Gold Lady,' fully double and golden; and 'Orange Lady,' an exciting bright, deep orange. The Gay Ladies packet is a blend of all three colors.

In the French marigolds, we find orange, yellow, and mahogany shades, 9 to 18 inches tall, and fully double. There are also dwarf single French marigolds and extra dwarf double French marigolds that are just 6 inches tall with a spread of 10 inches. 'Petite Gold,' 'Brownie Scout,' and 'Gypsy' are outstanding varieties.

MAGNIFICENT MARIGOLDS

Once planted, marigolds need little attention, just watering when the soil becomes dry, and the snapping off of flowers as they fade. For earliest bloom and greatest ease, buy marigolds as young plants from your garden center or greenhouse. Plant marigolds in full sun after all danger of frost is past, and space them a distance equal to one half their height.

Choose several varieties in increasing heights and varying shades for a most attractive, eye-appealing, glowing garden bed. When buying an American type, look for plants in bud or bloom because these plants are light sensitive, and may not otherwise bloom until late summer. Pinch out the center bud for increased bushiness; newer, stockier varieties won't need staking as tall marigolds formerly did.

41

Lastly, let's find out what a "mule" marigold is. This is the name given to triploid hybrids, crosses between the big American marigolds and the little French.

The little French marigolds have twice as many chromosomes as the big Americans, but they cannot mate normally. The resulting triploids have their chromosomes out of balance. That makes them mules, and like the mule animal, they cannot reproduce themselves. But like all living things, they try to do so. They keep on blooming and blooming and BLOOMING, but never go to seed, and they are the earliest blooming of all marigolds.

Perky Petunias

Petunias are one of the showiest and most versatile garden flowers. The range of colors and forms available is tremendous, and they are one of the easiest flowers to grow, with the longest season of bloom of any annual.

PETUNIAS CAN BE PLANTED EVEN IN MIDSUMMER

Petunias will grow well with minimum care, even in poor soils. A 15-30-15 fertilizer should be added to the soil when the plants are set in the garden; peat moss or compost is also helpful, although not absolutely necessary, unless you have very poor soil.

Two or three light applications of fertilizer should be made during the summer. Once the plants are established, they should be watered deeply at one- to two-week intervals, depending on the weather, and should get their Timely Tonic feeding every other weekend. Excessive water and fertilizer or too much shade can reduce their flower power.

MIX AND MATCH

Petunias mix beautifully with other flowering annuals. Try edging a walkway with white geraniums surrounded by multiflora petunias in pale lavender-blue and deep purple. For an unforgettable window box display, combine scarlet salvias with hot-pink double grandifloras. Zinnias, marigolds, and sweet alyssum also make good companions to petunias of all kinds.

42

Some gardeners prune the plants back in mid-season to encourage a heavier flush of blooms. Even without this pruning, they perform better than almost all other annuals.

Petunias have practically no pest or disease problems. Snails and slugs will eat newly set-out plants, but collaring them with cardboard tubes cut to stand 2 or 3 inches high will help to protect them.

Petunias flower heavily over a long season, from three to four months in northern states and Canada, to more than six months in milder climates. Plants should be set out after all danger of heavy frost has passed. They can also be planted later—almost until midsummer—and still make a colorful show.

Petunias can be used in almost any sunny spot in the garden, large or small, where you want a bright splash of color. Medium or large beds or border plantings of one or two colors give the most striking effect. Ten plants will quickly fill in to make 8- to 12-foot border of color.

Petunias can also be used to provide color in front of permanent shrubs. They are especially useful in new landscapes to fill in bare spots between small shrubs. Any spot a foot or more in diameter with at least a half day of sun is sufficient.

There are both single- and double-flowered petunias. Both types are divided into two classes or categories: multiflora (many-flowered) and grandiflora (large-flowered). The color range in both types includes red, violet blues, purple, shades of pink, white, and pale yellow. There are also interesting striped or starred bicolors in red and white, blue and white, purple and white, and pink

SUMMER REJUVENATING TONIC

August is the time to pinch your annuals back severely. You may think it's going to hurt, but it's in their best interest. Afterwards, feed them liberally with my Late Summer Rejuvenating Tonic:

**1/4 cup of beer,
1 tbsp. of corn syrup,
1 tbsp. of Shampoo, and
1 tbsp. of 15-30-15 fertilizer
per gallon of water.**

This little pick-me-up will stimulate the plants into producing at least one more dazzling display of color that season.

✦

and white. Two-toned pinks, blues, and purples with an interesting veined or lace pattern are among the newest colors available.

The multiflora, single petunias have flowers 2 to 3 inches in diameter. Although the flowers are smaller than most of the grandiflora, each plant produces more of them so that the color effect is equal to, or greater than, that of the grandifloras. They are sometimes called "carnation-flowered" because of their resemblance to that frilly flower.

Multifloras are useful in climates with wind or heavy summer rain because the flowers are more resistant to adverse weather. They are often used in parks for mass plantings; a clever homeowner can use them the same way.

The large, or grandiflora, doubles have the showiest individual blooms in the petunia kingdom. Its flowers are 3 to 4 inches in diameter, and most varieties have delicately fringed, ruffled, or serrated petals. The choicest variety, having the most consistently top-quality flowers and the widest range of color, is 'Fanfare.' 'Bridal Bouquet' is a brand-new pure white variety with a light spicy fragrance. 'Princess' is a medium pink with very large flowers.

DYNAMIC DUOS

Many annual flowers can be used in combination with zinnias to give instant color that lasts through frost. Most popular among these are the blue or white ageratum; white or violet sweet alyssum; shade-loving pink, red or white wax begonias; bright and bold geraniums; many-colored impatiens; sunny marigolds; cool-toned pansies; cascading petunias; bright red salvia and heat tolerant vinca and gazania.

Zesty Zinnias

In the plant world, zinnias got off to a slow start. But no one looking at them now would ever recognize these Cinderellas as the plants called *Mal de Ojos*, or eyesore, in their native Mexico!

Zinnias are now one of the most favored and best-performing annuals. Easily grown in full sun in almost any soil, they will make a striking and dramatic garden display in even the hottest weather.

The flowers are available in an enormously wide range of bold colors, which now even includes an exciting apple green—'Envy.' This lovely variety adds something never to be had before in a zinnia planting—coolness. It grows 2 to 2-$\frac{1}{2}$ feet tall, and has perfectly formed 3- to 4-inch wide dahlia-flowered blooms of good, long-lasting quality.

Until a few years ago, zinnias were all boldly colored, but now they are available in soft pastel shades. Don't pass them up just because you thought they came only in harsh colors.

You might find that the habits of some of the plants are not entirely fixed. Occasionally, they revert to single and semi-double forms. The colors may not be entirely true, and once in awhile the flowers may have little cones or "Mexican hats" in the center. This is because zinnias hybridize readily, and because plant habits may vary greatly among seedling plants obtained from the same flower head. Don't let this dismay you—if an occasional plant shows undesirable characteristics, simply discard it.

Another slight disadvantage of zinnias is that late in the season the foliage may become a bit unsightly from mildew or may shrivel because of prolonged dry weather. But in the face of their many advantages, none of these problems seem significant. Consider their long, continuous, prolific bloom, the ease of culture, and their adaptability to just about any climatic condition. They are extremely effective as bed or border plants.

Would you like to have a zinnia that is smaller still? Try 'Thumbelina;' these make the neatest possible edging for a walk or border. They grow only 4 inches tall, and the fully double flowers are 1 to 2-$\frac{1}{2}$ inches in diameter. They bloom early, and continue through the

ZINNIA TIPS

Tip #1—Although zinnias like moist soil, they are prone to mildew. So keep the leaves dry.

Tip #2—Use a fertilizer that is high in phosphorus (i.e. 5-10-5). This will really strengthen the root structure.

Tip #3—These flowers were known as "cut and come again" because they really respond to cutting. So keep the scissors handy—these plants are amazingly prolific bloomers!

season. If you want a low-carpet color, these are your zinnias. Try some of these adorable elves, and you will never be sorry!

HERE'S THE REST
OF THE CROWD...

We have talked about a number of annuals, their good qualities, and their special uses. The ones I have mentioned are by no means the only ones you should consider trying—there are many others that are just as worthwhile, just as beautiful, and just as interesting.

Even so, there are so many annuals out there that I can attempt only a partial list. The ones that I will now describe are generally considered to be the most popular, primarily because they are both lovely and easy to grow.

AGERATUM

IS GOOD

FOR EDGING

BORDERS

Ageratum

This is a multi-purpose, everblooming flower. Ageratum is equally at home in semi-shade or full sun. There are both dwarf types for borders, edgings, or rockeries, and tall types for cutting. By potting a few plants in fall, you may enjoy the bright blooms in winter. Ageratum begins to bloom three months after sowing. It is easily grown from seed, and a packet usually contains about 1,000 seeds. Plant tall varieties 12 inches apart; dwarf varieties 6 inches apart. Germination time is six to ten days.

'Blue Cap,' an elfin ageratum, grows 4 to 5 inches tall. The foliage is literally smothered with rich, blue flowers; it's a fine dwarf for edging.

'Blue Mink' has 6-inch trusses of powder blue blossoms on strong upright plants.

'Fairy Pink,' 5 inches tall, is a dainty fairy princess which blooms from early summer to late frost. Flowers are a delicate, soft, salmon-rose-pink.

Ageratum

'Midget-Blue,' a 4-inch dwarf with exquisite, tiny blue flowers, is just perfect to plant in front of 'Fairy Pink.'

'Snow Carpet' is very dwarf. It forms 4-inch mounds of pure white loveliness, and is an extremely free-blooming strain. It makes an excellent dividing plant to put between bright-colored annuals.

Alyssum

Even beginners will find this plant delightfully easy to grow. It will germinate and flourish under almost any condition, and is tolerant of both cold and hot, dry summers. It can be planted early in the spring, and will begin blooming in early summer and continue right up to frost.

Alyssums are particularly recommended for the hot, dry sections of the country. They are good for edgings, for bedding, to cover sunny banks and terraces, for pots, and as a quick filler for rock gardens.

They may also be used for indoor winter blooming. Sow some seeds in a flower pot in late fall, and keep the container in a sunny window. For anyone who longs for a bit of June in January, this obliging flower could be the answer.

Dwarf varieties should be planted 6 to 8 inches apart, larger varieties 8 to 10 inches apart.

'Carpet of Snow,' a new extra-dwarf spreading white, grows only 3 inches tall, as does 'Tiny Tim;' it, however, blooms several weeks earlier than other whites.

ALYSSUM TOLERATES COLD WEATHER, EVEN SOME FROST

HOME REMEDIES

Use bleach for cleaning and removing the white crust and green moss from clay pots. Mix 2 tbsp. of bleach and 1 tbsp. of liquid dish soap in a half gallon of warm water, and scrub the pots with a rough scouring pad until they are clean.

Alyssum

'Royal Carpet,' as its name implies, is a deep, vibrant purple. It makes a neat and well-behaved edging, and is a perfect companion for 'Tiny Tim.' It grows only a few inches high, but will be about 10 inches across.

'Rosie O'Day,' a deep rose-pink, grows 3 inches tall. This one is not only ideal for edgings, but is also delightfully fragrant.

'Violet Queen' is one of the older varieties—first introduced in 1941—but is still deservedly popular. It grows 5 inches tall, is neat and compact in habit, and deliciously fragrant.

Antirrhinum
(Snapdragon)

Ah, here's something to get really excited over! What's been happening to snapdragons is incredible, simply incredible.

GREEN THUMB TIP

Young snapdragons benefit from pinching because it helps them become stockier and bushier. Use your thumb and forefinger to take out the growing tip on the main stem.

Goldsmith's 'Little Darling' has the same leaves and spikes as normal snapdragons, but the flowers look like rows of butterflies rather than dragons' jaws. Because the flower petals have actually been opened up by the change in shape, there is more color exposed on each spike. What this really means is that there is more "flower" and less "snap!"

'Little Darling' plants grow only 12 inches tall, and have a vigorous, basal-branching growth habit. Each plant grows several short spikes suitable for cutting without time-consuming pinching or staking. Each time a flower is cut, the plant will produce several new ones giving continuous color in the garden throughout the summer.

The new azalea-flowered type, ' Madame Butterfly,' is also excellent. It has the showiest flowers of all the snapdragons. Each floret resembles a double azalea flower. Plants grow 2 to 2-$\frac{1}{2}$ feet tall.

The original variety of the butterfly type was 'Bright Butterflies,' which grows about 2-$\frac{1}{2}$ to 3 feet tall and is excellent for background planting in flower beds. It's also choice as a cut flower.

If you want to grow snapdragons from seeds instead of—or along with—purchased plants, start them indoors or in a coldframe. With the coldframe method, make your sowing a month before the earliest outdoor planting date. Sow the seed thinly on the surface of the soil in rows 3 inches apart. Do not let the soil get too dry. They won't germinate until the soil reaches 50°F. On fair days, raise the sash so the plants get plenty of fresh air. These seedlings can be set directly into a sunny spot in the garden without any intermediate transplanting; space them 6 to 10 inches apart.

Infant snapdragons are demanding, but once they're in the garden, they are very little trouble. Pinch back the tops to make the plants bushier. Rust was once a serious snapdragon problem, but it has been largely eliminated in the newer varieties.

Aster

Asters are among the most glorious flowers in the garden, but you'll have to try them for yourself in your own backyard. Many people grow them without the slightest difficulty; others find it impossible to raise them. This is not because of any actual difficulty with the asters themselves, for they are easy to grow. The trouble lies with two diseases which may attack them—fusarium wilt and aster yellows.

Fusarium wilt is caused by a soil-inhabiting fungus, and aster yellows by a virus disease transmitted by leafhoppers. I don't mean to frighten you away from asters by telling you this, but rather, to alert you to the need for extra care.

SNAPDRAGONS ARE SHAPED LIKE A DRAGON'S MOUTH

CUTTING ASTERS

Cut the bottom of the stems of asters diagonally so they have a larger area to absorb water. Do it underwater so that the vessels in the stems don't become blocked by air.

To prevent these troubles, don't plant asters in the same place more than once every three years.

Sow aster seeds in spring in a spot that gets full to partial sun. Thin the seedlings 15 to 24 inches apart; 15 inches for dwarfs, 24 inches for giants.

Asters are offered in a seemingly endless array of colors and sizes. They come in white, pink, blue, purple, creamy yellow, red, or lavender. Many have yellow centers. There are dwarfs such as the 6- to 10-inch high 'Kirkwell,' which has fully double 2-inch flowers; 'Giant Princess Aster,' with flowers 3- $\frac{1}{2}$ to 4 inches across on long stems; and 'Massagno Cactus Asters,' with well-formed flowers having airy, needlelike petals. And then there are the 'Super Giants,' which are wilt-resistant. The largest fully double asters known, they grow 3 feet tall. Their huge, "ostrich-feather" flowers are very striking, and they are superb for cutting.

Begonia

Looking for a colorful, graceful plant for that shady spot? If so, then why not try begonias? In recent years, hybridizers have been making major improvements in begonia breeding.

The fibrous-rooted, wax begonias have come a long way from the small-flowered, shade-loving bedding plants of your grandmother's day. Today, we can grow wax begonias with flowers up to 3 inches in width, profusely covering neat mounds of green, bronze-tinged, or dark bronze foliage.

BARE BEGONIA FACTS

Fibrous (including Wax)

Light	Bright
Water	Thoroughly
Temperature	65°-75°F days; 60°-70°F nights
Colors	red, pink, white
Winter Care	Can survive winter in south, if no frost
Extra Tips	High night temperatures cause flowers to drop
Uses	Shady or sunny garden; bright window indoors

50

New varieties have been developed to be weather-resistant and to perform well in sun or shade. They will bloom outdoors until frost, and can then be whisked indoors to provide color all winter long as house plants—they're truly ever-blooming.

European hybridizers have come up with the newest innovation in tuberous begonias. These seed-grown tuberous begonia hybrids produce vigorous, uniform plants that are abundantly covered with 3-inch, semi-double flowers in delicious colors. They have a neat habit, and stay small and mounded—perfect for hanging baskets.

While the fibrous begonias are undemanding and will grow in almost any garden soil, they do prefer to dry out slightly between waterings. Space them 12 inches apart.

Outdoors, in sun or shade, begonias are neat bedding plants and make spectacular specimens. So take another look at begonias—there's one that's right for you!

Calendula Officinalis
(Pot Marigold)

Calendulas are the marigolds, or "Mary's gold," flowers that come to us from Europe, having been grown there in Scottish and English gardens. One of the best annuals for the garden or greenhouse, they are easy to grow and will thrive almost anywhere. In the South, they will bloom almost all year; in the North, from May until frost. They are attractive as either border or bedding plants.

Plant them early in the spring in a spot that receives full sun so you can enjoy their long blooming period. Barely cover the seeds with $1/4$ inch of soil. Since you will be planting them in the soil while it is still cold, growth will be slow at first. Plants should be ready for thinning or transplanting in about a month. Thin them so they stand 8 to 10 inches apart.

If possible, transplant on a cloudy day or in the late afternoon. When first transplanted, you may notice that the plants

CALENDULAS

FOLDED

INTO SOFT

BUTTER

MAKE A

TASTY

SPREAD

Calendula

51

have a tendency to wilt, so be patient. Keep them watered. Also, shading with a shingle the first day or two will help, especially if the weather turns sunny and hot.

Calendulas require little care beyond keeping down the weeds and watering them during dry, hot weather. Cut off the old blooms so they won't run to seed.

A pixie you will love is 'Dwarf Sunny Boy.' The 6-inch, mound-shaped plants are covered with 3-inch, fully double, bright orange flowers. It makes a perky pot plant too.

Another small fry is 'Zvolanek's Crested,' which grows 18 inches tall. Each flower has a crested center made up of tiny rubes or quills, some of which are dark-tipped. The centers are framed by overlapping guard petals, which creates a lovely effect.

ANNUAL TIME SAVERS

Annuals are a must for every lazy gardener. So, in addition to selecting low-maintenance annuals, here are a few additional ways to save time while producing good quality plants during the growing season.

1. Transplant varieties that require similar moisture requirements into the same flower bed. For example, plant dusty miller with petunias or portulaca because they all prefer somewhat dry soil conditions, rather than with impatiens, which grow best in moist soil. This saves time because you do not have to spot water the individual plants that require more water.

2. Match each variety with its optimum light requirement. If you plant a tuberous begonia or coleus in full sun, they will "burn up." But if you put them in a semi-shady area, they should grow beautifully. Plant celosia, cosmos, or petunias in the shade, and they will stop blooming altogether. Plants that are grown in the correct environment thrive and therefore, take less time to maintain.

3. Mulch bedding plants soon after they have been transplanted. Not only does mulching reduce the number of times a flower bed needs to be watered, but it also reduces the time that has to be spent weeding it. Any way you look at it, mulching saves a lot of time in the long run!

Celosia

These are easy-to-grow, old-fashioned annuals that have been greatly improved in recent years by selective breeding. Late-summer bloomers, celosias provide long-lasting flowers in fresh arrangements, and may be dried attractively for winter enjoyment. Use them for edgings and window or porch boxes; the tall ones are good for solid beds or in the middle area of a mixed border.

Celosia

Both the crested *(C. cristata)* and the plumed *(C. plumosa)* varieties are extremely easy to grow. Just give the plants plenty of room to branch properly. This means pretty drastic thinning which must be done early. Water if the weather turns dry, but otherwise, no particular care is necessary.

After danger of frost is past, sow the seeds directly in your garden in an area that receives full sun; cover them with 1/4 inch of soil. Transplant the extras when the seedlings have 4 to 6 leaves. Thin them so they are 24 inches apart.

Celosias are very rapid growers, enjoy the heat, and resist drought. In other words, they are great for warm climates where the summers are long and hot!

The crested types, or cocks-combs, include dwarf and extra-dwarf sprites. They range in height from 10 to 18 inches. Among these are 'Empress,' 10 inches tall, with dark bronzy foliage and huge combs of crimson purple; 'Gladiator,' also 10 inches tall, with yellow combs up to 10 inches across—a sort of "Mr. Five by Five" of the plant world; and 'Fireglow,' a fairly tall type growing 20 inches with 6- 1/2 inch balls of the brightest color.

GREEN THUMB TIPS

Tip #1. Flowers planted around trees help protect them from lawn mower injury. Also, water deeply to help keep the tree healthy during dry periods. Choose shade-loving annuals such as impatiens, begonias, and coleus.

Tip #2. Many gardeners ask when is the best time to water their plants. The best time is in the morning, giving ample time for plants to dry before sundown. If plants are wet overnight, fungus troubles may develop. Water enough to soak the roots, but no more than once or twice a week. Rarely do you need to water daily.

Tip #3. Water gardenias with a mixture of 1 tsp. of vinegar per quart of warm water. This will make the soil slightly acidic, which is the way they like it.

Among the plumed celosias are the extra-dwarf or lilliput varieties, 'Golden Gem' and 'Scarlet Gem.' The dwarfs include 'Fire Feather' and 'Golden Feather.' The best of the semi-dwarfs is 'Forest Fire Improved,' which is 2 feet tall and early flowering.

One of the most unusual varieties now offered is 'Silver Feather,' a 16-inch tall, sparkling silver-white. Who said celosias only came in loud, bright colors? Not me!

Centaurea Cyanus
(Cornflower)

CORNFLOWER

SEEDS

ONLY

GERMINATE

IN THE

DARK

These hardy favorites are showy in the garden, and make beautiful cut flowers for the house. Growing from 12 inches to 6 feet tall, there are over 500 varieties of centaurea.

You can sow the seed in the fall, or early in the spring. Pick a spot that gets full to partial sun, and just scatter the seeds on the surface—the way self-sown seeds get planted—or cover them with about a $1/4$ inch of soil. If you are planting the taller varieties, it is better to cover the seed to give the roots better anchorage later on. Sow where you want them to grow because they don't transplant well. Thin the seedlings so that they are 24 inches apart; this will give them plenty of room to grow.

Centaurea

These undemanding plants will just about take care of themselves. They are hard workers, and will bloom abundantly. To keep them from going to seed, remove the faded flowers—you will enjoy their blossoms over a longer period of time. However, you might like to save some of the seed. In order to do this, you will have to let the plant have its own way and go to seed. Keep in mind, it may do so anyhow if you aren't very watchful.

Varieties offered include 'Blue Boy,' a bright cornflower blue; 'Pinkie,' an exquisite light pink; 'Red Boy,' a deep, glowing red; and 'Snow Man,' a glistening pure white; they range in height from 24 to 30 inches tall.

The dwarf variety, 'Snowball,' a delightful pure white. It grows just 12 inches tall, is very free-blooming, and makes an excellent border plant. It's also good as a cut flower, both fresh and dried.

Cleome Basslerana
(Spider Flower)

Cleome is a most unusual looking plant, being, in a way, both bulky and airy in appearance. The flowers are actually quite small. New petals form on the tops of the stems as the old ones fade and die. As this happens, long, narrow seed pods develop, and stand rather stiffly outward. Someone thought these pods looked like spiders' legs; hence the name—spider plant. Every afternoon, a new whorl of airy, orchid-like blooms open on every stem.

Cleome

Sow the seeds in May where there is full sun and sandy soil. When the seedlings get big enough, thin them so they stand 15 inches apart. They are the easiest of all flowers to raise and will self-sow lustily, even in poverty-stricken, waterless soil where you wouldn't think anything would stand a chance to grow. And they'll bloom from June until frost.

Because cleomes are so tall, they are principally used as a background or bedding plant, and are unequalled in either use. Even though some of the colors are not brilliant, the flower heads are so immense that they may be seen from a distance.

Probably one of the oldest, but still an excellent variety is 'Pink Queen,' which will blend beautifully with lavender asters and white alyssum in a bed or border. It grows 3 to 4 feet tall, and bears huge trusses of bright pink flowers all summer.

ROOTING ANNUALS

Before your annuals are killed by frost, take cuttings, remove flowers and buds, dip the cuttings in a rooting compound, and plant them in vermiculite or a mixture of vermiculite and peat moss. When established, repot in standard potting soil, place in bright light, water and feed regularly. Pinch back the plants to keep them bushy. Begonia, coleus, fuchsia, impatiens, marigold, and portulaca are among the easier annuals to grow indoors by this method.

Cosmos

These summer-blooming plants go right on making flowers into the fall. They are graceful and especially good for cutting, growing from 3 to 15 feet tall, depending on the variety. The early-flowering types are an especially prized value where growing seasons are short.

All varieties are easy to grow, and will thrive in even light, poorly textured soil. They're nice for first-year gardeners who have not yet had time to build up a supply of compost. They will do well either in sun or partial shade. Sow out-of-doors after all danger of frost is past. Thin the seedlings so they are 24 inches apart. When the plant is about half-grown, pinch it back so it will form numerous side branches. This will make the plant bushier and more symmetrical, and the additional branches and shoots will also bear flowers.

Some of my favorite varieties include: 'Radiance,' with deep-rose flowers; 'Pink,' a nice shade of rose-pink; and 'White,' noted for its purity.

The 'Klondike' strain is a bright mixture of yellow, golden orange, and vermillion red. 'Sunset' bears semi-double flowers of bright vermillion red over a long period. It grows 3 feet tall.

HOUSEHOLD HINT

To make a natural moth repellent, mix together equal parts of dried sage, rosemary, and thyme leaves in a mixing bowl. Place half a handful of the mixture in a loosely woven cotton bag, and sew the bag shut. You can hang the bags in closets, or lay them in drawers among your clothes.

Dahlia

It is easy and fascinating to grow annual dahlias from seed. They should be sown directly in the garden in a spot that receives full sun, and has well-drained soil after all danger of frost is past. They can also be started in a coldframe for earlier bloom. Thin the seedlings so they stand 16 inches apart. Dahlias will start blooming in ten to twelve weeks, and continue right up to frost.

They are virtually disease- and pest-free. The plant will produce a small tuber which can be stored indoors during the winter, and replanted the following spring. However, new plants grown each year from seed are more satisfactory.

There are over 15,000 varieties of dahlias, available in a veritable rainbow of colors. They can grow from 6 to 20 feet tall with flowers that range from 3 inches in diameter to the size of dinner plates. The elvin 'Pompon' dahlias form bell-shaped flowers that come in a wide range of colors. Dwarf dahlias include varieties such as 'Coltness Single Mixed,' 'Sunburst Mixed,' and the extra-early 'Early Bird Mixture.' Tall, giant-flowered dahlias are cactus and decorative type dahlias. Remove the weakest stems.

SUPER GROWING SECRET

You can double your dahlias by cutting the shoots once they are 6" tall. Cut them 1" above the base. Stick them in a 50/50 mixture of light sand and compost, water, and place in a plastic bag in a dark location. In 4 to 6 weeks, they'll be ready to transplant into the garden!

Delphinium
(Larkspur)

Something you must always keep in mind when growing these lovely spikes is that larkspur is a cool-weather plant. It needs cold weather for germination, and also while the seedlings are young. Plant the seeds either in the fall or very early spring in a spot that gets full sun. It reseeds itself profusely year after year, so it's a good idea to plant it, if at all possible, where it can self-sow. The double varieties will eventually revert to single-flowered strains, but for the first year or two, you will have many doubles in many colors.

The 'Giant Imperial' grows 4 to 5 feet tall with long spikes of closely spaced dephinium-like flowers. The colors are azure blue, violet-purple, scarlet, and salmon. The 'Regal' strain inculdes pink, white, and rose. Both bloom in July.

Dianthus
(Pinks, Carnation)

Dainty, fragrant dianthus are among the most adorable little people of the flower kingdom, blooming from June to frost. Like so many annuals, their culture is a simple matter. Dianthus may be grown from seed or purchased as pot plants. They actually do best in poor soil with plenty of sun. Dianthus are considered to be half-hardy, and can be either sown right in the garden about the date of the last spring frost, or grown in a coldframe and transplanted. In some mild climates (or with adequate protection), they will overwinter, and the second-year plants will bloom very early. Thin seedlings so they stand 12 inches apart.

The 'Queen of Hearts,' an F1 hybrid of brilliant scarlet red, grows 12 to 15 inches tall. It is covered with blossoms, and will overwinter in most climates.

'Snowflake' is an outstanding dwarf single dianthus suitable for borders, edgings, mass beds, and pot culture. This new hybrid grows 6 to 8 inches tall with a spread of 12 inches. The serrated white flowers are 2 to 2-$\frac{1}{2}$ inches across.

'China Doll' has double flowers in clusters. The range of colors includes shades of crimson red, red and white, and salmon. The plants have heavy, attractive leaves and a compact, basal-branching habit.

Dianthus

Eschscholzia
(California Poppy)

This carefree, spring-flowering annual grows just 12 inches tall. Sow the seed in fall in well-drained soil where the plants are to bloom. This little sprite, who loves to nod in the wind, resents transplanting. Just stir the top of the soil to make it rough enough to hold the seeds, broadcast as evenly as possible, and you're all set!

DIVIDE DIANTHUS EVERY FEW YEARS AT WINTER'S END

The original California poppy, *E. aurantiaca*, has single, rich, bright yellow blossoms. Mission Bells have lovely double- and semi-double flowers, many with crinkled petals and picotee edges. Color combinations include rose and white, scarlet and yellow, orange and gold, pink and amber, as well as the usual solid colors.

Geranium

Chances are every gardener has enjoyed the clear, lively colors of geraniums in their own garden—planted in window boxes, pots, hanging baskets, or beds.

These popular plants have showy, bright flowers in clusters held proudly above handsome foliage. They're available in a range of leaf shapes and flower colors, including red, white, pink, salmon, and fuchsia. Geraniums are compatible with almost any plant; they can be mixed with perennials and other annuals for quick color additions, or grouped with other plants in container gardens.

There are many types of geraniums to choose from: zonal, ivy, scented-leaf, and Martha Washington. The zonal, or common geranium, is the most popular garden geranium, with many varieties and colors to choose from. Named for its interesting "zoned" leaf markings, it's subdivided into two categories determined by the method of propagation: cutting geraniums and seed geraniums.

FLOWER FACTS

For fall color, look for bedding plants that will tolerate cool temperatures and shorter days. Some tried-and-true annuals that perform notably well in fall gardens are:

Northern Gardens:—Calendula, Dianthus, Ornamental (flowering) Cabbage, Ornamental (flowering) Kale, Pansy, Snapdragon, Viola.

Southern Gardens:—Bellis, Dusty Miller, Lobelia, Marigold F1 Hybrid (African or American), Phlox, and Poppy.

In frost-free areas such as Phoeniz, Arizona or Bradenton, Florida, typical summer annuals such as petunias, gazania, and zinnias can be grown. In the Southeast, the pansy is by far the most popular annual for fall color.

🌼

Cutting geraniums are propagated vegetatively from stock plants, and are generally noted for their tall height, great, early-season floral display, and flower heads with large florets. They are usually considered early spring potted plants.

DESIGN TIPS

When using flowers of one color in large open areas, keep the following two points in mind:

(1) Dark-colored flowers offer a more interesting focal point than light-colored flowers when planted toward the rear of a landscape.

(2) When the background setting is especially dark due to shade of a canopy or dark colored foliage, light-colored flowers add more contrast.

When combining colors in beds and borders, it's helpful to know that dark colors recede while light colors pop out. For this reason, you may want to allocate two to three times the space for dark flowers, such as deep red geraniums, bronze-leaved pink begonias or red zinnias, and one-third of the space for light colored flowers, such as pastel shades of petunias and impatiens, white alyssum, white salvia or dusty miller.

Seed, or hybrid, geraniums are grown from seed by commercial growers. They tend to be shorter than cutting geraniums, with beautiful flowers that last throughout the growing season. These plants are heat-resistant, and thrive in summer and early fall when many other garden plants have begun to decline. Since their introduction in 1965, seed geraniums have become true bedding plants. Available as small plants, seed geraniums can be used like petunias in mass plantings.

Whichever type you decide to grow, buying small bedding plants will give your garden colorful blooms early in the season. Start with healthy plants that have well-developed, dark green foliage. Bedding plant labels provide lots of information, so be sure to read them before you buy. The chosen location should provide at least five to six hours of full sun each day. If you cannot plant on the day of purchase, water thoroughly, and place them in the shade. Evenings or cloudy days are the best times to plant any bedding plant.

To prepare your flower bed, spade to a depth of 6 to 8 inches; loosen heavy clay or clay-loam soils by adding peat moss, ground bark, or compost. Fertilize with 2 pounds of 5-10-5 or one pound 10-10-10 fertilizer per 100 square feet. Turn the soil over, and rake smooth. For containers, fill the pots or window boxes with lightly moistened commercial potting soil. Do not use straight field or garden soil, since it may drain poorly and contain insects, disease, or weed seeds.

When planting, remove each geranium from its container with the root ball intact. Plants not in individual containers should be gently separated to retain as much soil around the roots as possible. Set them 12 to 14 inches apart. Water thoroughly immediately after planting, and then whenever the soil feels dry. Water early in the day, soaking at ground level; sprinkling the foliage isn't enough and may lead to disease problems.

Maintain geraniums by cutting off faded blooms to encourage more flowers, and by pinching the long stems occasionally to keep the plant compact and bushy.

In window boxes, containers, and gardens, the popular, showy geranium outshines and outblooms many other sun-loving plants. No matter how they're used, versatile geraniums add a bold accent to any garden setting!

Heliotropium
(Heliotrope)

This 30-inch tall plant is topped by huge (one foot in diameter) flower clusters in early summer. Best of all, it's very fragrant. 'Blue Bonnet' is the deepest blue. 'Marine,' a 2-foot-tall, semi-dwarf strain, has giant umbels of pure dark violet. Seeds may be sown in pots of sandy, well-drained soil in full sun in early spring, and then transplanted into the garden.

Heliotrope

Impatiens

Step outdoors to the shimmering colors of impatiens in those shady spots this year. Impatiens is the botanical name for the popular and pretty old-fashioned flower often called Busy Lizzie and sultana. Few other bedding plants bloom with so little sunlight; no other bedding plant offers the glowing, luminescent colors of impatiens.

Their radiant colors range from cool white to lavender-rose, intense pinks to brilliant orange-reds. 'Harlequin' bicolor flowers add spice to the sunshine-in-shade of impatiens. The 'New Guinea' hybrid impatiens add attractively variegated leaves, too; plant these hybrids in partial shade, since they need more sunlight than their shade-loving cousins.

Impatiens grow into colorful mounds that bloom all summer long. They come in several heights, from 8 inches up to 20 inches tall. The shorter ones make fine edging, hanging basket, or small-container plants; use taller impatiens for larger bedding displays.

It's best to wait until the weather has settled on the warm side of spring before planting impatiens. They are tender plants that grow fast in warm, hot weather. Ready-to-plant impatiens are available in spring and summer at your garden center. The young plants are offered in flats, trays, or peat or plastic pots.

Before transplanting impatiens to your garden or outdoor planters, condition them by placing the flats or pots

YOU CAN RAIN ON THEIR PARADE

The only thing undemanding impatiens require from you is water. Keep the soil moist, but avoid overwatering. Impatiens are one of the most rain-tolerant annuals. They thrive on rain and moisture. Rain doesn't harm impatiens' blooms, which is one of the reasons why the flowers always look fresh, new, and vibrant.

Impatiens have succulent stems which quickly signal their water needs. But don't wait for wilting stems and limp leaves because the continued stress of water deprivation will weaken plants. Impatiens may wilt temporarily if they're exposed to the direct midday sun. These plants, however, do not require more water if the soil is moist.

outdoors in a shady spot during the day; bring them in to the garage at night if it's going to be cool. And be sure to water them every day; plants in small containers have a tendency to dry out rapidly.

Impatiens are adaptable plants, not caring unduly about the type of soil in which you plant them, provided it's well-drained. To give them the best start in your garden, dig the ground to a depth of 6 to 8 inches. Work in plenty of organic matter such as peat moss, leaf mold, or compost; add perlite or ground bark to improve drainage where the soil is heavy and compacted.

You may need to replace the exhausted and root-laden soil under established trees with a fresh supply from elsewhere in the garden, or with a commercial soil mix. For hanging baskets, window boxes, and planters, use equal volumes of potting soil, peat moss, and coarse sand or perlite; or buy a ready-prepared mixture for your containers.

As you dig or mix the soil, add some 5-10-5 fertilizer at the recommended rate—about 2 pounds per 100 square feet— to boost fertility levels for your impatiens. Feed 'New Guniea' impatiens every month with my All Season Green-Up Tonic to maintain their vibrant colors. As growth slows in late summer, all impatiens will benefit from an extra shot of fertilizer.

Transplant impatiens in the late afternoon or evening, or on a cloudy day, so that the new plants aren't immediately subjected to full noonday heat. Carefully separate the plants from one another and from their containers. The stems are brittle, so handle them gently. Space impatiens 12 inches apart. Plants grown in peat pots can be set in the prepared ground, pot and all, but be sure to cover the whole peat pot with soil, folding under the top rim that rises above soil level. If the top of the pot rises above the soil, the pot will act as a wick—drawing moisture away from the plant's roots.

Water well to settle the transplanted roots into their new home. Check every few days, and water again when the soil starts to dry out.

IMPATIENS

WILL BLOOM

YEAR ROUND

IN FROST-

FREE AREAS

Your colorful impatiens will blossom and flourish all summer long in the shade and even in moderate sunshine if you give them enough water. At the end of summer, dig up your favorite ones and replant in pots—or take cuttings—for indoor decoration.

Lathyrus Odoratus
(Sweet Pea)

If I were awarding prizes for the best annuals, I would certainly say that those pretty dancing girls, the sweet peas, deserved one of the best. Though most can't bear the hot summer weather, sweet peas are a spring and summer delight. Many think them temperamental, but this is not really true if you understand their requirements which vary in different sections of the country.

Sweet Pea

Here are a few tricks worth knowing. First, of course, it goes without saying that for the climbing varieties you must provide support—wire or even thin shrubs or climbing roses. Planted on the latter, they won't be noticeable when they start to die back in the heat of the summer, leaving, as they would, a bare spot at a time when it is difficult to start something else.

HOME REMEDY

To relieve the burning of sunburn, windburn, or sunstroke after a long day in the garden, soak a hand towel in a cool garlic tea (chopped cloves in boiling water, simmer for 5 minutes, cover, and steep for 45 minutes), wring out the excess liquid, and apply it to the affected area.

Leave the towel on for about 20 minutes. Repeat with a fresh, cool garlic compress until relief is obtained.

Those of you who live in the South and have heavy clay soil should be especially careful to lighten it up with sand and compost. Northern gardeners with light loam or sandy soil will need to do very little soil preparation when sowing in the early spring; it can be done as soon as the soil starts to warm up. Southern or southwestern gardeners are best served if they grow their plants through the winter to obtain earlier flowers. October is a good month in which to plant the seeds. Sow the seeds in a spot that gets full sun. When the seedlings get big enough, thin them to stand 6 inches apart.

There are a number of frilly-skirted beauties, in almost any color, from which to choose:

The 'Galaxy' strain produces many-flowered giant sweet peas which will create a lovely massed effect. Each stem usually carries 5 to 7 well-formed, well-placed, fragrant flowers.

Other varieties include Burpee's 'Giant Spencer' sweet peas, which come into bloom after the spring-flowering type, thus extending the blooming period. They have large, long-lasting flowers.

'Knee-Hi' sweet peas are early, large-flowered and heat-resistant. With this variety, staking is not necessary.

'Little Sweetheart' makes small, compact, bushy mounds only 8 inches high. These minis are covered with ruffled blossoms.

'Bijou' sweet peas are a delight because of their low growing habit. They may be used in borders, beds, and window boxes and make excellent cut flowers. The profusion of flowers produced literally covers the foliage. The plants grow only a foot tall, but produce 4 to 5 ruffled pretties on each 5- to 7-inch stem.

If you are feeling patriotic and would like some majorettes, try the 'Americanas.' This class of sweet peas grows only 18 inches tall. They can be grown without staking, but if they are used as bedding plants, they may be trained on 3-foot stakes. The summer-flowering 'Americanas' do better than the 'Bijous' in eastern gardens, and will

SWEET PEA SOIL SECRETS

Here is a good recipe for preparing the soil for sweet peas. Dig a special 2-foot trench (it may be quite a narrow one), and move the soil to a low spot you want to fill in somewhere else.

Now make a mixture of one part soil, one part peat moss, and one part sharp sand. To each bushel of this mixture, add 2 ounces of bone meal, $1/5$ ounce of potassium sulphate, and $1\text{-}1/2$ ounces of super phosphate. For areas that are not alkaline, add 4 ounces of ground dolomite limestone and 3 ounces of ground chalk limestone. With soil preparation like this, you will get earlier and far superior results. For sustained performance, try one of the foliage fertilizers that is suitable for sweet peas and fairly low in nitrogen.

FOUR-O'-

CLOCKS

ATTRACT

AND POISON

JAPANESE

BEETLES;

THEY'RE

TOXIC TO

HUMANS

AS WELL

Mirabilis

flower longer. They are vigorous and prolific and, yes, these American beauties of the sweet pea world do come in red, white, and blue.

Mirabilis Jalapa
(Four-O'Clock)

Here's a comical fellow for you—a late, late, sleeper who refuses to get out of bed until four o'clock in the afternoon! Once open, however, he remains that way quite a while into the evening, and the blooms are abundant. This is a tuberous-rooted annual that is available in many colors. It grows 2 to 3 feet tall, blooming in June north of the Mason-Dixon line, and a little earlier further south. It develops best in the warmth of summer, planted in full sun to part shade. The name "mirabilis" means "wonderful" and refers to the color of the flowers. Sow the seed directly into the garden in spring.

'Jingles' is a mixture of striped colors of yellow, red, white, pink, and salmon. It is a bit on the dwarf side, and well branched. 'Petticoat,' 3 feet tall, has a flower-in-flower effect. It is a lovely rose color. The little gnomes are well represented by the 'Pygmy' mixture, which grows just 20 inches tall, and comes in many magnificent colors.

Phlox Drummondii
(Annual Phlox)

Here's an easy one for the beginner that's beautiful enough for the experienced gardener as well. No other flower can surpass its brilliant colors—reds, yellows, pinks, and whites. It is obliging enough to thrive and grow in a sunny location in almost any type of soil. When seedlings get big enough, thin so they stand 18 inches apart.

Annual phlox begin to bloom in early summer and continue until fall if the faded flowers are removed. It's great for bedding, borders, edgings, and cutting, growing 10 to 20 inches tall.

Portulaca

Often called moss rose or sun plant *(P. grandiflora)*, this is one of the very best annuals for a brilliant and continuous display of color—pink, red, white, yellow, and orange—over a long season, starting in early spring. Portulaca is great for rock gardens, growing 4 to 6 inches tall, but it will grow in almost any well-drained soil. Try using it between stepping stones.

Portulaca has a lot going for it, but you must not expect everything—it doesn't work at all as a cut flower.

Sow its seeds in a place that gets full sun. Thin seedlings so they stand 10 inches apart.

Portulaca

Scabiosa
(Pincushion Flower)

The old varieties of scabiosa were not particularly attrative, but the hybridizers, who just can't seem to leave anything alone, went to work on this ugly duckling and have come a long way toward turning it into a swan.

The 'Giant Imperial' is tall, with double, ball-shaped flowers 2-$\frac{1}{2}$ to 3 inches across. The blossoms are made up of broad, wavy petals without the usual pincushion center. The 'Dwarf-Doubles' are pretty, compact, rounded, free-blooming plants, with flowers that are up to 1-$\frac{1}{2}$ inches across.

Plant scabiosa seeds about the date of the last frost in a spot that receives full sun and has well-drained soil. Cover the seed with $\frac{1}{8}$ inch of soil. Once they germinate, they can be thinned or transplanted. Scabiosa is usually insect- and disease-free.

THUG BUSTERS

Let your flowers chase the bugs away: the most common good neighbor, thug-busting plants are marigolds, asters, nasturtiums, and mums. Plant some around your garden this year, and see if they don't keep the bugs away.

Verbena

Verbena, or vervain, is a deliciously fragrant flower in bloom from summer till frost. Fine for beds or borders, this little creeper will make a beautiful garden anywhere it's planted. The impish blossoms, available in white and shades of red and pink, are borne on terminal shoots which raise their perky heads 6 to 7 inches off the ground. The flower clusters are about 2 inches across, each composed of a dozen or more tiny florets.

Verbenas love the sun, but they will grow in partial shade. They will grow quickly and easily when the seed is planted directly in the garden after the last spring frost. Cover the seed lightly with about $1/8$ inch of soil.

Verbena

Give verbenas plenty of growing room; 10 square inches of space is about average for most plants. In mild climates, the plants, if given a light mulch, will sometimes live over the winter.

'Sparkle' is a dwarf, compact strain; varieties available are 'Crystal,' white; 'Delight,' coral; 'Splendor,' royal purple; and 'Dazzle,' red.

'Amethyst' is that lovely and much sought after shade of medium-blue. The 8- to 12-inch plants are very dwarf and compact.

Finally, there are the giant-flowered varieties, 'Ruffled Pink' and 'Ruffled White.' These are the multiflora gigantea type which bear semi-double, ruffled flower clusters 3 inches across.

GREEN THUMB TIP

Annuals don't like manure, and neither should you. Manure contains a lot of nitrogen, which produces too many leaves, too many stems, and too few flowers. So if you're going to use manure in your annual flower beds, make sure that it has aged (dried) for at least two years. By that time, some of the potency of the nitrogen will have dissipated.

Viola

(Pansy, Violet)

These are the real court jesters of the garden. Both flowers are so similar in culture that I will treat them together. Pansies succeed best in fairly rich, well-drained soil in the sun. They produce their finest flowers in the cool, early days of spring.

Keep the flowers picked, and the plants pinched back during the summer to produce new growth and flowers in the early fall. Seeds may be sown outdoors when the soil warms up. For earlier blooms, start seed indoors or in a greenhouse eight weeks before your usual outdoor planting time. When the seedlings are big enough, thin so they stand 10 inches apart.

In mild climates, pansies will not winter-kill. Even in colder climates, they may winter over if given some protection, such as leaves or hay.

Pansies come in all sorts of giant strains, and many, many different colors. They bloom so profusely that you will be doing them a real service if you pick them often—very often. Enjoy their funny "little old man" faces indoors.

PANSIES ARE COOL

Cold resistant—It's a term used to describe the first annuals we can plant in the spring, and those that will survive the nippy days of autumn. These annuals are also used for winter plantings along the Pacific Coast and in the Gulf States.

Pansies head the list. They are hardy and available in early spring in much of the country—even ready for late fall planting in the mildest climates. If you haven't raised pansies for several years, take a look at the newest hybrids—larger flowers and more of them, in clear pastels or rich, dark colors. Pansies come in single colors, with blotched faces and even tri-colors.

❀2❀

PERENNIALS
Year-After-Year Favorites

PERENNIALS

ARE A

LITTLE

INVESTMENT

WITH A

BIG RETURN!

For the life of me, I cannot understand why most new home gardeners have not discovered the advantages of using perennials in their flowering gardenscape. The initial investment of purchasing a perennial is but a few cents more than the cost of a packet of unusual flower seeds, and in some cases, no more than a single tomato plant.

Perennials can continue as a member of your garden virtually for life—yours! I have mums that are over twenty years old; a nice return on my initial purchase of $1.29—oh, and I almost forgot: I have traded, given away, or sold over 700 daughter plants from this same plant.

Perennials come in every color, shape, and height imaginable, and can be used for borders, dividers, backdrops, or solid beds. Perennials, however, tend to be rather complacent, and not much shakes them up, whether it be unexpected changes in the weather, a marauding band of bugs, or an overflight of disease spores. It has been said that if perennials were people, they would be considered to have low self-esteem, since they're always playing second fiddle to the flashier shrubs. I disagree. The perennials in my garden have always known that they were tops, and I couldn't get along without them!

DEVELOPING A BUDDING FRIENDSHIP

Their Part

If you know what to expect from each other—I mean you and your perennials—then your flowering friendship will last for years and years to come. Here's what they bring to the table:

1. Perennials are either flowering or foliage plants whose roots live from year to year. Depending on their variety, their tops may or may not die back in the winter.

2. Perennials give color to the garden in a shady spot and in front of shrubs. They can be colorful in spring, and throughout the growing season.

3. Some perennials flower the first year, but all need protection from drying winter winds. You can grow them as annuals, and eliminate the problem of protecting them in the winter.

4. Perennials usually will not flower unless they develop to a certain size, are exposed to low temperatures for a number of weeks, and then exposed to increasing day lengths and increasing temperatures. Their flowering time is the result of this sequence of day length and temperature.

A PLACE FOR EVERY PERENNIAL!

❀ Soggy spot—Marsh Marigolds

❀ Steep bank—Trailing Periwinkles

❀ Shade—Hostas

❀ Hot climate—Yuccas

❀ Cool climate—Delphiniums

❀ Height—Hollyhocks

❀ Foolproof—Daylilies

Your Part

Oh, yeah! This is a two-way street. If you expect your perennials to bloom from spring through fall, year after year, then you've got to perform a chore or two to ensure their comfort. Here's what you should keep in mind when you embark on this relationship:

1. Prepare the soil in your flower beds thoroughly.

2. Start with vigorous plants or seeds. The best plan is to buy started plants. Next best is to sow fresh seeds where you want the plants to grow. Usually, the least satisfactory plan is to start your own plants indoors because the seeds need the outdoor elements to best stimulate growth.

SEEDLINGS ARE BEST—GIVE THEM "ELBOW ROOM"

3. Set out plants or sow seeds at the recommended times. Plants set out too early may be killed by frost. Seeds will not germinate until the soil warms—and, if sown too early, they may rot. Early spring growth, however, is important for the survival of many perennials.

4. Provide the recommended distances between plants when thinning seedlings or setting out already started plants. Proper spacing is absolutely necessary for the fullest development of the plants.

5. Do not plant annuals that grow wildly in the same bed with perennials; they will crowd out the perennials.

6. Let the perennials stand out. Give them a background to show off against. Evergreens or wooden fences work very well.

Delphinium

7. Perennials are not maintenance-free plants; they are low-maintenance plants. Replanting, dividing old plants, and regularly improving their soil are essential for vigorous, flowering plants in your garden.

❀

FLOWER BEDS DON'T ALL HAVE TO BE <u>CIRCLES</u> & SQUARES

It Pays To Plan Ahead

In most cases, most home gardeners have a limited amount of time to spend in their gardens because of their busy lifestyles. So, before you stop in at the local garden center, look over the area you plant to landscape thoroughly—<u>very thoroughly</u>! Plan your garden, beds, or borders on paper first; graph paper works well. A rough drawing will do—you don't need to call in a landscape architect. And be very conservative; remember, one tiny little plant can spread out amazingly in a year or so, occupying all its own space, and maybe sneaking a little more from somebody else.

IT DEPENDS ON YOUR POINT OF VIEW

Place beds or borders where they can be readily seen and admired. Try to locate them in areas of high visibility, such as the front yard, near windows, the porch, or patio, while keeping in mind other factors such as soil type, drainage, pH, and light.

Also consider that certain trees, such as black walnut, produce a chemical in their roots that is toxic to many plants. Locate susceptible plants a minimum of 60 feet from such trees. Perennials with shallow root systems are less likely to be affected. Some trees, such as red maples, have a shallow root system, and will compete with nearby perennials for moisture.

Make Your Bed!

If you plan to do most of the gardening chores yourself, you will want your beds conveniently arranged. Don't make them too wide. A bed 6 to 8 feet long will allow for a wide variety of plants, some to bloom early, others in mid-season, and still others late in the year. Arrange your plants so you have a continuous display of color all season long.

Since most of the tall perennials flower in late summer or early fall, they should be in the back of the border, with the smaller ones placed toward the front. Don't exclude the tall plants from the middle—a few placed here and there will help avoid monotony, and make for a more interesting planting. "Tall" plants are those which usually grow to a height of 3 feet or more at maturity. The middle of the bed should consist primarily of plants that are 2 to 3 feet tall; these, for the most part, flower in mid-summer. The shortest plants, the spring-flowering ones which usually grow 2 feet tall or less, should occupy the front of the bed.

Look At Those Curves!

I think curved-line plantings are far more graceful and interesting than long, straight beds. Open areas of lawn provide nice contrast. Make your rough sketch fairly large. You can open up a big, brown paper sack if you have nothing else to draw on. Then use something to help you envision what the border will look like when it is planted. An old nursery or seed catalog that shows the various perennials you have in mind can help. Cut out the pictures, and place them on your diagram.

Move the pictures around until you feel they are pleasingly placed. They will be much easier to move now, on paper, then after the real McCoys have been planted and you decide they should have gone elsewhere. As you clip the pictures, jot down the information on each one—height, color, time of bloom, and growth habits.

Get The Big Picture

Consider all of your permanent fixtures, such as outbuildings, the garage, walls, walks, fences, and service yards that you will need to plan around. Some of these may be enhanced by perennial plantings, while you may want to partially screen others. Select perennials that are native or seem suited to your particular area. Notice what grows well in local gardens, consult nursery people, check with your state extension bureau, and choose those you find most attractive. The plants we discuss in this chapter will do well in most areas of the United States.

JOT DOWN PERTINENT INFO— HEIGHT, COLOR, BLOOM, & GROWTH HABIT

75

PERENNIALS FOR ALL PURPOSES

For Sunny Borders	
Under 12" (Edgings)	
Alyssum, Basket of Gold	Dicentra, Bountiful
Arabis alpina fl. pl.	Gaillardia, Dwarf
Artemisia, Silver Mound	Iberis sempervirens
Aster, Hardy Dwarf	Iris pumila
Campanula, Wedgewood	Phlox subulata
Chrysanthemum, Cushion	Platycodon mariesi
12" to 30"	
Chrysanthemum	Peony
Gaillardia	Pyrethrum
Geum, Lady Strathenden	Rudbeckia, Gold Sturm
Gypsophila	Shasta Daisy
Heuchera	Tritoma
Monarda	Veronica, Crater Lake
30" and Up (Backgrounds)	
Achillea, Coronation Gold	Hibiscus
Aster, Hardy Tall	Liatris, September Glory
Baptisia, False Indigo	Lupine, Russell Hybrids
Campanula, Brantwood	Phlox, Tall Border
Delphinium, Hybrids	Physostegia
Hemerocallis, Daylilies	Yucca

For Light Shade	
Ajuga	Helleborus (Lenten Rose)
Aquilegia (Columbine)	Heuchera
Astilbe	Hosta
Bleeding Heart, Old-fashioned	Primrose
Epimedium	Pulmonaria, Mrs. Moon
Fern	Trollius

PERENNIALS FOR ALL PURPOSES

For Poor (Light) Soil

Achillea	Lavender
Artemisia	Liatris
Catananche	Penstemon
Coreopsis	Sempervium and Sedum
Gaillardia	Spiderwort
Gypsophila	

For Cut Flowers

Achillea	Peony
Chrysanthemum	Pyrethrum
Delphinium	Shasta Daisy
Gaillardia	Statice
Gypsophila	Tritoma
Lily-of-the-Valley	Trollius

For Fragrance

Carnation	Peony
Dianthus, Old Spice	Phlox
Lily-of-the-Valley	Violet

For Rock Gardens

Alyssum, Basket-of-Gold	Dwarf Iris
Arabis	Epimedium
Campanula, Wedgewood	Moss Phlox
Cerastium (Snow-in-Summer)	Sempervium and Sedum
Dianthus, Tiny Rubies	

SPRINKLE

ASHES

AROUND

DELPHINIUMS

TO

DISCOURAGE

SLUGS

PERENNIALS FOR ALL PURPOSES

MUMS ARE

NATIVES OF

CHINA AND

JAPAN, FIRST

CULTIVATED

IN 500 B.C.

For Waterside (Damp But Not Wet)

Aconitum	Japanese Iris
Astilbe	Lobelia, Cardinal Flower
Cypripedium	Lythrum
Gentian	Thalictum
Helenium	Trollius
Hibiscus	

For Wild Borders

Anemone pulsatilla	Sanguinaria (Bloodroot)
Aquilegia canadensis	Tiarella
Cimicifuga	Trillium
Cypripedium pubescens	Violet
Fern	Yucca
Forget-Me-Not	

For Foliage Colors

Ajuga metallica	Pulmonaria, Mrs. Moon
Apple Mint	Ruta Blue Beauty
Artemisia	Sage (purple and green)
Chrysanthemum	Variegated Grasses
Hosta	

Continuous Blooms Throughout Growing Season

Aster frikarti	Dicentra, Bountiful
Campanula, Wedgewood	Gaillardia
Dianthus, Allwood Hybrid	Wonder of Staffia

Once you have a general design, you can gradually work toward your goal. Stagger your purchases over a period of time, even a year or two if need be. While you are waiting to buy the more expensive plants, fill in with bulbs and annuals.

Edge Your Bed

Non-living Edges

Down through the ages, gardeners have used various means to establish a line of demarcation between lawn and flower beds, using stone, brick, and wood. The best answer I have found to fix this problem is a strip of metal set flush with the grade; it is neat, clean, and unobtrusive, plus you can run your lawn mower over it.

Live Edges

For curved beds, I like the looks of living edges. **Daylilies** are a wonderful choice; their flexible, arching foliage is easy to mow under.

> ## LAYING OUT A PERENNIAL BED
>
> **I**f you want a straight-edged bed, simply drive small stakes into the ground at the corners, and stretch a string between them.
>
> For a curved edge, mark the shape you want with your garden hose. Then dig out the grass with a sharp edging tool.
>
>

Another good living edging is liriope, sometimes called **lilyturf,** which is an evergreen perennial that grows easily in full sun or deep shade, and is not particular about soil requirements. Liriope has flowers similar to those of grape hyacinth, but larger. These are borne abundantly in late summer, and are followed by polished blackberries. Mature plants grow about one foot tall, and have a spread just as wide. Liriope is propagated by dividing the clumps immediately after flowering.

Perennial **candytuft**, which grows only about a foot tall when in bloom, is another excellent choice for edging. As soon as the blooms fade, it can be cut down to a 6-inch height. While full sun is preferable, it will also grow reasonably well in half shade.

The lovely herbaceous perennial **thrift** *(Armeria maritima)*, or **sea pink** *(Armeria alpina)*, is exceptionally valuable for edging use, especially in sandy soils. It is an evergreen, and it looks good year-round. The foliage is delicate and grass-like in texture, and the deep rose-pink flower heads are borne on 6-inch tall stalks in the spring.

PERENNIALS FOR PROBLEM AREAS

Here's a quick, handy reference you can use to fill in those troublesome spots in your yard.

Wet Areas
Iris sibirica
Lythrum salicaria
Viola odorata

Fertile Soil
Astilbe
Chrysanthemum
Delphinium

Rocky Areas
Aquilegia
Armeria maritima
Aurinia saxatilis

Dry Areas
Achillea
Asclepias tuberosa

Infertile Soil
Asclepias tuberosa
Baptisia australis

For Naturalizing
Ajuga
Asclepias tuberosa
Cerastium tomentosum
Ferns
Grasses
Helianthus x multiflorus
Heuchera sanguinea
Tradescantia x andersoniana
Viola odorata
Wild Flowers

Low Plants
Artemisia
Dianthus

Shade
Astilbe
Heuchera sanguinea
Hosta

Tall Plants
Alcea rosea
Hibiscus moscheutos

PERENNIALS HATE A LUMPY BED

Get Them Ready For Bed

Proper soil preparation is extremely important to perennials. Annuals can grow and flower in poor soil, but perennials seldom survive more than a year or two if their beds are not properly prepared.

Properly prepared beds will have—

✓ **Good drainage**

✓ **Protection from drying winds**

✓ **Adequate water in the summer**

If you prepare beds carefully—by spading deeply, providing adequate drainage, and lightening heavy soil with sand and organic matter—the flowers grown there are almost certain to be outstanding. Water can enter well-prepared soil easily. Seed germinates readily; the plants grow deep healthy roots, strong stems, with late and abundant flowers. And the benefits of careful soil preparation carry over from season to season.

For new beds, begin preparing the soil in the fall before planting time.

Put Your Soil To The Test

Before preparation, test the soil's capacity for water absorption—your plants should never be under stress, either for lack of water or because of an overabundance thereof. To test the soil, dig a hole about 10 inches deep, and fill it with water. The next day, fill the hole with water again, and see how long the water remains in the hole. If the water drains away within ten hours, the permeability of the soil is sufficient for good growth.

81

Raise The Bed Up

If an appreciable amount of water remains in the hole after ten hours, it will be necessary to improve the drainage of the planting site; otherwise, water will saturate your prepared flower bed, prevent proper development of roots, and drown your plants!

To improve drainage, bed up the soil. By that, I mean to dig furrows along the sides of the bed, and add the soil from the furrows to the bed. This raises the bed above the general level of the soil. Excess water can then drain from the bed into the furrows.

You may find gullies in raised beds after heavy rains. You can prevent this by supporting the beds with wooden or masonry walls, making, in effect, raised planters of the beds.

The downside is that raised beds dry out more quickly than ground level ones; little moisture will move up into the bed from the soil below. So, you must be sure to water beds frequently during the summer.

A Run Of Spades

After you make your beds or determine that the soil's drainage is satisfactory without bedding it up, spade the soil to a depth of 8 to 10 inches. Turn the soil over completely. When spading, remove any branches, large stones, or trash, but turn under all leaves, grass, stems, roots, and anything else that will decay easily. This will provide nutrients for the young plants to grow on.

DON'T LET THE WEEDS WORRY YOU!

You must eliminate all weeds during this initial soil preparation period before plants are added or seeds are sown. Numerous problems arise when perennial weeds, such as bindweed or crabgrass, grow through a carefully planted bed. Due to the diversity among perennials, it is risky to chemically treat weeds in close proximity to valuable plantings. It may be possible, however, to treat individual weeds with an herbicide recommended for use on perennials.

The best course of action is to work the bed for one year before planting, so that all weed seedlings are killed as the seeds germinate.

Respade the soil 3 or 4 times during the fall at weekly intervals. If the soil is drying between spadings, water it with my Soil Prep Mix. As the weeds grow, pull them up before they get a chance to set seed.

In the spring, just before planting, spade again. At this spading, you should work peat moss, sand, fertilizer, and lime into the soil. For ordinary garden soil, incorporate a one-inch layer of peat moss and a one-inch layer of unwashed sand—both are available from building supply stores. If your soil is heavy clay, use twice this amount of peat and sand. Also at this time, saturate the soil once again with my Soil Prep Mix. By doing this, and adding peat and sand to the soil each time you reset the plants, you can eventually transform even poor subsoil into good garden loam. If you prefer, you can use well-rotted compost instead of the peat moss.

SOIL PREP MIX

1 can of beer,
1 can of regular cola,
$^1/_2$ cup of liquid dish soap, and
$^1/_2$ cup of chewing tobacco juice
applied with your 20 gallon hose-end sprayer.

Add A Twist Of Fertilizer And Lime

In order to determine how much fertilizer and lime you need, have your soil tested. Your state extension bureau will do this for you, and make the appropriate recommendations. Tell them that you are planning to grow flowers in the soil. Make sure you allow sufficient time to send in your sample, and get back the results in time for your planting.

For ordinary garden-type soil, I want you to add a complete fertilizer such as 5-10-5 at the last spading. Apply it at a rate of 1-$^1/_2$ pounds (3 rounded cups) per 100 square feet of bed area. Add ground limestone at a rate of 5 pounds (7 rounded cups) per 100 square feet. Then rake the soil surface smooth.

TO SEED OR NOT TO SEED— THAT IS THE QUESTION

The Fastest Way—Buy Seedlings

You can buy many perennial plants from your local nursery or garden shop. These plants usually are in bloom when they are offered for sale, which allows you to select the colors you want for your garden.

Here are a few of my buying tips:

Tip #1—Buy perennial plants that are compact in size and dark green in color. Plants sold in warm shopping areas are seldom vigorous. You can tell which plants were held in warm areas too long by their thin, pale yellow stems and leaves. Do not buy these plants.

Tip #2—Buy named varieties. Named varieties are most useful in the garden—useful because we know their disease resistance, their heat and cold tolerance, and their plant habit (height, color, and branching) since they are bred to have specific characteristics. They are the backbone of a good perennial garden. Named varieties are available most everywhere in the United States.

Put 'Em To Bed Quickly

Probably more plants have lost their lives because of delayed planting than because of all of the insect infestations and diseases put together. Plants that are mail-ordered, no matter how carefully they are wrapped, usually have two strikes against them due to the vagaries of mail delivery: their package has probably been crushed

TIMELY TONIC

To get your flowers off to a great start, mix:

4 cups of bone meal,
2 cups of gypsum,
2 cups of Epsom salts,
1 cup of wood ashes,
1 cup of lime,
1 tsp. of baking powder, and
4 tsp. of baby powder in a
bucket of dry peat moss.

Put a little bit of this mixture in the soil when planting perennials.

or traumatized by other, heavier packages during their journey; and in all likelihood, they have probably been stored in a close, warm room for many hours. So get them into the ground without delay. As a matter of fact, do this regardless of whether a local nursery delivers them to your home, or you buy them at a garden center, supermarket, or nursery. Don't let them languish in the back of your car—hot, tired, and thirsty!

Take Off Their Clothes And Give 'Em A Bath

Perennial wrappings can differ greatly. Some can be individually clothed in paper and moss, others in plastic pots or six-packs, and still others loose and bare-rooted. Here's what you should do to prepare them for their new home:

❁ Plant the individually-wrapped plants first, following your garden plan as you go to ensure you are planting them where you want them. A cloudy, humid day is always best for planting. Keep this in mind when you go out shopping for plants, or are ordering them from a local nursery. Always be sure to avoid exposing plants to drying winds when you plant them.

❁ To remove seedlings from flats, slice downward in the soil between the plants. Lift out each plant with a block of soil surrounding its roots, and set the soil back in a planting hole.

❁ When setting out plants in peat pots, remove the top edge of the pot to keep rain from collecting around the plant. Thoroughly moisten the pot and its contents to help the roots develop properly. Set the moistened pot in the planting hole and press the soil up around it. The pot will break down in the soil and improve the soil around the plant.

Whatever you do, I want you to drench the soil around the planting hole with a mixture of **1 tbsp. of Vitamin B-1 Plant Starter and 1 tbsp. of Shampoo per gallon of water** to stimulate root growth.

CLOUDY

DAYS

ARE

BEST FOR

PLANTING

PLANTING RHIZOMES

Rhizome

Soil mound

When planting most perennials, you should dig a hole a little wider than the plant and only as deep as it stood in its pot. For rhizome-rooted plants, such as irises, plant them with their roots below the surface of the ground, and the rhizome just on the surface. To do this effectively, dig a hole wide enough to accommodate the long rhizome, and then build up a little mound in the center. Set the rhizome on this so it will be about even with the surface of the surrounding bed. Let the roots hang downward, and cover them with soil, packing it down carefully. The rhizome-rooted plants must feel the kiss of the warm sun or they will not bloom well.

Plants which grow from a central crown should be planted with this crown just at the dirt line—much as you plant strawberries.

Allow plenty of space between plants because perennials need lots of elbow room to develop. Perennials usually show up and off when planted in clumps of the same variety.

Secrets To Starting From Seed

Many perennials do not grow true to type from seed, especially those harvested from cultivated, or named, varieties. You will have much better luck propagating these perennials from leaf cuttings or by dividing clumps.

Certain perennials, however, are best grown from seed each year. Many of the biennials—perennials that flower in their second year of growth—are grown only from seed; these include columbine, foxglove, hollyhocks, canterbury bells, sweet Williams, and delphiniums.

You can sow perennial seeds directly in the beds where the plants are to bloom, or you can start plants indoors early in spring, and set them out in beds after the weather warms.

Seed Buying Secrets

Be sure your seed is fresh. Do not buy it too far in advance of planting; for the best results, allow no more than a three-month interval. Old seed saved from previous years may lose much of its vitality when stored under fluctuating household temperatures and humidity levels. It also tends to germinate slowly and produce poor seedlings. Keep your seed cool and dry until you plant it. Special instructions for storage are usually printed on seed packets; make sure you follow them.

When buying seed, look for new varieties listed as F1 hybrids—they are widely available and are beginning to show up in perennials. The seed for these hybrids cost more than the seed for the usual inbred varieties, but its superiority makes it worth the extra price. These F1 hybrids are produced by crossing selected inbred parents. Plants of F1 varieties are more uniform in size and more vigorous than plants of inbred varieties and they produce more flowers.

Sowing Secrets

Don't be in a rush to start seeds or to set out started plants. As a general rule, delay sowing seed outdoors or

SOW

SEED IN

VERMICULITE

FILLED

FURROWS

GREEN THUMB TIP

If you put chemical fertilizer in the soil where seeds are about to be sown, and these "raw" materials come in direct contact with small roots, they are almost sure to "burn" them—that is, cause serious injury, if not actual death; it's only when they're dissolved in water that plants can absorb chemical fertilizers safely. The correct way to use this material is to dissolve it in water before the roots make contact with the mixture.

87

setting out plants until after the last frost. Most seeds will not germinate well until the soil warms to about 60°F anyway. If they are sowed in soil that is cooler than this, they will remain dormant until the soil warms and may rot before they get a chance to germinate.

Start seeds indoors no sooner than eight weeks before the average date for the last killing frost in your area. If you start seeds earlier than this, the plants will be too large to take well when they are finally transplanted outdoors.

Perennials seeded in the garden frequently fail to germinate properly because the surface of the soil cakes and prevents water from entering. To avoid this, sow the seed in vermiculite-filled furrows. Make the furrows in the soil about a half-inch deep. After filling them with fine vermiculite, sprinkle lightly with water. Then make another shallow furrow in the vermiculite, and sow the seed. I usually space my seeds according to the recommended spacing for the mature plant; this avoids having to thin them out later on.

However, if you're worried about all the seed not coming up, you may want to sow it more thickly.

Ready to thin

Growing Secrets

Cover the seed with a layer of vermiculite, and using a nozzle adjusted for a fine mist, water the seeded area thoroughly.

To retard water evaporation, cover the seeded area with sheets of newspaper or polyethylene film (plastic garment bags from the dry cleaners are excellent). Support the newspaper or plastic on blocks or sticks 1 or 2 inches above the surface of the bed. Remove the paper or plastic when seedlings appear.

When most outdoor-grown perennials develop two true leaves, they should be thinned to the recommended spacing, unless you already did so when you planted the seed. This allows the plants the light, water, nutrients, and space they need to develop fully.

ALL PERENNIALS NEED LOVE

Watering Is A Must

Correct watering can make the difference between a good flower display and a poor one. Don't rely on summer rainfall; water on a regular schedule. Water perennials throughout the growing season, particularly during dry weather. Allow the water to penetrate deeply into the soil; moisten the entire bed thoroughly, but do not water so heavily that the soil becomes soggy. Water again when the soil is dry to the touch and the tips of the plant wilt slightly at midday.

WATERING WISDOM

The best way to water perennials is with a soaker hose. The soft stems may bend if they're watered from above with a regular garden sprinkler. Give them about 1 inch of water per week.

Ways To Water

A soaker hose is excellent for watering perennial beds. Water from the soaker hose seeps directly into the soil without waste. The slow-moving water does not disturb the soil or reduce its capacity to absorb water.

If you water with a sprinkler, use an oscillating type. This will cover a large area with rainlike drops of water. Do not use a rotating sprinkler—it tends to tear up the surface of the soil, and only covers a small area. Run your sprinkler at least four hours in each place. This deep watering will quench their thirst, and allow for a longer interval between waterings.

The least effective method for watering is with a hand-held nozzle or watering can. Watering with a nozzle has all the disadvantages of watering with a rotating sprinkler. In addition, gardeners seldom are patient enough to do a thorough job of watering with a nozzle; not enough water is applied and the water that is applied is usually poorly distributed over the bed.

When To Water

Water anytime during the day except late afternoon. Even water in bright sunlight; just make sure you soak the soil thoroughly. If possible, water in the early part of the day; this will allow plenty of time for the flowers and foliage to dry before night. Night watering increases the chances of disease. Finally, be careful when watering flowers in bloom; the flowers tend to rot if they catch and hold water. You may want to give such plants a little shake after watering to dislodge some of the drops.

Mulch Is Mandatory

Mulch gives a nice look to the garden, cuts down on weeds and weeding labor, and adds organic matter to the soil. It will also retard water loss, prevent soil from baking, cracking, and splashing up on plants when you water.

Trim the plants of low foliage and stems before mulching. Mulch with buckwheat hulls, peat moss, salt hay, pine bark, pine needles, shredded bark, or wood chips. Select an organic material that will decompose slowly, that will allow water to penetrate to the soil below, and adds a neutral color to the soil.

Spread the mulch over the whole bed at least 2 inches deep. Be sure to do it before your plants have grown rather large. Then, water the mulch into place (dry mulch prevents water penetration). Be sure to keep your mulch free of debris—litter is very noticeable—as you will soon see.

❋

Winter mulching can be helpful in protecting newly planted or less hardy perennials. But be careful—it can sometimes do more harm than good. Apply mulch around the plants only after the soil temperature has gone down, usually in late fall, after several killing frosts. If the winter mulch is applied too early, the warmth from the soil will cause new growth to start. Severe damage to the plant can result from the new growth being frozen back when the really cold weather finally hits.

The best winter mulch is snow—if the bed has good drainage. A thin layer of peat moss is sufficient for a winter mulch. Keep winter mulch loose. It must be well-drained and have good air circulation to keep the plants from rotting. Winter mulched plants also should be screened from the drying southwest winds.

SNOW

IS THE

BEST

MULCH

Remove the winter mulch as soon as growth starts in the spring. If you don't, the new growth will develop abnormally as it tries to push through the mulch—your plants will have long, gangly stems due to an insufficient amount of chlorophyll.

If you have trouble carrying a particular plant over the winter, mulch can help. But remember, mulch is not a substitute for a coldframe. It may be better to grow the plant as a biennial, carrying it over the winter in a coldframe, and moving it to the flower bed in the second spring. In many of the colder areas of the United States, spring planting from coldframe-held plants is the only way to have a particular prized perennial in the garden.

THE BARE FACTS

A newly planted bed can look rather bare if plants are spaced at recommended distances for mature specimens. To avoid this bare look, initially space plants closer together, and then transplant a few out of the bed as they become crowded. This will also help to control weeds. Or, use annual plants in bare areas until the perennials grow into their allotted space. You also can cover bare areas with a 2- to 4-inch layer of mulch.

Feed 'Em Or Forget 'Em!

FEEDING FORMULA

Feeding perennials is like satisfying a child's appetite—make it sweet, and they'll eat themselves silly! Here's a formula for feeding your flowers that'll give them plenty of flower power:

In a five gallon pail, mix:

**2 lbs. of dry oatmeal,
2 lbs. of crushed
dry dog food,
1 handful of human hair, and
1/2 cup of sugar.**

Work a handful of this mixture into the soil, and then plant to your heart's content!

You must feed your perennials regularly because their extensive growing periods and sustained growing power rob the soil of its natural fertility.

Do not fertilize perennials heavily with inorganic fertilizers. A light fertilization program provides a continuous supply of nutrients. This produces plants that are easier to train or support on stakes, and that do not have foliage so dense it interferes with air circulation and the evaporation of moisture from the leaves. (Air circulation is also helped by the proper spacing of plants.)

If your soil has a lot of organic matter—like peat moss or compost in it, you can fertilize with a 5-10-5 fertilizer. Sprinkle a little fertilizer around each plant. If your soil lacks organic matter, fertilize with liquid fish emulsion or a sludge-type fertilizer like Milorganite.

The important thing is to set up a regular fertilizing program, and stick to it, fertilizing all along, a little at a time.

They Need Your Support

Many perennials are top heavy, so they will need to be staked. Plants like delphiniums and hollyhocks particularly need staking. If a plant falls over, the stem will function poorly where it has been bent. If the stem is cracked, rot organisms can penetrate the break.

Stake plants when you first set them out so that—

- They will grow to cover the stakes.

- They can be gently guided to face the front of the flower bed.

- They can better withstand hard, driving rain and wild, whipping wind.

You can use stakes made of twigs, wood dowels, bamboo, wire, or even plastic. Select stakes that will be 6 to 12 inches shorter than the mature height of the plant. Place them behind the plants, and sink them into the ground until they stand firm. Loosely tie the plants to the stakes, using strips of old pantyhose, velcro, twist 'ems or Plant Klips. Don't use string because it will rot over the course of the summer. Tie the plant, making a double loop of the pantyhose—one loop around the plant, and the other around the stake. Never loop the wire around both stake and plant—the plant will hang to one side, and the pantyhose may strangle the stem.

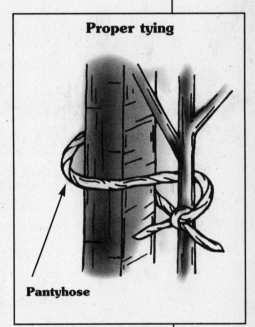

Proper tying

Pantyhose

Divide The Profit

The number one rule of perennial growing is never leave a perennial planted in the same place for more than three years. That's right! Divide them every three years. If you don't, the center of the clump will grow poorly, and the flowers will be sparse. The clump will deplete the fertility of the soil in which it is grown and the plant will crowd itself.

Divide mature clumps of perennials into clumps of 3 to 5 shoots each. Select only vigorous side shoots from the outer part of the clump because they will grow best. Be careful not to overdivide; too small a clump will not give much color the first year after replanting. Discard the center of the clump.

Divide perennials in the fall in southern climates and in the spring in northern areas.

Stagger your dividing to avoid having to dig up your whole garden at the same time; a good rotation will give you a constant display of flowers each year.

One final note—don't put all of the divisions back into the same space that the original plant occupied. That would result in too many plants being in a given area, with overcrowding and poor air circulation. Spread them out, move clumps to other parts of the garden, or give them away to friends.

Use a spading fork to dig up the clump of roots.

Dividing perennials

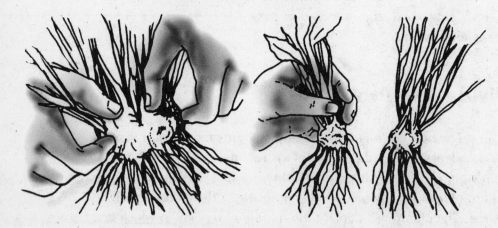

Pull the large clump apart into smaller clumps with 3 to 5 shoots.

Cuttings Are Part Of The Reward

Many plants can be propagated from either tip (or stem) or root cuttings. Generally, tip cuttings are easier to propagate. The best perennials for this type of propagation are new growth of dianthus, candytuft, and phlox.

A Big Tip

Make tip cuttings 3 to 6 inches long. Leave all of the foliage on the cutting, except the part that will be below the soil line. Treat the base of the cutting with Root 'n' Grow stimulant, and insert it into its own peat pot filled with a soil mix of **2 parts sand, 2 parts soil, and 2 parts peat moss.** Water thoroughly.

Place the cuttings in a lightly shaded place. Cover with a sheet of plastic and check regularly to make sure the cuttings do not dry out. When the cuttings do not pull easily out of the soil, they have begun to root. Make holes in the plastic sheet to let in air and to increase their exposure to air. This will harden the cuttings. Every few days, make those holes larger, or make new holes.

Finally, it's time to remove the cover. Pinch back the tips of the cuttings 10 days after the cover is removed—this will promote branching. Transplant the rooted cuttings to a freshly prepared bed in midsummer.

Get To The Root Of It

Root cuttings can be taken from phlox, baby's breath, and oriental poppies. To make root cuttings, dig up the plants in late summer, after they have bloomed. Select pencil-sized roots and cut them into 4-inch sections. Put each piece in its own peat pot with the same soil mix as for the tip cuttings. Water thoroughly. Then place the pots in a coldframe, and transplant them the following spring.

PERENNIAL

PROPAGATION

FROM TOP

TO

BOTTOM

Bugs And Blotches Are Facts Of Flower Life

One of my most frequently asked questions is what chemical control you should buy to get rid of bugs.

In nine out of ten cases, Dursban® for soil dwelling insects, and diazinon for above ground bugs should do the trick. Mix it at the recommended rate with 1 cup of liquid dish soap in your 6 gallon hose-end sprayer. Apply this mixture after 6:00 p.m. when the bugs are home.

NOT TOO CLEAN!

There is such a thing as cleaning up your perennial bed too thoroughly before the start of winter. All plant remains that are harboring insects and disease should be removed, and all dead stalks can well be cut off a foot from the ground so that they won't look unkempt. But leaving a reasonable amount of dead stuff (like leaves) lying on the ground around the plants will do the perennials more good than harm.

WHO'S WHO IN THE PERENNIAL WORLD

Most folks have little, if any, idea of what to expect when they buy a particular perennial. So here is a brief introduction to the upper crust of the flowering perennial world.

The following list of plants does not include all perennials. It is only a selection of some of the more commonly available ones. For more details on any particular plant, contact your local garden club, or plant societies, or check out the many gardening magazines.

I have included some of the plant's uses, height, and blooming time, to help you properly plan and plant your garden. As always, good luck and good gardening!

Achillea

Achillea millefolium (Yarrow) grows about 2 feet tall. It looks best in borders, and blooms from June to September. Achillea is grown also for use as a cut flower. Plant its seeds in early spring or late fall in a sunny spot in your garden, spacing them about 36 inches apart. The seed will germinate in seven to fourteen days. The seed is very small, so water it with a mister. Achillea is very easy to grow, and spreads very rapidly.

Althaea

Alcea rosea or *Althaea rosea* (Hollyhock) grows up to 6 feet tall, and is used for background screening. It blooms from late spring to midsummer. It does best in deep, rich, well-drained soil. Plant seeds anytime from spring to September in a sunny spot, spacing them about 36 inches apart. Seeds germinate in ten days. You will have to stake these plants to protect them from toppling over in the wind.

Alyssum

Aurinia saxatile (Gold-dust) grows 9 to 12 inches tall. It is used in rock gardens, for edging in borders, and as a cut flower. It blooms in early spring, and grows well in dry sandy soil. Plant seeds in early spring in a sunny spot, spacing them 24 inches apart. The seed will germinate in twenty-one to twenty-eight days.

HOLLYHOCKS ARE GREAT BACKGROUND PLANTS

LANDSCAPING TIP

Alyssum can turn a stepping stone or gravel pathway into a mini flower garden. Simply tuck the plants in among the stones, and then follow up with regular feedings. The plants love the heat that radiates from the stone, and will fill in quickly.

Anemone

Anemone pulsatilla (Windflower) grows about 12 inches tall. It is used in borders, rock gardens, and as a container plant. Anemone bloom in May and June, and is an excellent cut flower.

Aquilegia

Plant its seed in early spring or late fall in a sunny part of your garden. The seed will germinate in four days. Plant tuberous-rooted anemones in well-drained soil in September. Space both 35 to 42 inches apart, and cover with straw over the winter. Anemones are not hardy north of Washington, D.C.

Aquilegia

Aquilegia hybrid (Columbine) grows 2- $1/_2$ to 3 feet tall, and is used in borders and for cut flowers. It blooms in late spring or early summer. It needs fairly rich, well-drained soil. Plant the seeds anytime from spring to September in sun or partial shade, spacing them 12 to 18 inches apart. Seed germinates in about thirty days, though it can be irregular. Grow as a biennial to avoid leaf miner and rotting of the crown.

Arabis

Arabis alpina (Rock cress) grows 8 to 12 inches tall. It is used for edging and in rock gardens. Arabis blooms in early spring, and grows best in light shade. Plant the seed in well-drained soil anytime from spring to September. Shade summer plantings. Space plants about 12 inches apart. Seed germinates in about five days.

ROCK GARDENS

Arabis is a great choice for rock gardens. It adapts well to harsh conditions, and is accustomed to poor, quick-draining soil. Give yours a boost by mixing:

$1/_3$ **course sand,**
$1/_3$ **compost or leaf mold, and**
$1/_3$ **fine gravel**

into the soil when planting.

Artemisia

Artemisia stellerana (Wormwood, Dusty Miller) grows about 2 feet tall. It is used in flower beds, borders, and rock gardens. Artemisia blooms in late summer. Plant the seed in full sun from late spring to late summer, spacing them 9 to 12 inches apart. It will grow well in poor and dry soils.

Aster

Aster alpinus (Hardy aster) grows 1 to 5 feet tall. It is used in rock gardens, borders, and for cut flowers. Asters bloom in June. Plant the seeds in early spring in a sunny spot in your garden, spacing them about 36 inches apart. Seed germinates in fourteen to twenty-one days.

Astilbe

Astilbe japonica (Spiraea) grows 1 to 3 feet tall. It is used in borders, blooming in a mass of color in summer. Plant seeds in early spring in rich, loamy soil, spacing them 24 inches apart. Seed germinates in fourteen to twenty-one days.

Aster

Begonia

Begonia evansiana (Hardy begonia) grows 12 inches tall, and is used in shaded flower beds, providing handsome blooms in late summer. Plant seeds in summer in a shady, moist spot, spacing them 9 to 12 inches apart. Seed germinates in twelve days. You can propagate hardy begonia by planting the bulblets that grow in the axils (where the leaf and stem meet) of the leaves.

Bellis

Bellis perennis (English daisy) grows about 6 inches tall, and is used in beds, borders, and rock gardens. In cool climates, it blooms all summer long; elsewhere, from early spring to late fall. Sow the seed in fall in moist, well-drained soil in partial shade, spacing them about

UMBRELLLA PLANT SUPPORT

Save your old umbrellas because the ribs make excellent, long-lasting supports for flowers. Paint them green, and they will hardly be seen in your garden.

MOISTURE MAKER

Plastic film, aluminum foil, or a piece of moist burlap placed on the seedbed will help keep moisture in. Remove this as soon as the seeds begin to sprout (in about five to eight days). Shade the seedlings with a canopy for a few days, until they develop their first true leaves. The canopy (an inexpensive, makeshift one will do) should be arranged a foot or two above the bed to let the air circulate.

6 inches apart. Seed germinates in about eight days. English daisy needs plenty of water during the summer and should be protected in winter with cut branches of conifers.

Campanula

Campanula medium (Canterbury bells) grows 2 to 2-$\frac{1}{2}$ feet tall, and is used in borders and for cut flowers. Sow the seed thinly, about 15 inches apart, in partial shade anytime between spring and September; do not cover the seed with soil. Seed germinates in about twenty days. Be sure to shade the seedbed in summer. Divide mature plants every other year.

Centaurea

Centaurea cyanus (Cornflower) grows about 2 feet tall, and is used in borders and for cut flowers. It blooms from June to September. Plant the seed in early spring in a sunny spot, spacing them about 12 inches apart. Seed germinates in twenty-one to twenty-eight days. Remove the flowers as they fade (known as deadheading) to prolong the time of display.

Cerastium

Cerastium tomentosum (Snow-in-summer) grows about 6 inches tall, and is used in rock gardens and for ground cover. The plants form a creeping mat that blooms in May and June. Cerastium does well in dry, sunny spots. Plant the seed in early spring, spacing them about 18 inches apart. Seed germinates in fourteen to twenty-eight days. Cerastium is a hardy, tough plant and a rampant grower. Do not allow it to crowd out other plants.

Chrysanthemum

Chrysanthemum maximum (Shasta daisy) grows 2 to 2 1/2 feet tall. It is used in borders and for cut flowers, blooming in June and July. Plant its seed anytime from early spring to September in well-drained soil in a sunny spot, spacing them about 30 inches apart. Seed germinates in about ten days. Shasta daisy is best known as a biennial. It is winter-killed by a wet location or a heavy winter cover.

MUM MAKEOVER

The problem most folks have with their mums dying over the winter is too much moisture rather than the cold. So after the blooms fade, dig up the plants (with as much soil as possible), and set them on top of the ground in a protected area. Cover them lightly with mulch. Then next spring, divide them and replant as usual.

Coreopsis

Coreopsis grandiflora (Tickseed), an excellent border plant, grows 2 to 3 feet tall. It blooms from May through the fall if it is regularly deadheaded. Plant the seed in a light loam in early spring or late fall in a sunny spot in your garden, spacing them about 30 inches apart. Seeds take about five days to germinate. Coreopsis is drought-resistant. Grow it as a biennial.

Delphinium

Delphinium elatum (Larkspur) grows 4 to 5 feet tall, and is used in borders and for cut flowers. It blooms in June; if you deadhead it regularly, it will bloom twice more that season. Plant seed anytime from spring to September in a well-drained, sunny spot, protected from the wind; plants tend to rot in wet, heavy soils. Space the seeds 24 inches apart; they will germinate in about twenty days. Be sure to shade summer plantings and to stake the plants to prevent their falling over when they reach mature height. Their foliage tends to mildew.

Delphinium

Dianthus

Dianthus barbatus (Sweet William) grows 12 to 18 inches tall; a dwarf form is also available. It is used for borders, edging, and as a cut flower. Sweet William blooms in May and June. It is very hardy, but grows best in well-drained soil. Plant seeds any time from spring to September in a sunny spot, spacing them about 12 inches apart. Seed germinates in five days.

D. caryophyllus (Carnation, or Clove pink; Hardy garden carnation) grows 18 to 24 inches tall, and is used in beds, borders, edging, pots, and rock gardens. It blooms in late summer. Plant seeds in late spring in a sunny spot, spacing them 12 inches apart. Seeds germinate in about twenty days. Cut plants back in late fall, pot them, and hold them over winter in a coldframe.

D. deltoides (Maiden pinks) and *D. plumarius* (Cottage pinks) grow 12 inches tall, and are used in borders, rock gardens, as edging, and for cut flowers. They bloom in May and June. Plant seeds anytime from spring to September in a well-drained, sunny spot, spacing them 12 inches apart. Seeds germinate in five days. Dianthus is best when grown as a biennial. It is winter-killed in a wet location and very susceptible to rotting at the soil line.

LANDSCAPING TIP

Keep your dianthus border neat and tidy by dividing them every three years in late winter. Remove the root clumps, and cut them into several segments. Replant at one foot intervals.

Dicentra

Dicentra

Dicentra spectabilis (Bleeding heart) grows 2 to 4 feet tall, and *D. cucullaria* (Dutchman's breeches) grows 1 foot tall. They are used in borders and as container plants, and are very striking when shown off against an evergreen background. Dicentra blooms in late spring. Plant seeds in late autumn, spacing them 12 to 18 inches apart. Seeds take a long time to germinate—upwards of fifty days or more.

Digitalis

Digitalis purpurea (Foxglove) grows 4 to 6 feet tall, and is used in borders and for cut flowers. It blooms in June and July. Plant seeds any time from spring to September in light, well-drained soil in sun or partial shade, spacing them 12 inches apart. Seeds germinate in about twenty days. You <u>must</u> shade summer plantings. Select—and propagate—strains that bear flowers at right angles to the stem; discard those with drooping flowers.

Echinacea

Echinacea purpurea (Purple cornflower) grows 2-$\frac{1}{2}$ to 3 feet tall, and is used in borders and naturalized settings, and for cut flowers. It blooms midsummer to fall. Plant seeds any time from spring to September in well-drained soil in a sunny spot, spacing them about 30 inches apart. Shade summer plantings. Seed germinates in twenty days.

Gaillardia

Gaillardia x grandiflora (Blanketflower) grows 12 to 30 inches tall, and is used in borders and for cut flowers. It blooms from midsummer to frost. Gaillardia is easily grown from seed, which you can plant in early spring or late summer in well-drained soil in a

BE CREATIVE

Many perennials are fine plants to grow in tubs, window boxes, and other containers on the terrace, porch, or patio. The shorter and medium height perennials are best suited to container growing. Some good ones are agapanthus, gaillardia, columbine, summer phlox, candytuft, coralbells, and vining perennials like the perennial pea. They grow best in a light soil mix, one that retains plenty of water too. Provide protection (mulch) against freezing in winter.

sunny spot in your garden, spacing them 24 inches apart. Seed germinates in about twenty days.

Gypsophila

Gypsophila

Gypsophila paniculata (Baby's breath) grows 2 to 4 feet tall. It is used in borders, and for cut and dried flowers. Gypsophila blooms from early summer to early autumn, and does best in a deeply prepared soil that has a high lime content (alkaline). Plant seeds any time from early spring to September in a sunny spot, spacing them about 4 feet apart. Seeds germinate in about ten days.

Hemerocallis

Hemerocallis (Daylily) grows between 1 and 4 feet tall, and is used in great masses in borders, or placed in smaller groupings among shrubbery. To have flowering daylilies throughout the growing season, plant various species. Plant seeds in late fall or early spring in well-drained soil in full sunlight or partial shade, spacing them 24 to 30 inches apart. Seeds germinate in fifteen days, although divisions are best for propagating.

DIVIDING DAYLILIES

Daylilies have fleshy roots which are great for taking root cuttings. Do it when the plant is dormant; lift a clump from the ground, and cut back all top growth. Thoroughly wash the roots, and separate the young ones from the parent plant. Cut the roots into 2 inch sections, and plant them below grade in a sandy potting mix. Don't water until new shoots appear.

Heuchera

Heuchera sanguinea (Coralbells) grows up to 2 feet tall, and is used in rock gardens, borders, and as a cut flower. It blooms from June to September. It grows best in soil with a high lime (alkaline) content. Plant seeds in early spring or late fall in partial shade, spacing them about 18 inches apart. Seeds germinate in about ten days. Propagate by dividing in spring.

Hibiscus

Hibiscus moscheutos and *H. oculiroseus* (Mallow rose) grow 3 to 8 feet tall, and are used in flower beds or as background plants. They bloom from July to September. Plant seeds in spring or summer, in full sun or partial shade, and in moist or dry soil. Space the seeds at least 24 inches apart; they will usually germinate in fifteen days, but may take much longer.

Iberis

Iberis (Candytuft) grows about 10 inches tall, and is used in rock gardens and for edging and ground cover. It blooms in late spring. Candytuft does well in dry places. Plant seeds in early spring or late fall in a sunny spot, spacing them about 12 inches apart. Seeds germinate in twenty days. Deadhead (snip off) the flowers as they fade to promote full growth.

Iris

Iris

German, Japanese, Siberian, and dwarf iris are the most commonly grown types. They grow from 3 inches to 2-$\frac{1}{2}$ feet tall, and are used in borders and as cut flowers. Planting a variety of irises will ensure flowers throughout spring and summer. Plant their bulbs or rhizomes in well-drained soil in a spot that gets full sun in late fall, spacing them 18 to 24 inches apart. They germinate the following spring.

Kniphofia

Kniphofia (Tritoma) and *K. uvaria* (Red-hot poker) grow 3 to 4 feet tall. They are used in borders and as a cut flower, blooming from August to

IRIS TIPS

Siberian iris are great for controlling erosion. Their tough, fibrous roots bind soil, even on slopes. Plant the rhizomes in a deep hole with plenty of manure.

✍ For maximum bouquet display, cut iris when they're still in bud. The blooms only last a few days.

✍ To divide, trim back foliage, lift the clump, and break it into sections with several shoots on each one.

October. Plant seeds in early spring to late fall in well-drained soil in a sunny spot, spacing them about 18 inches apart. Seed germinates in twenty days. In northern climates, dig and store roots over the winter.

SWEET PEA SEEDS

Sweet pea seeds have a hard shell that must be penetrated before they will germinate. To do this, soak them in a very hot, weak tea water solution overnight, and then sow after drying them off.

Lathyrus

Lathyrus odoratus (Sweet pea) grows 5 to 6 feet tall. It is used as a background vine, trained onto a fence or trellis, or as a cut flower. Sweet pea blooms June to September, and will succeed almost anywhere without much care. Plant seeds in early spring in a sunny spot, spacing them about 24 inches apart. Seed germinates in twenty days.

Liatris

Liatris pycnostachya (Gayfeather) grows 2 to 6 feet tall, and is used in borders and for cut flowers. It blooms from summer to early autumn. Liatris is easily started from seed; plant the seeds in well-drained soil in early spring or late fall in a sunny spot, spacing them about 18 inches apart. They will germinate in twenty days. You can propagate new plants by cutting their thick, fleshy roots into pieces and planting them.

Lunaria

Lunaria annua (Money plant or Honesty) grows about 4 feet tall. It is used in cutting gardens as a source of seedpods for use in everlasting bouquets. Lunaria blooms in summer and is easy to grow. Plant seeds in early spring in a sunny spot, spacing them about 24 inches apart. Seed germinates in ten days.

Lunaria

Lupinus

Lupinus polyphyllus (Lupine) grows about 3 feet tall, and is used in borders and for cut flowers. It blooms in summer. Plant them in early spring or late fall in a sunny spot that has perfect drainage, spacing them about 36 inches apart. Plant the seed where the lupines are to flower because they do not transplant well. Seed germinates in about twenty days.

THE COLD SHOULDER

Lupine seeds need to be given the cold shoulder treatment before sowing them in soil. Soak the seeds in a weak tea water solution in the refrigerator for at least a month before planting. This will coax them into germinating properly.

Lythrum

Lythrum (Loosestrife) grows 4 to 6 feet tall, blooming in July and August. Use lythrum scattered in gardens and yards, or among trees and shrubs. Plant seed in late fall or early spring in a moist, lightly shaded area, spacing them 18 to 24 inches apart. Seed germinates in fifteen days.

Monarda

Monarda didyma and *M. fistulosa* (Bergamot, Bee balm, Horsemint) grow 2 to 3 feet tall. They are used in borders and massed for color. Monarda blooms all summer long. Plant the seeds in spring or summer in an area that gets full sun to medium shade, spacing them 12 to 18 inches apart. Seed germinates in fifteen days. If you cut the plants back after flowering, they will bloom again the same season.

Monarda

Paeonia

Paeonia (Peony) grow 2 to 4 feet tall. They are used in borders and for cut flowers. They bloom in late spring and early summer. They are difficult to grow from seeds, so plant tubers in late fall at least 36 inches apart and 2 to 3 inches deep.

Papaver

Papaver nudicaule (Iceland poppy) grows 15 to 18 inches tall, while the *P. orientale* (Oriental poppy) grows 3 feet tall. Both are used in borders and for cut flowers. They bloom in the summer. Plant seeds in early spring in their permanent location; poppies do not transplant well. Choose a sunny spot, and space seeds 24 inches apart. Seed germinates in about ten days.

Phlox

Phlox paniculata (Summer, or garden phlox) grows to be about 3 feet tall, and is used in borders and for cut flowers. It blooms in early summer. Plant seeds in late fall or early winter in a sunny spot, spacing them about 24 inches apart. The seed must be kept in the refrigerator for one month before sowing. Keep soil moist. Germination takes about twenty-five days, but can be very irregular. Plants grown from seed will vary greatly in color and form.

Phlox subulata (Moss, or mountain phlox) grows 4 to 5 inches tall. It is drought-resistant, and is used in borders and as edging. It blooms in the spring. *P. subulata* is normally grown from stolons, planted in a sunny spot and spaced about 8 inches apart.

PHLOX FACTS

- A sunny position.

- Temperate climate.

- Rich soil low in clay.

- Lots of water.

- Cut to ground in winter.

- Easy to grow.

Physalis

Physalis alkekengi (Chinese lantern) grows about 2 feet tall. It is used in borders, and as a specimen plant. The "lantern" is borne the second year in September and October; it dries well, and will keep nicely for several weeks in a winter bouquet. Plant seed in late fall or early winter in a sunny spot, spacing them about 36 inches apart. You can plant Chinese lanterns in the spring if you keep the seed in the refrigerator over the winter (the seeds need the cold to germinate). Seed germinates in about fifteen days.

Platycodon

Platycodon grandiflorus (Balloon flower) grows about 2 feet tall, and is used in borders and for cut flowers. It blooms from spring until frost. Plant seeds any time between spring and September in a sunny spot, spacing them about 12 inches apart. Seed germinates in ten days. In the fall, dig up the roots and store in moist sand in a cool (but frost-free) coldframe. Replant them in early spring.

PERENNIAL PROTECTION

In the north, alternate freezing and thawing are your perennials' worst enemies. So, protect your plants with discarded evergreens or evergreen branches, and top with shredded (oak) leaves.

Primula

Primula x polyantha (Primrose) grows 6 to 9 inches tall, while *P. veris* (Cowslip) grows 6 inches tall; both are used in rock gardens, and bloom in April and May. In early spring, pot up some soil, and sow the seeds on the soil's surface. Then, water with a mister, cover the pot with glass, and place it outside to freeze; once it has done so, bring it inside to germinate. Seeds can also be planted outside in the spring if they are first frozen in ice cubes. Usually the seeds are planted in late autumn or early winter. Choose a spot in partial shade and plant the seeds about a foot apart. They will germinate in about twenty-five days, but they can be very irregular.

Primula

Pyrethrum

Pyrethrum roseum, also known by its botanical synonym, *Chrysanthemum coccineum* (Painted daisy), grows about 2 feet tall, and is used in borders and for cut flowers. It blooms in May and June. Plant seeds any time from spring to September in a sunny spot, spacing them about 18 inches apart. Seed germinates in twenty days. If grown in wet soil, pyrethrum will be winter-killed.

HUMMINGBIRD ALERT!

Salvia is a great addition to a hummingbird garden. Plant it along with bee balm, zinnia, and red-hot poker—the birds love the red, orange, and bright yellow colors!

Salvia

Salvia azurea grandiflora (Blue salvia) and *S. farinacea* (Mealy cup) grow 3 to 4 feet tall, blooming from August until frost. Use salvia in borders. Plant seeds in spring in a sunny spot, spacing them 18 to 24 inches apart. Seed germinates in fifteen days.

Stokesia

Stokesia laevis (Stokes' aster) grows 15 inches tall, and is used for borders and cut flowers. If planted as soon as the soil is workable, it will bloom its first season—in September. Plant seeds in a sunny spot any time from spring to September, spacing them 18 inches apart. Be sure to shade summer plantings. Seed germinates in about twenty days.

Trollius

Used in borders, *Trollius ledebourii* (Globeflower) grows about 20 inches tall. It blooms from May to July. Trollius requires a lot of moisture, so water regularly. Plant seeds in late fall in well-drained soil. If you want to plant in early spring, you must soak the seeds in hot water for thirty minutes before sowing. Sow the seeds about a foot apart. They will germinate in fifty or more days.

Veronica

Veronica spicata (Speedwell) grows about 18 inches tall. It is used in borders, rock gardens, and as a cut flower. It blooms in June and July. Veronica grows very easily. Plant seeds any time from spring to September in well-drained soil in a sunny spot, spacing them 18 inches apart. Seed germinates in about fifteen days.

Viola

Viola cornuta (Tufted, or horned, violet) grows about 6 inches tall, and is used for bedding, edging, and in window boxes. It blooms all summer if you deadhead it regularly. V. cornuta is easily grown from seed any time from spring to September in well-drained soil in partial shade, spacing them about 12 inches apart. Seed germinates in ten days.

HOSTAS

ARE THE

PERFECT

PERENNIAL

FOR PARTIAL

SHADE

HOSTING
HOSTAS

Having introduced you to the flowering perennials, now let me tell you about the best of the bunch. Even though it flowers and in the early days of popular home gardening it was called the shade lily, the hosta is known for its size, shape, and the luxuriant color and growth of its foliage. All by itself, it can make a complete garden!

For sun, partial shade, or full shade; for ground cover, edging, mid-border, background, or specimen planting, you'll find a variety of hostas to suit your needs. Hostas provide long-season landscape interest; their foliage delights flower arrangers.

Hosta

Hostas will flourish under a wide range of light conditions, with those on the blue side coloring best in deeper shade, while the yellows prefer more sun (partial shade). Their main requirements are ample moisture, and soil that is well fortified with

111

organic matter. They are virtually free of insect pests (with the exception of slugs) and disease. Hostas may require a couple of years to establish themselves before they show their beauty to the fullest; after that, they simply get better and better with each passing year.

HARDY BIENNIALS

The biennial always seems like the hidden sister, the Cinderella of the flower family. She's not an annual, and as a general rule, she only lives for two years. But when she is in bloom, she is the beauty of the flower garden!

The difference between annuals, biennials, and perennials is somewhat relative to climate. Petunias, for instance, may be grown as annuals in the North, but often live over the winter in the southern states, where they may be grown as perennials. A biennial, generally speaking, is a plant which may be expected to grow for two years, producing leaves the first year, and flowers or fruit the second.

The hollyhock is one of the garden's most important biennials, though in some climates it's considered a perennial. The English daisy is—how confusing can you get?—a perennial which is usually treated like a biennial. Foxgloves, canterbury bells, forget-me-nots, and pansies are also considered biennials.

Listed below are the top hostas offered today in the United States. All of them are hardy in Zones 3-10.

'BIG DADDY.'—Deep blue puckered leaves on fast-growing plants, perfect for the back of the border or for architectural use in the landscape. It produces white flowers in early summer. Grows well in shade to half-shade.

'CELEBRATION.'—A rapid grower, with lance-shaped leaves of cream with striking green margins, this is among the earliest hostas to leaf out. It produces late summer flowers of delicate lavender. Good for rock gardens or as a ground cover. These beauties do well in full shade to three-quarter sun.

'DAYBREAK.'—An impressive specimen type from Paul Aden, with deep gold leaves emphasized by prominent textured veins. The leaves are extremely heavy to withstand adverse weather. Grows well in shade to half sun.

'FRAGRANT GOLD.'—A Paul Aden specimen that produces extremely fragrant lavender flowers in mid-August. The foliage is golden with prominent ribs; it flourishes in shade to three-quarter sun.

'GOLD MEDALLION.'—A selected clone of *H. tokkudama* 'Golden,' with round, cupped, puckered golden leaves that hold their brilliant color all season. An exceptionally heavy producer of white flowers in early summer. Grow in half sun.

H. VENTRICOSA 'AUREA-MARGINATA.'—Its large, heart-shaped, green leaves are accentuated by broad, irregular margins of yellow to white. A splendid ground cover, it produces mauve flowers in midsummer. Does best in full shade to three-quarter sun.

'HALCYON.'—This is considered by many to be the best of all the introductions by the late Eric Smith of England, famed for his blue hostas. Its chalky blue leaves form a medium-sized clump. Abundant soft blue flowers in June. Grow in shade to half sun.

'INVINCIBLE.'—A fine plant with exceptionally shiny, bright green, light-tolerant foliage. Grows less than 10 inches tall—a fine ground cover, with light lavender fragrant flowers in midsummer. Grow in shade to three-quarter sun.

'JANET.'—This chameleon-like plant often varies from chartreuse to yellow to white, offset with green margins. In our shady garden, it remained a striking combination of yellow and white all summer—a truly magnificent sight! It produces delicate lavender flowers in June. Grow in shade to three-quarter sun.

'SAMURAI.'—A handsome plant with blue-green leaves with wide, irregular yellow margins. White flowers adorn it early in the summer. Excellent for background plantings. Does best in full shade to three-quarter sun.

SLUG BUSTER

You've heard me talk about beer in the garden, but did you know that grape juice is also an effective slug killer? Simply add it to a shallow pan that is placed at ground level in your garden, and then remove the dead (drowned) slugs the next morning.

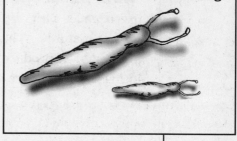

'SEA DRIFT.'—Truly different and delightful, this variety has leaves so ruffled they give a pie-crust effect. It produces lavender-pink flowers in June. Grow in shade to three-quarter sun.

'SEA SPRITE.'—Excellent for the front of the border, this rapid grower has wavy yellow to cream leaves outlined in green. It bears pale orchid flowers in midsummer. Plant it in shade to three-quarter sun.

'SHINING TOT.'—A lovely dwarf, mound-shaped plant with lustrous deep green leaves and lilac flowers in midsummer. Very vigorous; it thrives in shade to three-quarter sun.

ADD ASHES

In spring, generously apply wood ashes from your fireplace all around your perennials, several inches deep. This will help to enrich the soil.

You can also use dried dog food for the same purpose. It contains many of the same nutrients found in organic fertilizers, such as blood meal and bone meal. For an added boost, work it into the soil when planting, or sprinkle it around growing plants.

'SHOGUN.'—This vigorous grower matures to a height of 18 inches and a width of 30 inches. Its bold, wide, white-leaf margins provide outstanding contrast—a very choice and much-sought-after variety. Does best in full shade to half sun.

'TRUE BLUE.'—Many experts consider this the best of all blue hostas. It is a large plant, excellent in the back of a border where it will form a large, flaring mound. The leaves are heavily textured and will readily withstand sun. Its flowers are orchid, edged in white, a very unusual combination, and are produced in June. Grows best in one quarter to three-quarter sun.

'WIDE BRIM.'—Truly a magnificent specimen plant, with blue-green leaves with very wide, irregular margins of cream tinted with gold at maturity. This is a fast grower that is a favorite of flower arrangers. It produces soft lavender flowers in midsummer. Best in full shade to three-quarter sun.

❀3❀

BULBS
Darling Dutch Dandies

"BULB"

CAN ALSO

MEAN

TUBER,

CORM, OR

RHIZOME

When you say "bulbs" to a knowledgeable gardener, it's like opening Pandora's box because we tend to lump the corms, tubers, true bulbs, and bulb-like plants all together.

Most of you are familiar with the spring-flowering bulbs from Holland, and many of you receive at least one catalog from one of the main sources that offer them by mail. If you don't, then send away for a few. These catalogs will give you an idea of the wide range of colors, shapes, heights, and bloom times that are available to you.

You can plan a bulb garden that will bloom from the gray days of winter in the north, when the snow is still on the ground, throughout the summer, fall, and in some instances, into the early winter. In warmer climates, you can have flowers virtually all year round. Don't ever think that flower gardening is limited to the hazy, lazy days of summer—not when there are bulbs to be had!

ALL BULBS AREN'T BULBS

My first step to a lifelong love affair with bulbs was discovering that everything that looks like a bulb and acts like a bulb isn't necessarily one. Only about half the 3,000 types of plants ordinarily called **bulbs** are true bulbs. The others are **tubers, corms, tuberous roots,** or **rhizomes**.

115

All 3,000 types are alike in one way, though. During the growing season, they all gather food from their foliage, and store it in their built-in underground pantry for future use when it's once again time to wake up and grow.

Only an awfully mean person would risk putting his plants to sleep permanently by treating every type alike. So go ahead, and call them "bulbs" until you're alone with them. Then let your hair down, and call each one by its own first name. Think about your own family. There's moody Aunt Molly, sensitive Uncle Arthur, and good-time Cousin Charlie.

Here is a brief introduction to each of the major bulb groups.

ALL BULBS NEED TLC

When you realize that a small but perfect plant is inside each dead-looking bulb, you'll understand why you can't treat your bulbs roughly. Never carelessly drop a bulb into the bottom of a shopping bag—bruised bulbs seldom recover! Neither will bulbs with mushy, gray spots on them. They're not worth carting home, so if you find some at your local garden center, just let them die in peace where they are, not in your plant bed. If you buy pre-packaged bulbs, and find that some of them are mushy, take them back, and demand a refund or exchange.

Bulb dealers ship bulbs all over the world when they are dried out, in their dormant stage. Don't be fooled—although the bulbs look dead, they're very much alive, and living off their built-in food supply.

True Bulbs

In each true bulb, there is a perfect miniature of the mature plant that will ultimately blossom. At the bottom of

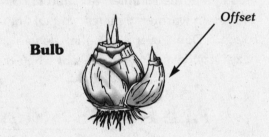

Bulb

Offset

each, you'll find a basal plate which really holds the bud and the storage tissue (layers or scales) together. It's from this plate that new roots develop. If you inspect the inside of a cut-open tulip bulb carefully, you'll see a dark spot near the bottom. That's the new bulb, or offset, already forming.

Corms

The solid, starchy corm does not have layered scales like the true bulb, but it does have a basal plate from which roots develop. At the risk of hurting feelings, I must point out that the corm is a greedy little fellow who eats himself up every growing season. What starts out as a swollen, firm stem is only a shriveled shadow of its former self by the end of the growing season. Unlike the true bulb, the corm doesn't have an embryonic flower in its center. It does, however, have one or more growing points from which the plant develops.

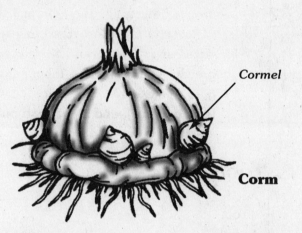

Cormel

Corm

As the plant grows, the corm shrivels—but don't think it's done for! After the plant blooms, it gets busy building a new corm on top of the old basal plate. Baby corms, called cormels, grow around or on top of the old corm, too. The cormels will take two or three years to bloom, but the new corm will produce for you the following season.

Corms come in all different shapes and sizes. Some are rounded like the crocus, but others are flat at the top like the gladiolus.

Tubers

A tuber is a rough hombre, partner! It's different from the true bulb and corm in that it has no dry outer leaves and no basal

GLADIOLUS

ARE

EXAMPLES

OF CORMS

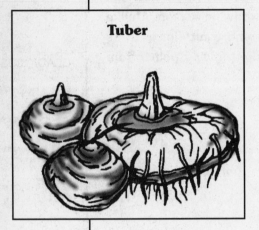

plate. If you're judging a beauty contest, a tuber is not your number, at least not in the bulb stage—but it makes up for lost time when it blooms. Few flowers can equal the tuberous begonia for beauty and grace, and it has very humble origins. The begonia tuber looks like a miniature version of the Creature That Ate New Jersey!

Tuber

Tubers have tough, lumpy skin. The lumps are actually buds, or "eyes," from which roots and shoots will develop. Tubers are usually fat. Some, like the potato, lose weight as the plant grows; others, like the tuberous begonia, get even fatter. More new tubers are produced every year, and if you're feeling greedy, you can cut a tuber into pieces (just make sure each piece contains at least one eye), and plant each one.

Tuberous Roots

Will the real root please stand up? To tell the truth, tuberous roots are the only true root in the bulb family. Growth buds don't form on the tuberous root itself, as they do on tubers, but grow on the root's neck or crown. It depends on its fingery root system to draw food from the surrounding soil.

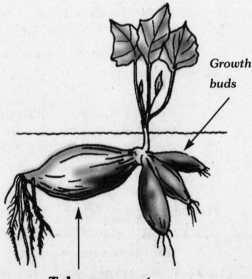

Growth
buds

Tuberous root

The dahlia is the most famous member of the tuberous root family, and rightly so. It comes in every hue except blue, and will grow anywhere in the United States and Canada—as long as its toes don't get frostbitten!

The glory lily, another tuberous root that, like the dahlia, has to be taken indoors for the winter, makes an excellent potted plant. The glory lily's breathtakingly beautiful blooms will brighten up anyone's patio or front porch.

Rhizomes

The rhizome is an underground stem that creeps along just beneath the surface of the soil. Every now and then, it sends up a stem. I think it does so for the same reasons submarines send up periscopes, to take a look around. There are little buds on the sides and tops of the rhizomes, and it's from these that the plants grow. The roots grow from the bottom of the rhizome.

Rhizome

The lily of the valley and some of the other rhizomes send up very small stems with their own roots—these are called pips.

THE BLOOM CALENDAR

If you ever wonder where the flowers "is," you'll find the bulb bunch up long before the grass has "riz." I just cannot say enough in praise of the whole bulb group, and their ability to blend into any gardenscape. From late winter in the North, and early winter in the South and West well into the fall, they spread blooms of beauty and joy.

No matter what your preference is, every season is bound to offer something that's just your cup of tea. Take a good look at a list of available bulbs, and you'll discover a range of sizes that you never dreamed of finding in the flower world. Just take the versatile dahlia, for example—its blooms, depending on the variety, vary from less than an inch across to more than a foot wide.

Every season has its special treats to offer, and if you look through a few catalogs, you'll have to admit that there's something in the bulb world for nearly everybody. Even when the outdoor bulbs stop blooming, you can cultivate bulbs indoors, and replace winter's dullness with a splash of color.

Maybe, just maybe, I can show you skeptics who have always thought bulbs were for parks and/or pictures that they will fit into your little corner of the world. Here is a sneak preview, season by season.

Spring Bulb Festival

Bulb Varieties

The snowdrop, winter aconite, and crocus all try to beat the groundhog up every spring. Soon afterwards, you can look for daffodils, chionodoxa, grape hyacinths, early tulips, and narcissus. As these bulbs begin to fade, the late tulips, including the show-off parrot tulips and quaint cottage tulips, will start brightening your landscape, along with hyacinths, anemones, and still more daffodils.

Choosing bulbs to celebrate spring with you is no easy task. Daffodils come in eleven different categories alone! Crocuses, hyacinths, and tulips can't be neglected. I always grow lots of these old favorites—they're dependable and colorful.

FORCING CROCUSES

Crocuses can be forced in water. Get yourself a narrow-necked bulb vase that holds the crocus bulb just above the water. Keep the vase in a cool, dark place until the roots develop. When the sprout is 2 inches tall, you can move the vase into a warm, sunny room.

But don't limit yourself to the old favorites. Why not surprise your neighbor next spring by including some of the lesser-known bulbs such as chionodoxa or snowdrop? If you really want to make his eyes pop out with envy, plant some anemones and ranunculuses.

Allium

If you want to spice up your spring bouquets, try allium, a beautiful and sophisticated member of the onion family. When you first cut the stem of the allium, hold your nose. It smells like its humble relatives (onions and garlic), but this odor will disappear once the stem is in water. In spite of the scent, alliums make excellent cut flowers—they come in many colors, and last a surprisingly long time. They're also lovely in a planting of other bulbs. A friend once said they looked like balloons floating above the rest of the flowers.

A Show-off

There are lots of other guests you can invite to your spring festival, including dwarf irises, ixias, Stars-of-Bethlehem, and fawn lilies. But if you really want something different, let me give you a tip. The checkered fritillary is the court jester of the bulb kingdom, and he'll really put on a show in your garden! The small, bell-shaped blossoms are purple and white checked.

When To Plant

You'll have to start to work in autumn and winter to prepare for your spring festival. From the Atlantic to the

ALLIUM LORE

Allium moly is an ornamental allium, or flowering onion. It is a close relative of the famous edible alliums: *Allium sativum* (garlic), and *Allium cepa* (the common cooking onion).

Onions also have been used medicinally for centuries. In the Middle Ages, the onion was used as a charm against evil spirits, the plague and infection. The onion was a favorite spring food of American Indians, so it provided the enterprising frontiersman who had a good nose with a telltale means of locating an Indian encampment.

❀

Pacific, spring-flowering bulbs will grow if planted at the proper time. The crocus, scilla, and snowdrop—the little bulbs—should be planted as soon as they are available from suppliers in snow country. Early December is a good time to plant in the South and West. Tulips, however, are ready for bed when they feel the first chilly breezes of fall. Rome wasn't built in a day, and you won't grow a tulip in a day either! Plant them early in the fall to be sure of strong root growth. I always try to have all my fall-planted bulbs in the ground a month before the ground freezes.

MAILBOX MAGIC

Here's a neat idea to brighten a lamp post or mailbox: turn these simple structures into eye-catching centerpieces by encircling it with a parade of flowers from earliest to latest spring. Plant purple and gold crocus; dainty white snowdrops; pink-and-white narcissi; blue hyacinths; bright white anemone blanda, and several colors of tulips. Position rocks or boulders around the posts to create added interest.

Watch 'Em Grow

As soon as you drop your bulbs into well-prepared soil, they begin to release their pent-up energy. Roots and stems start to develop from the embryonic flower inside the bulb. Then, just out of sight beneath the surface of the soil, the bulb waits like a lunar rocket ready for lift-off. The moment the temperature starts to climb upward, the bulb begins its countdown. When all systems are "go," it blasts its way through the ground, and continues its upward thrust. In a few days, it will accomplish its primary mission—a bud will explode into bloom for you to enjoy!

Summer Flowering Carnival

Spring can't last forever, and neither can your spring bulbs. You won't have much time to mourn their demise, though. Your summer will burst into bloom before you've had time to shed a tear if you've planned your garden wisely.

Lilies

Like your mother-in-law's annual visit, you can expect your hardy lilies back summer after summer. Most of them are hybrids, bred to withstand extreme weather conditions. For June through August blooms, choose the varieties carefully, and plant them in the fall or early spring. For example, you might choose coral lilies and star lilies for an early-summer show; meadow lilies for midsummer; and Japanese goldband lilies for the last days of summer. Other groupings will work just as well.

Dahlias

Dahlias, long the darlings of summer-flower lovers, will stay in bloom from July until Jack Frost nips at your windowpane. You can't overcut dahlias, so keep on cutting those blooms the whole time. One plant is capable of bearing between fifty and one hundred blossoms a season. That's a lot of bouquets! The dahlias you grow today aren't like your grandmother's—they've been improved, thanks to horticulturists, so the stems are much stronger. You're less apt to have too many blooms for their stems.

Caladiums

I want to introduce you to another fine summer porch plant—the caladium. You've probably already met him. This is a fancy-leaved plant that seems determined to shame the

BULB BUYING TIPS

Gardening experts have a rule of thumb: "the bigger the bulb, the bigger the flower." When planning your buying strategy, remember that bigger doesn't necessarily mean better. It depends on the usage you have in mind. Choose the larger bulbs to accent a walkway or plant around a lamp post (areas that will be seen up close). These will give the most impressive show. Consider smaller bulbs to create cost-effective mass plantings (especially ones designed to be seen from a distance.) Yellow and white daffodils add a romantic touch along rock or brick walls, or along wooded areas.

rainbow with its display of colors. You can pot the tubers, or start them outdoors when it warms up. I have experimented with leaving the tubers in the ground after the weather turned cold, but they rotted. I haven't made that mistake twice, and you shouldn't make it at all. Let your caladiums spend their winters indoors.

Gladioli

Gladioli are one of the hardiest summer-flowering bulbs, and one of the most popular. If you're growing them to exhibit —either in a show or in your home—you want straight flower stems with no spaces between the individual blossoms. My judge friends also tell me that they look for flowers with uniform color, and no faulty streaks or thinned out spots. You should hope for an equal number of open flowers, buds, and closed flowers on each stalk. Look at your glads, and who knows, you might have some winners!

GLAD TIP

Plant gladioli corms between 4 and 8 inches deep (depending on their size) to keep the top heavy flowers from pulling out of the ground in sandy soil or on windy days.

In general, you should plant gladiolus corms as soon as all danger of late spring frosts is over. Cormels (small, developing corms) may be planted earlier. In any climate, the planting ought to be staggered so that all of the flowers don't bloom at once. Wherever you live, you will have a tremendous range of colors and sizes to choose from in the glad world. If you can't find room for all you want in your yard, plant a row or two for cutting in your vegetable garden.

Begonias

Do you have a front porch, a patio, or a deck? If you're like most of us, you probably don't use it very often. Tuberous begonias may help you with that problem. Plant some in pots or hanging baskets, and arrange them attractively on your porch. You might add a few ferns, too. If all of those beautiful, lush blossoms and the cool, green foliage don't lure your family away from the television set on a warm summer evening, nothing will!

And finally...

While you're planning for summer, don't neglect some of the other sun lovers, such as gloriosa lilies, cannas, hardy amaryllises, calla lilies and tuberoses.

Fall Bulb Party

Bulb Varieties

The last rays of summer don't have to leave you flowerless. Dahlias bloom until frost, and some bulbous flowers hold their flowering display until fall.

Dahlias, however, don't dally in the frost. They want to be out of the elements before old Jack's premier performance.

The colchicum, also known as the meadow saffron, can be planted in August to bloom late in fall. The pale lilac blooms are always a surprise when they pop up from the ground with scarcely a leaf to protect them from the cold.

Cannas are good choices for the canny garden planner. They keep blooming all through the summer, and don't slow down for fall.

Cyclamens

Cyclamens are a lot like the proverbial bad penny that keeps turning up, but you'll be glad that they do. You can find

CREATIVE CONTAINERS

Tulips, daffodils and other bulb flowers are the stars of the spring garden. But even "yard-less" gardeners can enjoy colorful spring flowers in containers suited for entryways, decks, patios, and balconies.

Antique stores, flea markets and even some creative rummaging through the attic or cellar can often yield other usable options, especially when you use your imagination. Try objects quaint or odd, such as old wooden wheelbarrows, retired truck tires, or wash tubs, a child's wagon, milk crates, wooden boxes, or old fixtures.

some in bloom in almost every month of the year. Indoors, the florists' cyclamen thrives in the coldest months. The fall-flowering cyclamens include the Neapolitan and European species. The former is known for its white or rose-colored blooms and unusual silvery leaves, while the latter has fragrant, crimson blossoms. These plants always remind me of a cloud of butterflies hovering over the grass when they flower. I wouldn't be a bit surprised to see a near-sighted collector sneaking up on them with a butterfly net one bright autumn day.

CROCUS TIP

Chipmunks love crocuses. So to protect yours, plant them in wire baskets, spray them with a commercial bulb protector, or sprinkle moth crystals on top of them. This will keep the critters from getting to them.

Crocuses

Fall-blooming crocuses will brighten up your rock garden until the last leaf falls. When the crocuses stop blooming, you can leave them in their warm bed, and cover them with a warm blanket of mulch. In spite of their small size and fragile-looking flowers, they're really tough little guys that don't bat an eye at icy winds and freezing temperatures.

Lycoris

If you really want to work a little autumn magic, plant one or more bulbs from the Lycoris family. The foliage appears in spring, then dies down—but don't turn up your nose just yet. In the last sweltering days of summer, a bud will stick its nose above the ground, but you probably won't notice it. Then one day, when you come home from another day at the office and are ready to snarl at your family about the traffic, you'll see it—a 2-foot-tall stalk topped with gorgeous blossoms. And that, my friend, is why they call one species of Lycoris the "magic lily." The blossoms can be red, yellow or pink, depending on the species you choose. Most are trumpet-shaped. The spider lily *(Hymenocallis)*, however, has a delicate, graceful blossom surrounded by long curving stamens.

Winter Bulb Parade

Bulb Varieties

If you live in a frost-free climate, you can enjoy the amaryllis outdoors all year long, as well as the white-capped tazetta narcissus. If you're not so lucky, you can still enjoy them—both can be forced in any climate.

Don't be greedy, though, and bring all your spring-flowering bulbs indoors at once. Space them out so you can enjoy a succession of blooms.

If you're like me, and can't stand to be cooped up all winter, you'd better think about some plants to enjoy outdoors, too, unless you don't mind carrying a potted tulip with you on your walks. Snowdrops will bloom before winter is over. I've often seen them nodding their pretty little heads over a blanket of snow. If the snow is very deep, you may not see these early birds at all.

SELECTION— CHOOSE YOUR BULBS WISELY

Selecting just the right bulbs for you and your garden can be a puzzle, but with a little knowledge and luck, you can choose the right ones for you.

Bulbs are big business, and if you fall in love with bulbs, you're messing around with a million-dollar baby. Over $400 million is spent throughout the world on bulbs every year. The United States buys more glads than any other kind, perhaps because these flowers are so popular in cut bouquets.

BULB FACTS

Americans buy one-third of their bulbs (36%) through mail order catalogs.

Garden centers (in non-urban areas) account for 24% of sales. Supermarkets and other non-traditional outlets account for 16%. Small garden and seed shops (in urban areas) for 15%. It is the supermarket and non-traditional outlets that have witnessed the most dramatic shifts in consumer buying patterns.

Purchases in these outlets are up over 40% in the past several years.

You may feel pretty small in the world of big bulb business, but you can get as good a bargain as the biggest bulb tycoon on Wall Street if you learn something about the when-, what-, and where to-buy end of business.

The Catalog Concept

Many bulb growers buy only from catalogs because they feel they get a greater variety and better quality bulbs. That may be true, since few nursery facilities are equipped to keep unusual, seldom-bought bulbs on hand during the purchasing season. Catalogs offer varieties seldom seen in your local bulb market, and the photographs (which can be deceiving as to color and size) may stimulate your thinking and inspire you to buy new exotic varieties.

Once you buy from a reputable catalog dealer, he'll keep you on his mailing list, hoping that you won't be able to resist that new species of tulip or that dazzling new dahlia he's planning to offer next year. If you're not receiving catalogs regularly, write to several dealers in early summer and ask for their newest catalog. You have to plan ahead of time to receive your bulbs in time for fall planting. If you wait too long, all the other bulb lovers will have beaten you to the punch, and there won't be any catalogs left!

If you're going to plant in the spring, you should plan on getting your catalogs early in the fall, so you'll have all winter to decide.

BULB CONSIDERATIONS

Before you order or buy any bulb, make sure you consider the following:

#1. The color of the flowers;

#2. The months they will bloom;

#3. How tall they will get; and

#4. How deep you'll have to plant them.

Home-Known Bulbs

Your local garden centers usually know their business. Now, I'm a great believer in word-of-mouth advertising, so if you're new in town and don't know which bulb dealer can order that new hybrid you want, find somebody who plants a lot of bulbs.

The best reason for buying your bulbs locally is that you get to see and feel what you're buying. You can pick the fat, healthy-looking bulbs out from the shriveled, anemic ones. Pick them up, one at a time, and inspect them carefully. Make sure that you put any bulbs you reject back in the proper bin—which brings me to one of the disadvantages of local bulb buying. Not all bulb browsers are as considerate as you and I. I've seen people take bulbs out of one bin, inspect them, then put them down—in the wrong bin! The next unsuspecting bulb buyer who comes along to buy a batch of tulip bulbs will have an unpleasant surprise a few months later. She'll discover that her all-yellow tulip bed looks as if it has a case of the measles.

SEASONAL COLOR

For a full season of color next year, plan ahead and plant accordingly. The following is a list of bulbs and perennials that bloom at different times during the growing season. So keep this list handy when you're ordering your bulbs.

Early Spring
Crocuses
Grape Hyacinths
Early Tulips
Windflowers
Early Daffodils

Mid-Spring
Darwin Hybrids
Triumph Tulips
Daffodils
Hyacinths
Trumpet Daffodils

Late Spring
Exotic Tulips
Single Late Tulips
Dutch Iris
Anemones
Pink Parasols
Crown Imperials

Early Summer
Ornamental Alliums
Daylilies
Asiatic Lilies
Peonies
Irises
Ranunculus

Late Summer
Chrysanthemums
Oriental Lilies
Dahlias
Dwarf Asters
Dwarf Daylilies

Crocus

129

Yes

The bulb on the left will always be a good buy; avoid bulbs like that on the right, with cracks, dents, or broken places in the skin where diseases and pests can get in.

Bulb buying is a lot like playing the stock market. It's better to invest in a few dependable blue-chip bulbs than in lots of cheaper bulbs that may or may not give you a good return on your investment. So, in two words—buy quality.

So how do you pick a blue-chip bulb without a broker? Just look at it and feel it. Does it feel fat and firm, as it should? Look for mold and other signs of disease. Small cracks, dents, or other broken places in the skin can let diseases and pests into the bulb, so discard any bulbs with bruised or scratched complexions. Check to see how many "noses" each bulb has—the more, the better. Each "nose" will grow into a flower stalk.

Dutch Treat

Windmills, wooden shoes, and tulips usually pop into my mind when I think of the Netherlands. Nowadays, though, more and more bulbs have "Made in Japan" tags. I still prefer the Dutch bulbs, partly because of the fascinating history behind them, and because I honestly believe Dutch bulbs produce stronger plants with larger, longer-lasting blooms.

When I mention Dutch bulbs, I mean tulips, hyacinths, crocuses, narcissi, grape hyacinths, snowdrops, and wood hyacinths for the most part. All of them provide an abundance of beauty without an abundance of work, indoors or out.

The Japanese are number two in the bulb export business, so I suppose they do try harder. Even though I prefer to go Dutch, I must tell you that Japanese bulbs have been greatly improved in the last few years. And Japanese bulbs tend to be cheaper than Dutch bulbs.

Not all the bulbs you buy are from faraway lands. Lots of them are born and raised right here in the good old U.S.A. Holland, Michigan, produces a good many tulip bulbs. Washington State, Oregon, and northern California specialize in lily and daffodil bulbs. Florida is a leading producer of the world's caladiums, and California is a leader in begonia bulbs.

THE PRICE OF BEAUTY

Today, a handful of tulip bulbs costs a dollar or two. But in times gone by, incredible sums were paid for the chance to own a tulip bulb.

In Holland in the early 1600's, groups of hard-nosed traders filled the smoky air of taverns with sky-high bids for bulbs. At one point, a single 'Semper Augustus' bulb could command nearly 3,000 Dutch guilders ($1,500 U.S.). Just a short time later, a similar bulb fetched a whopping 4,500 guilders ($2,250), plus a horse and carriage!

LANDSCAPING— BULBS DON'T GROW IN BAGS

No matter where your bulbs come from or what their background is, they'll do you no good until you plant them. So with bulbs in hand, you must now decide if you want to set them in beds or naturalize them. This is entirely a matter of personal preference.

Do What Comes Naturally

If you prefer to naturalize your bulbs, simply follow the lay of your land. If you have sloping hillsides, you can set clumps of crocuses, daffodils, tulips, or anything else you happen to like up and down the sides of the hills. Perhaps you have a rock garden laid out by yourself or Mother Nature. In either case, you have an ideal location for naturalizing small, strategically placed clumps of bulbs. The key to successful naturalizing is planting everything so that it seems to have grown wild. What you're really doing is fooling around with Mother Nature again—and enjoying every minute of it!

A Bed With Style

The natural lay of your land will influence your choices in making bulb beds as it does in naturalizing, but there is no limit to the patterns and designs you can enjoy if you use a little imagination and plant wisely. If a corner of your garden is very sunny, you'll want to plant your first-blooming spring flowers there as well as some of the heat-tolerant summer bulbs. Shady areas call for some of the more delicate beauties that are susceptible to sunburn. Just remember not to force your bulbs to live in conditions they can't tolerate. If you do, your beds will never look as attractive as they might, no matter how much hard work you put into them.

USE A

HOSE TO

LAY OUT

A BED

Ferns Fill In

I like to mix ferns with bulbs whenever possible, so it's difficult for me to think of laying out bulb beds without sketching in some ferns, too. The ferns serve a double purpose—they make a perfect backdrop for bright blossoms, and they do an admirable job of hiding the bulbs' unattractive foliage until it dies away. I use them as a sort of all-purpose gardening cosmetic to highlight beauty spots and hide bad features.

Look At Those Curves

If Andrew Jackson's wife could shape her front lawn like a guitar, I have the right to design my bulb beds to suit my own tastes. So do you, but being on the lazy side, I avoid laying out any flower beds that have sharp corners or 360 degree circles; I suggest you do likewise. I'd much rather mow around flower beds than get down on my knees, and clip their sideburns by hand. Hard-to-mow areas might result in plant damage, too, so lay out your beds in gently curving lines. One of the best ways to do this is to lay a garden hose in the line you want your bed to follow. Stand back and look at it, then test it with your mower, experimenting until you find something that works.

Small Flat Yards

If your yard is small and flat with no distinctive features, you'll have to create your own beauty spots from scratch. Try a mixed border along your sidewalk or driveway. This is a conglomeration of annuals, biennials, perennials, and bulbs. Stick to tall, brightly-colored bulbous flowers, like crown imperials and dahlias, so they'll stand out from the rest. Scatter your bulbs here, there, and everywhere among the border plants. Lump only a few bulbs together in each spot for best effect.

No Yard

But what if you live in a house with almost no garden area? Don't throw in the trowel! Plant some moderately tall bulbs in front of your foundation. Hang some baskets of tuberous begonias from the eaves of your house, or plant tulips and hyacinths in pots and window boxes. Use your imagination, and your life can be filled with flowers no matter where you live!

Recipes For Mixing Flowers

You can create your own mixtures of plants, but I'll share some of my own recipes for garden beauty. Tulips, spaced farther apart than usual, are gorgeous with pansies tucked in between them. The color patterns are unusual, and you'll be surprised every time you look out your garden window and see the two mixed together.

GREEN THUMB TIP

When your spring flowering bulbs are in full bloom, take pictures of them or make a diagram of where they are for 2 reasons: first, it'll help you decide where you need more of the same, or a different color next year, and second, you'll know right where the bulbs are so, you don't damage them when planting more bulbs this fall.

133

In the early spring, you can sow California poppies between your bulbs. Other annuals that fit nicely among your spring-flowering bulbs include clarkia, annual larkspur, phlox, and portulaca. Later in the spring, you can set out sweet alyssum, pansies, daisies, or wallflowers between your flowering bulbs. And if you like anemones as well as I do, you'll have to include some in your bulb bed. Their jewel-like colors look especially beautiful with tulips.

Warm Shades

DON'T

PLANT

BULBS

TOGETHER

IF YOU

DON'T

KNOW THEIR

COLORS

If you're tired of staring at the redwood fence you built, get out your palette of bulb colors and make it the frame for a summer masterpiece. Plant cannas, tigridias, daylilies, dahlias, glads, and lilies, all in shades of red, orange, and yellow. For still more zing, throw in some zinnias, and plant a row of yellow marigolds and red geraniums along the front of the arrangement. But be careful—the exuberance of this arrangement is catching! If you don't exercise some self-restraint, you may find yourself obsessed with a mad desire to fill your whole yard with red, yellow, and orange flowers. And believe me, there are plenty to choose from!

Cool Colors

If your tastes are more sedate, you might like a fence planting in the pink, lavender, and purple color range, accented occasionally with white and crimson. You might train a crimson or white climbing rose to grow up the fence, and serve as a backdrop for dahlias, glads, Japanese irises, and lilies, all in pink, purple, or lavender shades. Add some of the new double-flowered hollyhocks and foxgloves to fill in the background. In the front of the planting, you could use pansies, violas, violets, sweet alyssum, phlox, or even carpet bugle.

There is no "right" planting for a particular spot. Instead, you have to choose among a multitude of possibilities according to your own likes and dislikes. The first time you plan a flower bed and plant it accordingly, don't be surprised if you're not entirely satisfied with the results. Planning attractive gardens, like any other creative endeavor, takes a lot of practice. You can't pick up a paintbrush and create a masterpiece on your first attempt.

PROFESSIONAL TIPS FOR GARDEN COLOR

Spring gardens can be based on a one-color approach, a carefully selected combination of colors, or just a wild riot of color. It all depends on your personal taste.

The biggest mistake that people tend to make is to plant just a few bulbs. Then they're disappointed come spring. One of the reasons for this is that in fall, there is still some color in the garden. It's important to imagine what the garden is going to look like after winter, when no other flowers are out.

The other mistake people make is to plant one tulip here and another there, or to plant their bulbs too far apart. Mass tulips together. Whether you're planting 20 or 2,000, you'll get the greatest impact by planting bulbs close together in groups or 'color blocks.' Think of creating little (or large) bouquets in the garden. What's most important to remember is that fall is the time to think of spring color. The best investment you can make on a crisp fall afternoon is to plant bulbs. Then stand back, and dream of a beautiful spring!

YOU CAN FOOL BULBS INTO BLOOMING INDOORS

You don't have to be a Houdini to force spring bulbs to grow indoors, but you do have to be pretty good at faking it. Bulbs have to think that it's time to go to sleep, so you'll need to regulate the inside temperature just as Mother Nature does outdoors. Cold is essential to bulb development; bulbs need a resting or "dormant," period. Afterward, you can give them an artificial "wake-up" call by putting them in sunlight or artificial fluorescent light.

135

CROCUSES,

HYACINTHS,

AND

PAPERWHITES

ARE BEST

FOR

FORCING

Buy Early

I try to be the first one in line in the late summer and early fall to buy my bulbs for indoor planting. That way, I'm sure to get the healthiest, largest bulbs available, even if it means bribing my garden dealer with a slice or two of homemade cake. I rush home, and plant my bulbs as soon as possible. But if something prevents immediately planting them, I store them at 60°F until I can put them to bed in their pots.

Going To Pot

1. I use a good house plant potting soil mixed with perlite or vermiculite. Some people add a bit of garden loam to the mix.

2. Plug up the drain hole in the pot (plastic or clay, whichever you prefer) before adding the soil. Half fill the pot, then gently place the bulb on top of the soil. Continue filling the pot, firming the soil in place. Leave about an inch between the soil and the top of the pot to make watering easier.

3. Always make sure your bulbs have breathing room. Leave from one-half to one-fourth of each bulb out of the soil.

4. Drench the soil thoroughly after you're through planting. You know how thirsty you are after a hard day's work. Well, bulbs undergo a tremendous upheaval at planting time, so they need a long cool drink! Besides that, their hardest work is just ahead.

5. Gather up some of those old newspapers you've been saving, and wrap the whole pot in newsprint. I bury mine 6 to 8 inches deep in my garden, and mark the spot with bamboo shoots. Some of my friends store their pots in their garage; if you park your pots there, keep

SUPER GROWING SECRET

Indoor sprouting of bulbs is stimulated by moving the bulbs into a warm spot with indirect sunlight. Keep them well watered, and when the sprouts turn green, move them into direct sunlight.

them in a dark, damp, location where the temperature is between 40° and 50°F for ten weeks.

6. Your wife (or husband) will thank you profusely when you dig up your planted pots after ten weeks because you'll be able to discard the dirty newspaper and reveal clean pots. Put the pots in your basement or in a dimly lighted room that's not warmer than 65°F. When the foliage is about 3 inches tall, place the plants in direct sunlight, and keep them moist. The blossoms should appear soon.

7. As soon as the blossoms appear, take the plant out of direct sunlight so the blossoms will last longer. Keep them in a cool place; turning back the thermostat at night suits the plants just fine. With proper care, you can expect your blooms to last seven to ten days.

8. When the last blooms shrivel, cut back the flower stem and set the plants in a cool, sunny place. <u>Do not cut back the foliage!</u> Gradually water the plant less and less. When the leaves finally wither, let the soil dry completely. I then store my pot, bulb and all, in a dry, airy place until the next time around.

Amaryllis—The Queen

If you're easily addicted to things, you'd better not start growing amaryllises *(Hippeastrum)* indoors. They'll grow on you, and before you know it, you'll have pots and pots of them all over your house. No flower surpasses the amaryllis in beauty, and what home couldn't use a little cheer when the kids have been snowed in from school for a week, and the television set is on the blink?

Soil Secrets

Use a good potting soil for amaryllises, as well as for most other spring-flowering bulbs. If you begin with a good, rich soil, you can expect to have a healthy plant for several years. You can

AMARYLLIS

DO BEST

WHEN

FORCED

TO REST

buy packaged potting soil or you can mix garden loam, peat moss, and perlite or vermiculite in equal parts to make your own. If you have any fertilizer (preferable 5-10-5) left over from your garden, stir a little into the potting soil before planting, but don't go overboard—a teaspoon to a 6-inch pot is plenty! I would suggest that further fertilizing be done with a liquid formula, but don't use it more than once a month, and then use it sparingly, at 10 percent of the recommended rate.

AMAZING AMARYLLIS

Amaryllis now come in several different types. Hybrid Dutch Amaryllis come in red, pink, orange, and white varieties with blooms up to 8 inches across. There are also Double and Miniature varieties that are colorful and long lasting. These come in shades of white, yellow, red, salmon, and apricot.

Contain Yourself

For amaryllis, you can use plastic or clay pots. I like some of the new brightly colored plastic ones and, of course, you can still buy beautiful ceramic pots and jardinieres as well as the old standbys—unglazed red clay pots. Unglazed pots should be soaked overnight in water, or they will deprive your plants of much-needed water by drinking it themselves. If you use hand-me-down pots, clean them thoroughly with soap and hot water so your amaryllis bulbs won't catch any leftover germs.

Put Them In Their Place

I like to pot my amaryllis around September or October, but I've known people who have successfully potted them right on up to spring. They like to crowd a pot with their large bulbs and roots, so don't give them too much extra room. Set the bulb in place, spreading the roots carefully. Then add a little potting mix, and gently pack it around the bulb, making sure the bulb is centered in the pot. Keep filling and firming until one-third of the bulb is above the soil. (Amaryllises like to keep their noses clean, well above the soil level.) Pat down the soil around the bulb, and water generously. Don't water again until growth begins.

Treat It With Warmth

Place your amaryllis in a warm, visible place so you can watch its progress. It shouldn't be placed in bright sun, though, until growth begins. I imagine you'll have at least a month's wait from planting time to blossoming time, but you'll think it's worth it when you see the glorious blooms.

Don't Give It Too Much To Drink

STOP

WATERING

AMARYLLIS

WHEN THE

FOLIAGE

YELLOWS

Don't plant your amaryllis in a pot that drains too freely. If you can't beg, borrow, or buy a pot without a drainage hole, plug the hole up with a piece of broken pottery or a bottle cap. If you're used to watering your house plants, and letting the excess water drain into the bottom dish and onto your coffee table, you'll have to practice some self-control. Overwatering is one of the fatal mistakes of amaryllis growers. Another mistake that Amy Amaryllis won't forgive you for is exposing her to the cold. Temperatures below freezing are enough to make her give you the cold shoulder—and she'll certainly refuse to bloom! Here again, you've got to have heart, and consider the feelings of your plants. I'm sure, though, that once you're in love with Amy, you'll always be in love with Amy—Amaryllis, that is.

Taking Care Of Amy

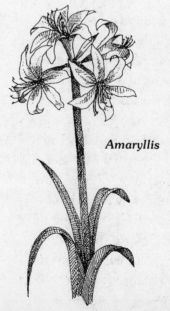

Amaryllis

After the flowers die, cut the stems down to 2 inches, leave the pot in direct sunlight, and continue to water and feed the plant. You need to allow it to build up an adequate food supply for next year's bloom. When summer comes, you can set it outside, pot and all. Feed it regularly until August or September, then stop feeding, but keep on watering moderately. When the leaves have dried out, stop watering the plant altogether. Let the

139

soil dry out thoroughly, and then just before frost, move it, pot and all, to a dry, well-ventilated place kept at 60°-70°F, like your garage or basement. Leave it there until new growth starts. It'll need a dormancy period of about 10 weeks.

Although I have cut an amaryllis bulb and successfully grown a plant from each segment, you'll get blooms sooner if you don't cut them. Since the amaryllis is a true bulb, you can collect the bulblets that develop beside the bulbs and grow new plants from them if you have the patience to wait until they reach flowering size each season.

AMARYLLIS BULB FACTS

The Netherlands produces approximately nine billion flower bulbs annually. Evenly distributed, this number would allow for two flower bulbs for every person on the planet. Tulips alone account for about two-and-a-half billion bulbs, which if placed roughly four inches apart, would circle the equator six times. This is quite an output for a country of only 16,042 square miles (about half the size of Maine) of which 1,638 square miles is under water!

Tulips are the most widely grown bulbs, with about 17,500 acres under production. Tulips are followed by lilies, with just over 5,500 acres under production; gladioli, with more than 5,300 acres; and daffodils, grown on nearly 4,300 acres.

The Pebble Beach Bunch

Tazetta narcissi grow exceptionally well in water and pebbles. Most people appreciate this method of indoor forcing because the dish used for growing doesn't have to be a plain-Jane clay pot or plastic pot. You can use your best china or that lovely vase Aunt Matilda bought you in Sweden. No drainage hole is necessary. Actually, the slightest crack would be disastrous because these plants live by water alone.

By the way, you don't have to add pebbles or shells to the water when forcing these indoor plants. They can live in water alone, but the pebbles make it easier to maintain the proper water level, and add to the attractiveness of the plant. They also keep the roly-poly bulbs from toppling over.

After choosing your planter, fill it almost to the top with pebbles or gravel. I like to buy the colored gravel that is used in aquariums and fishbowls. In the sunlight, the tiny stones actually sparkle, and the colors make both the container and the blossoms look even prettier. If you prefer, of course, you can use plain perlite or vermiculite.

A Big Drinker

Leave three-fourths of the narcissus bulb above the water, and allow at least an inch of breathing room between the bulbs. Do not submerge the whole bulb unless you're growing water lilies. Paperwhites or any other bulb grown in water will rot if water-soaked for too long; it's the roots that are avid swimmers, not the bulb itself. Keep the bulbs in dim light.

Whoever has the job of watering your plants—I'm the official rainmaker at my house—should keep the water level just even with the bottom of the bulb. The roots have to be covered with water at all times, so if you go on vacation, ask your next-door neighbor to baby-sit. Leave written instructions, as any good parent would, telling them exactly how to care for your bright-eyed darlings. And be sure to tell the baby-sitter their names!

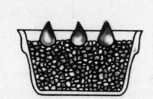

Set bulbs on gravel

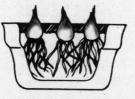

Fill pot with water so that three-fourths of the bulb is above water. Roots will grow down into the gravel.

In a few weeks, you'll have a fragrant pot full of paperwhites!

The Living End

When the stems are about 3 inches tall, move the container into curtain-filtered sunlight. Wait until the flowers are ready to appear before you give the plant full sunlight. Move the plant to a shadier area when it does bloom. I know you'll want to put it in the brightest, cheeriest spot in the house, but don't. Direct sunlight shortens the life of blooms.

The tazetta narcissi give you a big bang for your buck because each stem bears from 4 to 8 blossoms. The paperwhites are the most popular, but two other varieties—Soleil d'Or and the Chinese sacred lily—are also excellent for forcing in water.

Although I try to look on the cheerful side, and remember all of the happy memories the water-grown bulbs bring, they do have sad endings. By the time these bulbs stop blooming, their lives are finished. They use up all their stored energy producing blossoms for us. As I throw away the spent bulb, I just tell myself and the bulb that it isn't the length of a life that counts, but what it has accomplished in its living. I certainly think the water-grown bulbs are well worth the investment.

Hyacinth Glass

Plain Water Hyacinths

Gardeners of all ages enjoy watching plants grow in plain water. Besides enjoying the seldom-seen beauty of roots floating in the water, you'll be the hit of the garden club meeting when you show off a lovely hyacinth or other bulbous plant grown in a hyacinth glass. This vase looks like an hourglass, and works just as you think it would. Set your bulb, nose upward, in the top of the glass. The bottom part of the glass should contain plain water or water and pebbles. I don't use pebbles in my hyacinth glass because I like to see the intertwined roots. Also, I think the whole arrangement looks more delicate without pebbles.

Once you've bought a hyacinth glass and top-quality bulb, you're ready to begin. First, clean up the bulb. Remove any soil, dead skin, and shriveled roots that you see on the bottom of the bulb. If you don't, this debris will rot, and cause the water to look and smell foul. Fill the glass with water up to the base of the bulb, and set it in a cool, dark place until roots reach the bottom of the glass and the top starts to grow. Then move the glass into a cool, bright room until the plant blooms. Hyacinths are my favorites for this type of forcing, with crocus running a close second. Started in late fall, either makes a worthwhile addition to my Christmas blessings.

HYACINTH LORE

Hyacinths, it is believed, were first cultivated in Europe by the ancient Greeks and Romans. Both Homer and Virgil describe their fragrance.

In eighteenth-century France, Madame de Pompadour, mistress to King Louis XV, filled the gardens of Versailles with them. Inside, she forced hundreds of lush hyacinths "on glasses" to sweeten the palace air in midwinter.

The hyacinth was very much en vogue in Europe in the later eighteenth and early nineteenth centuries. Not only were they grown indoors and out, but they were also used as ornaments for women's fashions, and even used as a pharmaceutical. Labeled "the scourage of the Arabs," hyacinth juice, mixed with wine, was touted as a retardant of beard growth.

Even today, Europeans remain heady over hyacinths. And even though it has taken us a while, Americans too are gaining interest in this delightful garden denizen.

THE FACTS OF OUTDOOR BULB LIFE

Soil: It's A Dirty Business

If you buy a good-quality bulb, you are almost always assured of a healthy plant and blooms in the first season. What happens after that depends on the attention you give to your plants.

DON'T

PLANT

BULBS

IN HEAVY,

MOIST

SOIL

How you treat your plants, however, will matter little if you're going to stick them into soil that is sick itself. Wouldn't it be foolish to buy a bulb, plant it, and then leave it to fight the world of insects, rodents, malnutrition, and poor drainage alone? As your personal friends, your bulbs deserve the best lodgings you can give them. And I don't mean the guest room! They want a bed of well-prepared garden soil.

If In Doubt, Test Your Soil

In the interest of healthy bulbs, I wouldn't take Uncle Joe's word about the acidity of your soil, nor your mother-in-law's. Both are probably wrong, and your bulbs would suffer. So would you when you thought of your investments dying in the ground.

Bulbs do best in slightly acidic soil; the pH should be between 6.0 and 6.8. Only a soil test can measure the acidity of your soil. You can have your soil tested by the nearest extension service laboratory for a small fee, or you can do it yourself with one of the many kits available. Take samples from several different locations, always digging down to a depth of at least 4 inches.

When you receive the results of the test in the mail or when you complete your own testing, you ought to be prepared for the next step.

Let's suppose you discover that your soil is too acidic and you need to reduce the acidity so that the pH registers 6.0 to 6.8. Your soil needs to be sweetened, and lime is generally the first remedy that comes to mind. As I'm sure you know, lime is strongly alkaline and quickly neutralizes acids, thus lowering the pH rating of over-acidic soil. I like to think that it's a lot like taking an antacid for heartburn.

I've known people who thought lime was a plant food, and that their bulbs needed no other food. This is not true.

You can use calcite or dolomite, the two kinds of ground limestone, in an amount recommended on the package. The smart gardener will work this into his soil well before bulb-planting time so that the soil can prepare itself. I always try to lime my soil at least two weeks before planting time.

You'll discover, possibly through trial and error, that heavy, clayey soil will require a little extra lime.

Humus Your Bulbs

Organic material comes from decaying vegetable and animal remains. If your garden happens to be in a wooded area, you'll have plenty of rich organic material in your soil. Dear old Mom Nature will provide fallen leaves, twigs, and branches to keep the soil rich and fertile with decomposing organic matter, known as humus.

WHICH IS WHICH?

There are 4 kinds of lime that you can use in the garden. They are:

❧ Ordinary (calcitic) lime—calcium carbonate, used to provide calcium, decrease soil acidity, and condition clay soil.

❧ Dolomitic lime—a mix of calcium and magnesium carbonate; it adds an essential nutrient—magnesium—to the soil.

❧ Burnt or quick lime—calcium oxide, used as a wash on tree trunks.

❧ Hydrated or slaked lime—calcium hydroxide, used as a pesticide or fungicide.

Out of the woods, it's a different story. Your garden might be in a beautiful location, but sadly deficient in organic materials. Maybe you don't care about the organic materials in that lovely setting, but your bulbs do! Consider those little darlings, and you'll immediately perk up your ears at the mention of organic material.

Humus holds water in the soil so the root system can use it. It also keeps water from running off and taking your soil with it. I had a friend who stood at his picture window and watched the first real gullywasher run off his lawn after a long dry spell. He said his "sense of humus" left him right then and there, but I don't think any humus had ever been applied to his soil, or the water would have soaked in well. Why? Because humus acts like a sponge, gulping up moisture when too little is present, and releasing it a little at a time when the soil is dry.

HUMUS INCREASES THE SOIL'S CAPACITY TO HOLD WATER AND AIR

Humus How-To's

After breaking up my soil and removing the rubble, I spread a 3-inch layer of humus over the soil, and work it in thoroughly. I usually use peat moss, but if you're lucky enough to have enough compost or manure, you can use that, too. Be sure to work the humus in deeply. A tiller will save you a lot of work and probably a Monday morning backache, but a spade and a little elbow grease will work just as well.

After planting my bulbs, I put a blanket of leaves or light bark chips over the ground for looks, and to keep the soil moist.

If you have a shredder, you'll enjoy munching up a mulch. I ask my neighbors to rake their fall leaves into my yard, then I shred them up into a lovely leafy salad for my flowers. I'm not above asking them for their leaves if I see them bundled in plastic bags beside the garbage dump. When I have enough on my flower beds, I put the rest in my compost heap. Pride doesn't stand in the way of providing for the needs of my flower children!

STOP THROWING MONEY AWAY!

You throw three bucks right down the garbage disposal each day; this adds up to $1,095 a year, and that's quite a bundle!

You guessed it—I'm talking about table scraps. Why not make garden swill (a nice name for liquid compost) out of it instead? This rich, robust, tasty treatment is just what your garden is waiting for each evening for two reasons: first, when you pour this mushy mess onto the soil, it doesn't have to break it down, and second, the growing plants will begin to receive the direct benefits from it within a week.

Simply take your vegetable and fruit peels, leftover salad, potatoes, etc. (no meat, bones, grease, or salt), and place them in a blender. Fill it up with water, and add a cupful of ammonia or beer, or a shot of whiskey. Now blend, go directly to your garden, and let the growing party begin. Pour the mixture onto the soil. If you use it enough, who knows, your crops may just rotate themselves!

Drainage: Bulbs Can't Swim!

James Russell Lowell said, "One thorn of experience is worth a whole wilderness of warning." I've been pricked with more than enough thorns in the bulb business, so maybe my advice can save you from wandering in the woods. One of the things I've learned beyond the shadow of a doubt is that bulbs demand good drainage. A few are real daredevils who'll plunge right into the water, root, bulb and all, like the calla lily, but most of them are real dry-weather friends.

I believe you can get by with poor soil easier than poor drainage when you're dealing with bulbs. Just keep in mind that it's the roots of the bulbs that need water, and not the bulbs themselves, which rot easily when kept wet. Remember the hyacinth glass and the paperwhites grown in water? Their roots needed water, but the bulbs themselves were kept high and dry.

Here's The Dirt On Soil

There are several types of soil, as you probably have realized just from poking around your backyard. Some soils are sandy, and are made up of coarse mineral particles. These soils are usually low in nutrients and organic matter, and must be fortified with humus or compost.

Clay soils hold water too well. Bulbs are apt to rot in clay soils. You can pick up a dab of clay soil between your fingers, and it will almost feel damp, even in relatively dry weather. Clay soil packs down hard, too, and makes it difficult for tender roots to stretch and grow. The addition of sand will make clay soil workable, and improve the drainage, too. Your old standby—compost or other organic material—is good for clay too. In fact, it's an excellent tonic for almost any soil.

DRAINAGE TESTING TIP

How can the amateur gardener decide whether or not his soil drains properly for bulb growing? You won't believe how difficult this experiment is! The next time it rains, have the good sense to go out into the rain; then stand there and observe your soil. Move around and check several places because the drainage will differ according to the lay of the land and the types of soil. If you have a lawn plugger, take a few samples, and inspect them. You can't tell anything about drainage by looking only at the top of the soil. Drainage is not determined by how fast the water runs off your ground, but by how well the water seeps into your soil. To be fair to you, I guess I should tell you that you could try this experiment on a fair day, too, by soaking several areas of your yard with a hose laid on the ground.

You Can't Dampen Some Bulbs' Spirits

Some bulbs will thrive in moist soil; this does not mean, however, that you can plant them in an area that is a miniature version of the Dismal Swamp. If you do own some marshy, mucky ground, you can set out **calla lilies.** They will grow well in very damp soil with partial shade. Planted in the spring, they can even remain in the ground through the winter if you mulch them, and if the climate isn't extremely cold.

If you have moist places that present problems even after you've treated them for drainage problems, don't despair! Experts have come up with several varieties of bulbs which may turn your eyesore into a beauty spot. Many **crocuses** thrive in moist soil. **Clivias** enjoy a moist soil, and produce lovely orange or scarlet blossoms with a delightful fragrance. Numerous types of **irises** will grow in moist spots, as well as **caladiums, cannas**, and **white fawn lilies.**

I told a cousin once that **schizostylis** grew well in damp soil, so she ought to plant some down by the stream in back of her house. She later informed me that that particular plant couldn't be found anywhere in her little town, but that she did set some crimson flags out, and they were flourishing. I'm still hoping to get up the nerve to tell her that they are one and the same!

IRREPRESSIBLE IRISES

Irises that grow in and around water and swampy type soil include the Japanese iris, yellow flag, and several native American species including the Virginia iris and blue flag.

You might try the **wild hyacinth**, which is available in blue, white, or cream. This easy-to-please plant will grow in shade or full sunlight where the ground is wet. The sweet-smelling **lily of the valley** likes moist soil and full to partial shade—no garden is quite complete without this fragrant old favorite.

If you have small children in your family, I suggest that you plant an **elephant's ear**. No—it will not grow an elephant! Elephant's ear is the very appropriate common name for *colocasia*, which is also known as taro. The leaves of this plant reach giant proportions.

Putting Bulbs In Their Place

Sunshine Is Their Life

Bulbs nap when it's dark and cold, and grow when it's light and warm, so sunlight is essential to their development. If some of your tulips always bloom earlier than the rest, you can bet they're the ones smiled upon by the sun. So don't scold the later bloomers—they're not being lazy.

You can tamper with Mother Nature by planting your spring-flowering bulbs in a warm, sunny spot, perhaps against a wall; you'll get blooms a week or so earlier than usual. Later in the season, the same spot might be too hot for growing anything else, so spring is the best time to make use of it.

If you want to risk fooling Mother Nature again, you can delay the blooming time of some bulbs by planting them in a cooler spot—a northern hillside perhaps.

TOO MUCH
SHADE MAKES
PLANTS LEGGY
AND WEAK-
STEMMED

The Shady Characters

I've told you several times that bulbs are an eager-to-please lot. So it shouldn't surprise you to learn that there are quite a few bulbs that will be very happy in shady locations. I guess you could call them shady, underground characters.

By shade, I don't mean a total eclipse. If you plant a caladium under your evergreen trees where no sun has shone for fifty years, you won't be very happy with the results. Partial shade means just what it says. Bulbs do need some sun, filtered through tree foliage or from the early morning or late evening sun, if they are to develop properly.

Keep A Weatherly Eye On Your Bulbs

Remember Dorothy in The Wizard of Oz? She was uprooted and blown away by a Kansas tornado. Even if you don't live in Kansas, the same thing can happen to your tall plants if you don't provide them with some protection—and I don't mean a pair of ruby slippers, Glinda!

The early flowers, such as daffodils, snowdrops, and crocuses, seldom suffer much serious wind damage. But any flowers that come along in March and April risk their lives. That old

150

saying that "March comes in like a lion, and goes out like a lamb" still often proves itself to be true. While we're quoting things, you may also recall that those "April showers that bring May flowers" often ruin tulips, daffodils, hyacinths, and other plants with mud damage. Did you ever try to stand up clumps of daffodils, sturdy though they be, after a hard rain? It's tougher than putting Humpty Dumpty together again!

Windbreak Ideas

Windbreaks are exactly what their name implies—structures that break the force of the wind, and keep your plants from losing their heads on the first gusty day. You should always try to place tall, top-heavy plants near the house, the garage, a wall, a hedge, or anything else that will provide protection.

Our old pal Mother Nature provides her own windbreaks, and since she is the one who sends the rain and wind, she ought to know how to protect her children from them. The next time you go for a walk in the woods, look around at her handiwork. Small, fragile plants nestle up against their larger, stronger cousins, and against boulders and hillsides. When you go home, look around your yard for similar windbreaks. You can even safely plant bulbs that thrive in hot, dry areas under tall, high-branched trees. The shade they provide is light, and they will protect the flowers when winds or storms come.

Surely you have an empty-looking wall or fence somewhere on your property. I like to see tall glads growing beside a garage, or in a border that curves against the wall of a house. If you have a mailbox on a large post, you can plant tall

RECYCLING ROUND-UP

You can recycle many things around the yard by using them as windbreaks. Milk jugs, paper bags, clay pots, milk cartons, and newspaper are just a few that come to mind.

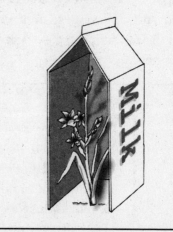

glads, dahlias, or tulips at the base of the post, and thrill the post-man daily with the blossoms that will greet him. At the same time, the post will protect the flowers in a storm. If you really want your plants to feel secure, you can tie them loosely to the pole.

Stakes: Something To Lean On

I've already told you that bulbous plants, especially tall ones, can suffer a lot of damage if they have to stand unprotected in storms and high winds. Planting them near a windbreak is one way to keep them from getting battered by rain and wind. If you've already planted your bulbs in the open, or if you're planning to because you happen to like the sight of plants growing in solitary splendor, then you'd better plan on staking your tall beauties.

Any plants that are over 2 feet tall ought to be staked, or protected by a windbreak. Dahlias, irises, lilies, glads, and a few others fall into this category. For prize seekers, staking is not a suggestion, it is a command! Don't expect your beloved, much-nurtured glads to bring home any ribbons after they've weathered a couple of Mother Nature's temper tantrums.

WALLS,

FENCES,

AND ROCKS

CAN BE

USED AS

WINDBREAKS

STAKING SECRETS

For near invisible staking, paint your stakes green. Use green "twist 'em" ties, or if you need extra support, use green nylon netting.

A lot of folks use bamboo shoots for plants, but I've found that they don't sway with the wind as they should. I prefer 8- or 9-gauge galvanized wire stakes because I think they're easier to use, and less conspicuous in the garden. They're also good in extremely heavy winds because they sway a little, and aren't as likely to cause the plant's stem to snap.

Plant your stakes when you plant your bulbs. Count Dracula may deserve a stake through the heart, but not your bulbs—and that's what you risk if you wait to stake the plant until it's tall. One small miscalculation can damage the bulb, and allow disease or insects to enter it. Planting the stake with the bulb will also help you remember where your bulbs are. The stakes aren't going to interfere with mowing if you've been smart enough to leave mowing lanes between them and your lawn. If you don't want a lot of tall stakes in your landscape, use short ones at first, and replace them when necessary.

For actually tying the plants to the stakes, nothing works as well as strips of old nylon pantyhose. They're more durable than garden twine—and cheaper.

A Bath Before Bed

Bulbs have rough, unappealing faces, but inside, they're very sensitive. After all, they have a flower for a heart. Bulbs can be severely damaged or destroyed by insects and burrowing animals, though they usually suffer fewer problems than other flowers. To be sure that they are pest-free, I treat my bulbs before planting them. There's nothing a bulb loves more than a warm bubble bath before bed.

I carefully drop the bulbs into the Timely Tonic, stir them gently, then remove and plant them. Quick and painless, this preventive medicine is just what the doctor ordered to keep insects away from your bulbs.

Planting Is A One-At-A-Time Job

When it comes to planting your bulbs, give each the individual attention it deserves, whether you plant it in a clump or in a bed individually. Make sure you know when to plant it, how deep to plant it, and which end is up. Being dropped in a hole and covered with dirt is traumatic enough without having to stand on your head at the same time!

TIMELY TONIC

To get your bulbs, tubers, and corms off to a great start, before planting, soak them in a mixture of:

**2 tsp. of Shampoo,
1 tsp. of antiseptic mouthwash, and
1/4 tsp. of instant tea added to 2 gallons of warm water.**

When you're done with this mixture, don't throw it out! Your trees, shrubs, and evergreens would love a little taste, so don't let it go to waste!

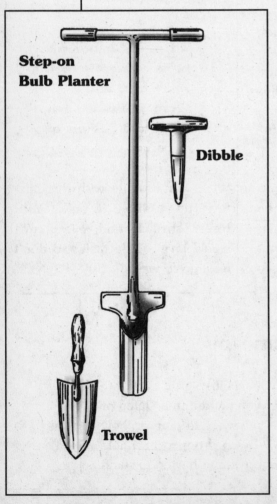

Bulbs will grow if you chuck them into the ground upside down, but they'll grow in spite of your treatment, not because of it. Learn what each kind of bulb looks like, and how to tell the nose from the toes. Then plant it nose up so that the roots will grow downward, and the foliage and plant will grow up and out as they should. Plants will develop and grow the long way around if you plant the bulb upside down, but this wastes energy that could better be spent on flower production.

Tooling Around

1. Step-on Bulb Planter

A step-on bulb planter would make a great Christmas present for an avid bulb fan. This little tool lifts out a 6-inch cylinder of soil, and is ideal for making individual plantings. After you've removed the soil, you can easily break it up, and work in a handful of compost and bone meal. Replace enough soil to make the bulb set at the proper depth, set it in the hole, and cover it. What could be easier?

2. Shovel

For larger clumps of bulbs, remove a section of soil with a shovel. Make the hole wide enough to house all of the bulbs, and at least 6 inches deep. Break up the soil, add compost and a quarter cup of bone meal, mixing it into the soil thoroughly.

Step-on Bulb Planter

Dibble

Trowel

For your birthday, you could suggest that someone get you a dibble. Some folks call it a dibber. Whatever you call it, it's a tool that punches holes of whatever depth you want for bulb planting. A dibble has a rather pointed end, so most bulbs don't fit exactly into the hole. Therefore, you have a worrisome space between the bottom of the bulb and the bottom of the hole. When the roots start growing, they'll be reaching out into nothing if you leave that air space there. Some people carry a pail of sand around with them, and drop a little into the point of the hole before placing the bulb in it. Watering the bulbs immediately after planting will accomplish the same thing.

4. Trowel

You probably own several trowels already. I have one that is notched, not to show how many bulbs I've planted, but to indicate the proper planting depth for several different kinds of bulbs. This little trick has saved me many trips back to the garage to pick up the ruler I forgot to take with me.

A Deep Subject

This leads me to an important point in planting bulbs. I have already told you any old hole in the ground won't do, and that goes for the depth at which you set your bulbs in their holes. The following are general guidelines on how deep to plant them.

BULB PLANTING TIPS

You can have a succession of flowering plants from the same bed by planting your bulbs in layers, with late bloomers at the bottom, and early bloomers topside. Here's what you should do:

1. Dig your bed about 8 inches deep, replacing the soil with a mixture of 25% bone meal, 25% gypsum, and 50% peat moss.

2. As you set each layer down, note where you've placed the bulbs because you don't want to plant later layers directly over any of the bulbs that you have already planted.

3. Cover each layer of bulbs with a layer of the soil mixture, being careful not to plant too shallow.

4. Finish by mulching with leaves, light bark, or wood chips, and scatter moth crystals over the top to keep varmints away.

155

Bulb	Planting Depth
Amaryllis	5"
Anemones	2"
Begonias (tuberous rooted)	1-$\frac{1}{2}$"
Calla lilies	2"
Crocuses	4"
Daffodils	8"
Dahlias	7"
Gladioli	5-$\frac{1}{2}$"
Hyacinths	4"
Hyacinths (Grape)	3"
Lilies	10"
Tulips	9"

MAINTENANCE: SPECIAL ATTENTION, PLEASE!

Webster must have been a gardener because his dictionary says that the word "cultivate" means "to give special attention to." When you cultivate your plants, that's exactly what you do— you give special attention to them once they're established in the homes you've chosen for them. You make sure they're well fed and healthy. You keep their greedy neighbors, the weeds, out of their front yard, and you make sure they're snug and cozy in the winter. Basically, you treat them like very welcome guests who will provide you with a great deal of pleasure in return for a little hospitality.

Bulbs are among the easiest guests to entertain. They're not as susceptible to attack from insects and diseases as most other flowering plants, and they require no pruning to keep them trim and fit. Some bulbs, such as crocuses and narcissi, will be very happy if you just treat them like family. Others, including dahlias and tuberous begonias, need a little extra care if they're to be happy and productive.

Don't become overconfident and lazy if your bulbs produce gloriously beautiful blossoms during their first blooming season. You can take credit for buying fat, healthy bulbs and planting them correctly, but the first blooms are really courtesy of the grower who produced the bulbs, and gave them the grow-power that produced the blossoms. After the first season, however, it's all up to you. You have to make sure the bulbs stay strong and healthy so they'll continue to produce those glorious blossoms. If you take care of the foliage and allow it to mature properly, the blossoms will take care of themselves.

Your Turn To Buy The Drinks!

You've seen photographs of Holland bulb fields, I'm sure, but have you ever stopped to wonder why bulbs do so well there? Well, one reason is that they get plenty of water. The water table is constant and not far below the surface—which is just a fancy way of saying that you can dig down a few feet, and hit water or water-saturated soil just about any place in the Netherlands.

You don't have to pack up your bulbs and move to the Netherlands, though. You just have to make sure they get enough water when they need it most. Have you ever been so thirsty you felt as if you could drain the city reservoir in five minutes? Chances are you'd been working hard on a hot day. And that's when bulbs need extra water too—when they're working hard to produce foliage and blossoms in spring and summer.

There's usually enough rain in the spring to provide spring-flowering bulbs with the water they need to produce blossoms. However, if Mother Nature is stingy with the April showers, or if she's feeling sulky and cooks up a prolonged

WATERING WISDOM

A soaker hose is best for watering bulbous plants. You can use a sprinkler, but you run the risk of burning foliage if you water on a sunny day. Sprinkling is especially hazardous for tuberous begonias and tulips.

Whichever method you use, be sure you water deep. A shallow watering does more harm than good. When you're watering your bulbs, get to the root of the matter—don't just sprinkle their uniforms! Remember, shallow watering will cause a shallow root system, which does neither you nor your bulbs any good.

dry spell, you'll have to give your bulbs a drink yourself. Even after the spring bulbs have stopped blooming, they're still producing foliage, and if it dries out and dies before it matures properly, your bulbs will put on a poor show the next spring. So don't be a fair-weather friend and neglect your bulbs after they've stopped blooming for you.

CHOW TIME!

When I plant my bulbs, I pack an organic lunch for them just to keep them from getting hungry. Here are some ideas:

🐾 For bed plantings, I spread at least 10 to 15 pounds of well-rotted manure or compost, and 5 pounds of bone meal over every 200 square feet of soil.

🐾 If you have a fireplace in your home, and have been wondering what to do with the ashes in the bin, put them on your bulb bed—up to 15 pounds per 100 square feet. They supply potassium, which helps your bulbs develop good, strong stems and flowers, and fat, firm bulbs.

🐾 If you're fresh out of wood ashes, you can buy muriate of potash, but use it sparingly—no more than 1 pound per 100 square feet of soil.

Lunch Time

Having house guests wouldn't be much of a problem if you didn't have to feed them. I'm sure you ladies will agree with this since you're the ones who often do the extra cooking and dishwashing. And it's not just a matter of quantity, is it? You don't want your in-laws or your son's girlfriend to think you're the original burger queen, so you have to prepare something a little special three times a day. And that's a lot of trouble!

Well, ladies—and gentlemen—let me reassure you! Bulbs are perfect house guests. I've already said you can treat them like family, and that goes for feeding too! Bulbs don't need a lot of fancy feeding and they don't demand, or even particularly like, hard-to-get gourmet food.

Unless you have very poor soil, your bulbs could probably do without an initial feeding, but I like to make sure they're off to a good start—particularly the fall-planted bulbs that have a long, cold winter ahead of them. You mothers know how good it makes you feel to give your children a good hot breakfast before

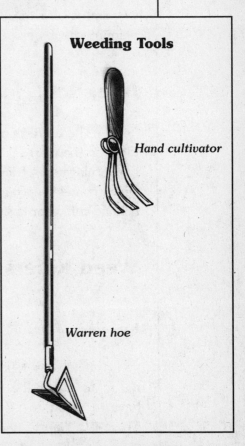

sending them off to school on a cold winter day, don't you? You'll feel the same way when you give your fall-planted bulbs a good feeding.

Don't neglect to feed individually planted bulbs, either. Work a handful of compost and a teaspoon of bone meal into the soil in each hole before setting in the bulb.

The only other feeding I give my bulbs is a light snack in early spring. When I notice that they have begun to stick their noses out of the soil, I go outside to admire their progress and spread half a handful of garden food, 4-12-4 or 5-10-5, over the soil at the same time. Of course, I also tell them how glad I am to see them again and encourage them to do their best for me.

WEED WEAPONS

Have you ever grown onions from sets? If you've done any vegetable gardening at all, you probably have. This humble but delicious bulb is one of the easiest and most surefire crops in the vegetable garden—if, that is, you keep the rows free of weeds. If you don't, the onions you pull will be so scrawny and anemic that you'll end up running to the grocery store to buy some decent ones.

Glamorous flowering bulbs are no different from their humble cousins when it comes to weeds. They don't like to compete with weeds for the soil nutrients they need to produce strong foliage, fat bulbs, and lots of blossoms. Since bulbs can't defend themselves, you'll have to do it for them. So check your arsenal of anti-weed weapons, then get out there and fight!

Weeding Tools

Hand cultivator

Warren hoe

There are three weapons available to you in your war on weeds: by hand; using a hoe or other tool; or applying one of the pre-emerge weed killers

Whichever method you choose, the key to success is getting an early start. If you wait until the weedy intruders have completely invaded your bulbs, the battle will be twice as hard. Never let weeds get a foothold in your bulb beds! They grow faster than other plants (or seem to anyway), and they're real robbers and scoundrels. You just can't afford to leave them in your bulb beds, or you'll be sorry!

Give 'Em A Hand

When I find a stubborn weed growing very close to a bulb, I usually engage in a little hand-to-hand combat. That way, I don't have to worry about cutting up the bulb or its delicate roots. Hand weeding is also the best way to clear weeds out of a naturalized planting where you don't want a lot of bare soil showing.

Hoe, Hoe, Hoe

There are many different kinds of hoes and hand-weeding tools on the market, but my favorites are the Warren hoe and the hand cultivator. The Warren hoe has a pointed, triangular blade which makes it easy to work between plants without injuring them. A hand cultivator is simply a three-pronged claw.

Weed Killers

Kneeless Weeders

If all this talk about weeding has just strengthened your desire to avoid the task altogether, don't despair. You don't have to resort to plastic tulips and daffodils planted in asphalt. There is a way to have lovely flower beds without ever having to pull or chop a weed, thanks to the pre-emerge weed killers which I call the kneeless weeders.

These chemical wonders will protect your flowers from weeds for months, and they're not as dangerous to non-target plants as other types of weed killers. In the spring, after you've planted your bulbs or after you've stirred up the soil in an already-established bed, just spread your pre-emerge chemical over the soil. It will prevent the weeds from sprouting. It will not kill any plants which are already above ground, so you must remove all existing weeds before applying the chemical.

Mulch Beats Weeds

A good mulch is a lot like a Swiss army knife—both will take care of a lot of different jobs. First and foremost, a good thick layer of mulch will keep weeds from rearing their ugly heads in your bulb bed. Once you've spread on a mulch, you can forget about hand weeding, hoeing, and pre-emerge weed killers. You'll have to add a little more mulch now and then, and you might have to pull out an occasional weed that's slipped through your defenses, but that's all!

An All-Purpose Protector

As if a weed-free bed weren't enough, a mulch also protects your bulbs from winter frosts and freezes, enriches the soil with organic matter as it decomposes, keeps the soil cool and moist in summer, and makes your beds look neat and well groomed all the time. What more could you ask?

Lilies are especially fond of having their feet covered in mulch. If you're planting them late, just before frost, use a mulch to keep the ground frost-free as long as possible. Then, once the surface soil has frozen, pile on more mulch to make sure the ground stays frozen. In the spring and summer, a mulch will keep your lilies' feet moist, cool, and comfortable.

A WEEDER

CAN EASILY

DAMAGE

BULBS AND

THEIR

ROOTS

Many materials are available for mulching. Perhaps you'd like to try a live mulch in the form of low-growing ground covers, such as ivy or vinca. I like to use ground covers, around short plants like crocuses and grape hyacinths, to keep their little faces from becoming mud splattered. Ground covers also protect the bulbs against alternate freezing and thawing in winter, which can cause heaving of the soil and root injury. Actually, such heaving is the only thing that spring bulbs need to be protected from.

MULCH ALERT

I want you to be aware of the fact that some mulches, like wood chips and sawdust, actually take nitrogen out of the soil, away from the plants, as they decay. So if you're going to use any of these as a mulch, work ammonium nitrate, blood meal, or rotted manure into the soil before spreading them.

If you've naturalized your spring bulbs in grassy areas, you don't have to worry about mulch. Mother Nature has provided one for you in the form of grass. To protect spring bulbs in beds, spread on a blanket of mulch after the ground has frozen to a depth of about 2 inches. You can use salt hay, pine needles, wood shavings, bark, or evergreen boughs. Remove the mulch in spring before the bulbs sprout.

If you and I have been garden friends for long, it should come as no surprise when I say mulch is still the easiest way to beat the weeds.

WHAT'S BUGGIN' YOUR BULBS?

I want you to make it plain right away to all insects that you mean business! Shower your young plants with soap and water before they flower. Then dust the soil with diazinon granules if there are any signs of insect damage.

For disease control, keep your bulbs free from weeds and litter since both carry diseases. Look at your plants, too, and learn to spot the first signs of insect or disease damage. Then immediately tackle the problem with the proper control.

Mice eat any bulbs except daffodils, which contain a slightly poisonous sap. Mice, chipmunks, and moles will eat bulbs right out of the garden if you don't do something to curb their appetites. Since traps give only partial control, and various poisons will pollute the soil, try planting your bulbs in mesh baskets set into the ground. You also can surround your bulb beds with half inch wire mesh, buried a foot deep. I guarantee this will drive the rodents nuts!

To heat up the action, mix a little Cayenne pepper with crushed paradichlorobenzene crystals (moth crystals), and spread it about your bulb bed—it'll keep out dogs, moles, and surface insects on the outside looking in.

Here's a quick look at a list of the usual suspects:

DAFFODIL PATROL

Moles, chipmunks, squirrels, and deer can't stand the taste of daffodils because of its slightly poisonous sap. So, use this to your advantage. Plant your tulips wherever you want to, then ring them with a protective border of daffodils.

Aphids

Aphids are very small, soft-bodied insects that come in many species and colors. They suck the plant's juices, reducing its vigor. Aphids cause various deformations, spread virus diseases, and secrete honeydew, a sticky substance which attracts ants. Sometimes they hide away with stored bulbs.

Malathion is usually recommended for a severe infestation, but you should try spraying them off with water from a garden hose first, paying special attention to the undersides of the leaves. A mixture of Shampoo and antiseptic mouthwash at a rate of 1 tsp. per quart of water will also do the job.

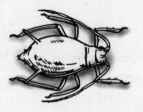

Aphid

THUG BUSTER

Don't plant your bulbs without babying them. Dust them with medicated baby powder before planting, and the varmints will stay away. This one simple step could save their lives.

Bulb Mites

Minute white, spider-like creatures, bulb mites infest the rotting bulbs of many plants. They also eat cavities into healthy bulbs, transmitting the organisms that produce bulb rot, which is a soft, mushy condition.

Amaryllises, crocuses, daffodils, freesias, gladioli, hyacinths, lilies, and tulips are among those bulbs damaged by this pest.

Infested bulbs should be discarded. Healthy bulbs may be sprayed or dusted with Diazinon. Care should be taken to store the healthy bulbs in airtight containers until you're sure they've beaten the bulb rot.

Gladiolus Thrips

These tiny insects are, at maturity, about the size and color of a lettuce seed. Host plants show silvered leaves and/or streaked flowers. Sometimes, they attack stored bulbs.

Thrips favor gladioli, but they also go for freesias, irises, and lilies.

Diazinon or Sevin spray or dust are effective against thrips. Dusting bulbs with Malathion before storing them also provides good, extra protection.

Japanese Beetles

Japanese beetles are about a half inch long and metallic bronze in color. Although they feed on the foliage, stems, and flowers of many plants, cannas and dahlias are among their favorites.

Sevin seems particularly effective against adult beetles on flowers. You can also fight heavy infestations with sprays of carbaryl, Malathion, or Methoxychlor. A sure cure is hand-picking or knocking them into a can of water covered with a thin film of anti-freeze.

Japanese Beetle

Narcissus Bulb Fly Larva

These are fat, yellow maggots which eat into bulbs, and encourage decay. The narcissus, tulip, and Easter lily are all susceptible to this pest. Successful control is difficult to accomplish; however, a good preventive measure is to dust the trench and bulbs with Diazinon granules before planting. Soft bulbs should be discarded. After the plants are finished blooming you can sprinkle naphthalene flakes around them to keep the flies from laying eggs.

Damage caused by the larvae of the narcissus bulb fly.

Slugs

Slugs are fat, legless mollusks, 4 to 5 inches long. They mostly feed at night, leaving a slimy trail behind them. Dahlias

Slug

SLUG CONTROL

- Set out boards or newspapers as traps. Check them daily.
- Beer, grape juice, and cider vinegar mixed with sugar all attract slugs.
- Copper strips make effective barriers—slugs get an electric shock when they touch it.
- Cut up coarse hair and sprinkle it around. It can kill snails.
- Aluminum foil wrapped around plant stems makes an effective barrier.

and lilies are among their prime targets.

Leaving out shallow containers of beer or grape juice will lure these pests to an untimely death. A border of Diatomaceous earth, coarse sand, or cinders around your bulb bed is another good protection from slugs. For heavy infestations, metaldehyde bait is standard control. Dusting or spraying the soil with metaldehyde is also recommended.

Stem And Bulb Nematodes

These transparent, microscopic worms leave the tissue they inhabit scarred, stunted, or distorted. Their pattern is to enter new shoots and feed upward, then return to infest the bulb, leaving rings of brown damaged tissue in their wake.

Plants affected include daffodils, dahlias, gladioli, hyacinths, irises, lycorises, snowdrops, and tulips.

Dig up and burn all infested bulbs. Practice clean cultivation, and dip your tools in alcohol to avoid spreading the infestation.

Wireworm

Wireworms

Wireworms grow up to 3/4-inch long. Their segmented bodies are yellowish-brown in color. They are the larvae of click beetles, and develop from eggs laid in the soil. After they tunnel into bulbs, they hollow out the plant's stem, causing it to fall over.

Dahlias, gladioli, and tuberous begonias are most susceptible to this pest.

In order to eliminate wireworms, it is best to pre-treat the bulb bed before planting. Apply diazinon and work it into the top 6 or 8 inches of soil. After the bulbs are set in place, you may spray or dust them as well with diazinon before covering them up with soil.

AFTER THE BLOOMIN' IS GONE

Who gives a hoot about a plant after it has stopped blooming? People who love the total plant, not just its beauty when in bloom, that's who! And what happens to your spring-flowering bulbs next season depends on the care they get this season.

You should never leave dead blooms on your plants, except the ones with lovely seed pods, like the Jack-in-the-pulpit or the blood-lily. Dead blooms can rob your plant of much-needed nutrition.

Don't Forget The Foliage

The foliage is the bulb's food-manufacturing factory, trying to build up a food supply to be stored in the bulb during the dormant season. If you have deficient foliage, you'll have an unhealthy bulb. Water the foliage if it begins to dry out, gradually decreasing the amount as the foliage reaches maturity. You can even feed anemic-looking foliage a little plant food now and then, up until you stop watering.

Foliage sometimes gets messy toward the end, but don't get impatient with it, or hostile toward it. It's just doing what comes naturally. Some people plait or braid the long leaves of daffodils and similar plants after the blooms are gone. I personally like the ponytail look—on the plants, not myself—so I turn the fading foliage down, and make little ponytails. I tie the little bunches together with rubber bands saved from my daily newspaper. This prevents the foliage from sprawling all over my bulb bed.

WITHER AWAY!

Once the petals have fallen, remove all stems with withered flowers at the first leaf so that no unwanted seeds will form. Then let the foliage yellow on the plant naturally.

A Formal Affair

Years ago, when more formal bed designs were the rage, foliage could not be left to die a natural death. The foliage of tulips, hyacinths, and other bulbs used in formal settings was ruthlessly chopped back after the blooms withered. If you use a formal design in your garden today, take up your bulbs as soon as they stop blooming, and immediately replant them elsewhere. I can't guarantee you that the bulbs will develop normally, but they stand a better chance. If you merely take them up, and let the foliage die, next season, you'll have to buy new bulbs or do without flowers. So replant immediately in a shaded area, preferably in a trench lined with peat moss. Water thoroughly and cross your fingers. An apology might help, too.

Although those bulbs may not be the healthiest ones on the block next season, they should produce blooms that won't disgrace you. And maybe by the next season you will have learned to like more casual planting patterns.

You've Got To Dig For Surprises

Bulbs will multiply as surely as children will grow. Look at your daffodils. You'll probably notice that their blooms aren't as large and pretty as they were a few years ago. Chances are, the bulbs are overpopulated, and need dividing. The longer you wait to replant the bulbs, the harder the job will be, and the smaller your bulbs will be. Bulbs can't grow large if they've got no place to go.

Some people keep daffodils for ten or more years without ever seeing their bulbs, but yours may need to be divided sooner. The best way to tell is to look at the size of the blossoms.

Dig When?

It's best to dig up your bulbs for dividing at the beginning of the dormant period, just after the foliage dies back. Some bulbs, like the colchicum, have very short dormant periods, much like my vacations have always been. The colchicum is dormant from about the Fourth of July to the middle of August, which means you have to make hay while the sun shines to divide these cookies. As soon as the foliage is dried up, go to work moving them.

JUST BE PATIENT!

You should never remove tulip and daffodil foliage until at least half of the leaf surface has turned brown. This indicates that the bulb has completed it's growth for the following year. If you need the bed for a follow-up planting, remove the bulbs with roots and foliage intact, and heel them in a convenient spot until the maturing process is complete.

Divide And Conquer

The best tool for dividing bulbs is the spading fork. I like one with large tines so that I can get the fork under a clump of bulbs, and not in the middle of it. I don't want to lie down at night with speared bulbs on my conscience, and I wouldn't wish that fate on you either.

Try to lift out the whole clump at once. Then find a cool, dim place for separating the bulbs—don't let them dry out any more than necessary. Replant them immediately. I put my larger, parent bulbs in the most conspicuous place, with their smaller offspring behind them. If you prefer, you can put the babies in a nursery bed until they reach adulthood and begin to blossom heavily. Then they can be moved into the limelight with Mama and Papa.

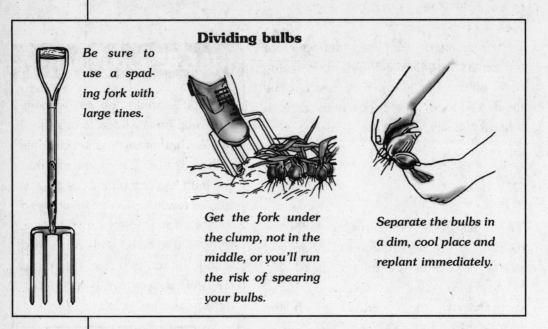

Dividing bulbs

Be sure to use a spading fork with large tines.

Get the fork under the clump, not in the middle, or you'll run the risk of spearing your bulbs.

Separate the bulbs in a dim, cool place and replant immediately.

Store Them Cozy, Clean, And Cool!

The bulbs of dahlias, gladioli, tuberous begonias, and often cannas, must be dug up and stored during the freezing months. I like to wait until the foliage has been blackened by the first frost. If you want to jump the gun, go ahead and dig them up a little early. Tag the bulbs, and temporarily put them in glassed-in cold-frames or a ventilated shed for a few weeks. The idea is to keep them out of the frost. When the bulbs are dry, shake them in a bag of fungicide powder to prevent storage rot. Then place them in their winter home. Few modern cellars have ideal temperatures for bulb storage anymore (55°-60°F), so look around for a place where the bulbs will be safe and comfortable.

HOME REMEDY

Dust bulbs in a paper bag filled with medicated foot powder to prevent disease before storing for the winter.

You'll notice that bulbs in storage will separate by themselves, so you won't have to pry them apart. If you have a small number of bulbs, you can store them in plastic bags filled with peat moss, perlite, or vermiculite. Once you've packed your bulbs up, don't worry about them. If they're stored properly, they'll keep until it's time to replant them again.

Two Special Cases

Dry tender dahlia roots for a couple of hours before storing them in plastic-lined shallow boxes. Blanket them with perlite, vermiculite, or peat moss. Store at about 45°F. A higher temperature might cause sprouting.

Tuberous begonias should be dug up and given a bath. Dust the begonia bulbs in sulfur, and store them in shallow, open trays. If everyone in the family agrees, tuck tuberous begonias away in the vegetable bin of your refrigerator— just don't eat them by mistake!

In all cases, cover the sorted bulbs with fine mesh wire or plastic to keep out mice and other rodents.

BULB STORAGE

Store bulbs in a cool (45-50°F), but frost-free environment during the winter. An unheated garage or root cellar will do. Most bulbs will rot unless kept dry, so store them in mesh or paper bags. Never store bulbs in plastic bags; good air circulation is necessary to prevent rot.

For the few bulbs that must be kept slightly moist, shallow pans filled with damp sand, vermiculite, or peat moss are perfect winter homes. Occasionally sprinkle the mix with water to keep the bulbs barely moist.

PROPAGATION:
GROWING YOUR OWN

Propagation of new babies that you helped bring into the garden world is the greatest satisfaction of any gardener. Why not give it a try? I don't suggest growing bulbs from seed unless you don't mind waiting a long time—up to six years for daffodils! There are, however, several easier and faster ways to propagate bulbs.

Even though I own more bulbs than I can possibly keep an accurate account of, I am always trying to get my hands on more. Sometimes, friends give me new bulbs, especially if I've hinted enough. My family sneaks bulbs into the house, and makes a big to-do about surprising me with a new hybrid. Mostly, though, I collect my bulbs from offsets (smaller bulbs) that form on true bulbs, or from sections that I've cut up.

What we are concerned with here is the bulbs, corms, tubers, tuberous roots, and rhizomes that are most commonly propagated. Ask the average daffodil grower how he propagates new plants, and he'll tell you that he collects the offsets at the daffodil bulb's side. Talk to the dahlia enthusiast, and he'll show you how to cut the dahlia root to grow new ones.

If you are interested in increasing your bulb crop, the ways to do it are easy to understand and easy to put into practice. No hocus-pocus or magic tools are needed, just know-how and a little bit of work. The offspring of spring-planted bulbs can either be set outdoors when the soil temperature is above 50°F, or started earlier indoors in peat pots filled with professional potting mix. Fall-planted baby bulbs should be set into the soil after the first heavy frost.

Bulbs

The most common method of propagating true bulbs is by removing the offsets, which are small bulbs that develop within the parent bulb, and then split off from it. Bulbs which produce offsets can simply be dug up and divided every few years.

Daffodils

Daffodils, which should be left alone unless they are overpopulating an area, probably won't need to be dug up more than once every five years. Dig them up only if the blooms decrease in size, or if you absolutely have to move them.

Lilies

Lilies are more complex than daffodils—they can be propagated in three different ways besides growing them from seed. Since lily bulbs are usually pretty expensive, I'm glad that they're so willing to produce offspring.

Offsets

The easiest way to propagate lilies is to lift the bulbs and pick off the bulblets, or offsets. These should produce flowering plants in about two years. Some experts debud their lily plants, which simply means they strip the plants of their buds before they open.

TOP OF THE CROP

The tulip remains the most popular and recognizable bulb flower among American consumers. Seventy-seven percent of all Americans think first of the tulip when they think of bulb flowers. The tulip is followed in popularity by the daffodil and other narcissi, the gladiolus, the lily, and the crocus.

Trends in the most popular tulip colors tend to follow fashion colors. Over the past several years, there has been a definite move towards pastel colors. Yet, red has always been and continues to be the tulip color of choice among many of the world's consumers. Keeping up with the fickle tastes of fashion is not always easy for the Dutch bulb industry. For example, it normally takes twelve to fifteen years (and can take as long as twenty-five) to bring a new variety of tulip to market.

173

That sounds cruel, but it apparently increases the number of bulblets that form on the parent bulb.

After picking the offsets off your lily bulbs, clean, dry, and store them for the winter. Next year, plant them at the proper time.

Scales

You know that fish must be scaled before cooking, and that mountains are scaled by adventurers. Singers sing scales, and you weigh on scales. But did you know that scaling is a good way to grow more lilies?

Look at your lilies in the spring, and you'll see the thick fleshy scales that wrap around the center of the true bulb. Carefully break off the outer, strong scales, but don't be greedy. Take only 5 or 6 scales to be sure your bulb will have all of the food it needs in spite of the scaling. Dust the scales and parent bulb with a fungicide. Then place all of the scales in a plastic bag of damp peat moss, sphagnum, or vermiculite. Fasten the bag, and store at about 70°F for a few days. Peek in on your babies every now and then. After the bulblets form roots, put the bag into the refrigerator until early fall, and then plant. Place them in your nursery bed, and in a couple of years, you'll have several new flowering-size lilies.

Amateurs and pros alike get excellent results with this method, so don't be afraid to try it.

Scaling lilies

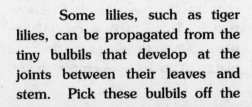

Scales

Bulbils

Some lilies, such as tiger lilies, can be propagated from the tiny bulbils that develop at the joints between their leaves and stem. Pick these bulbils off the

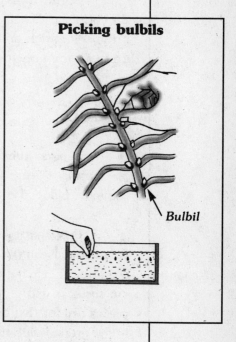

plant when they are ripe, which is always sometime after the plant has flowered. When they're ready, the bulbils will snap off easily, but don't rush them!

Plant the bulbils about an inch deep in a mixture of equal parts loam, coarse sand, and peat moss. Store them in a cold-frame over the winter. When they sprout in the spring, move them to a new home, either in your garden or in a nursery bed.

Corms

Unlike bulbs, corms don't fatten up during the growing season. When you gently tug the plant out of the ground in the fall, you'll see that the original corm is dead. It has dried up, having gobbled up all of its energy during the growing season. In its place, however, is a nice new corm, surrounded by several smaller corms, or cormels.

Dry And Store

After you've dug up your corms, let them dry for two or three weeks in a shady place before you start picking off the cormels. (Women, save those snagged nylon stockings you usually throw out. They're perfect for storing corms and cormels. The open-mesh bags that pota-toes, onions, and citrus fruits come in are good, too.) Keep the corms cool—no warmer than 50°F, but not in danger of freezing.

Picking bulbils

Bulbil

Remove Corms

When they're dry, carefully clean off any soil that's sticking to the bulb, and remove the cormels, which will be clustered around the basal plate of the old, dead corm. I know this sounds heartless, but there's nothing you can do to save the old corm. You can, of course, say a few kind words over it before you throw it in the wastebasket!

Separate Mom And Babies

I always separate my corms and cormels according to size just after I divide them. This makes it easy to decide where to plant them the following spring. I put the fattest corms in the spotlight, and the cormels in my nursery beds. When they reach blooming size in two or three years, I'll give them their chance to take center stage.

Corms multiply rapidly. One gladiolus corm will produce 25 cormels. Crocus corms multiply even more rapidly than glads if the soil is rich and cared for. I don't recommend digging them up more than once every three years.

Tubers

Tubers, tuberous roots, and rhizomes, unlike true bulbs and corms, do not form small "offspring." Neither do potatoes, the most beloved of all tubers.

Propagating tubers, such as gloxinias, gloriosa lilies, and caladiums, is simple. Just cut them up the same way you would a seed potato. Make sure each piece has at least one eye. Dust all cut surfaces with a good all-purpose fungicide powder, and let the pieces dry for two or three days before you plant them. Set them in the ground with the eyes looking upward, 3 to 4 inches deep for the small bulbs, 4 to 6 inches deep for the larger bulbs.

Tuberous Roots

Tuberous rooted plants, such as dahlias, are also propagated by cutting, but with them, the operation is a little more difficult. All the eyes on tuberous roots are in the same place, at the base of the original stem, so you'll have to include a piece of this stem in every section you cut. Cutting the sections apart is a little tricky, but with a little practice, you'll be able to do it like a professional horticulturist. Just remember that no horticulturist would use a dull knife for anything but separating butter. Dip each cut piece in medicated baby powder, and plant them 4 inches deep with the eye looking up. If they're planted in the spring, they'll bloom the same year.

ALWAYS

USE A

GOOD,

SHARP,

CLEAN

KNIFE

Rhizomes

Rhizomes are propagated by cutting too. As I told you, rhizomes are really fat, underground stems that creep along just below the surface of the soil, sending down long, branching roots. All the eyes are on top of the rhizome. When you cut them up, make sure there is at least one eye per section. (I usually include 2 or 3 just for good measure.) Dust each piece in medicated baby powder first.

If you live in the northern half of the country, you'll want to start your lilies of the valley and other rhizomes indoors in damp sand or peat moss. If you live in one of the warmer parts of the country, you can set them outdoors, 4 inches deep, with the eye looking upward immediately after dividing them. Wherever you plant them, rhizomes will usually produce a flowering plant in their first full growing season, unlike their slow-poke cousins who may loaf around for four or five years before producing one bloom.

Rhizomes are propagated by cutting. Make sure there is at least one eye per section.

177

SOME OF MY BEST
BULB FRIENDS

Don't get all excited, I'm not going to introduce you to all 3,000 varieties of bulbs! I'm just going to let you meet some of the more common ones you can easily find and count on. I again want to remind you to get your hands on as many catalogs as you can so that you can better understand—and take advantage of—the vastness of the bulb family.

Achimenes
(Magic flower, Widow's tears)

Achimenes are hanging-basket and strawberry-jar favorites. From spring until fall, they bear small, colorful, trumpet-shaped blossoms on graceful, trailing stems. They are available in many colors, including purple, pink, yellow, blue, and red; some of the newer varieties have contrasting veining or brightly colored throats.

Achimenes require warm temperatures throughout their growing period. They are very susceptible to cold; even one light frost can kill the rhizomes for good. For these reasons, they are usually grown in containers or as house plants.

Achimenes rhizomes look like tiny pine cones, and are very fragile, so handle them with great care. In late winter or early spring, pot them in a mixture of **2 parts peat moss, 1 part potting soil, and 1 part clean sand.** Cover the rhizomes with 1 inch of soil, and water from below. Set them in bright indirect sunlight, and keep moist. After they've sprouted, you can move the container outdoors to a spot in light shade.

BASKET BULBS

Achimenes are ideal bulbs for hanging baskets. Plant bulbs 1 inch deep and 3 inches apart with the tips facing outward.

When the plants stop flowering, let them die back. The rhizomes can be stored in the pot, or can be sifted out and stored in dry peat moss or vermiculite. Keep them at about 60°F until February, when you should move them to a window, and start watering them again.

BULB.COM

The Dutch flower bulb industry is now making their 400 years of bulb cultivating experience available on the Web through a home page at

http://www.bulb.com

There is a huge amount of information on the site, ranging from lists of the best performing perennial tulips and the most fragrant daffodils, to technical cultivation information and statistics.

Amaryllis
(Belladonna lily, Naked lady)

The true amaryllis, or belladonna lily, is often confused with the amaryllis *(Hippeastrum)* grown as a house plant, and with the hardy amaryllises of the *Lycoris* genus. It differs from both. This unusual lily grows long, flat leaves in early spring. These die back, and are followed by a leafless flower stalk in early summer. A month later, clusters of fragrant, trumpet-shaped blossoms unfold on the 2-foot-tall stalks. The flowers, which bloom for 6 to 8 weeks, may be mauve, white, pink, or rosy red.

Belladonna lilies can be grown in all but the northernmost states. Plant in well-drained soil enriched with compost or well-rotted manure. In the Deep South, cover the bulbs with 1 or 2 inches of soil; elsewhere, cover with 5 to 8 inches of soil, depending on winter temperatures. Apply a 5-10-5 fertilizer when the foliage appears.

Leave the bulbs undisturbed until you're ready to propagate from offsets. This should be done in the spring.

Begonia

BULB BUYING TIPS

Many bulbs come back year after year. Others, however, diminish over time. To get the most bang for your buck, look for bulbs marked on their packaging "Good for Naturalizing" or "Good for Perennializing." As a rule, naturalizing means that the bulbs will multiply and their flowers become a permanent, seasonal feature in your garden. Daffodils and other narcissi, crocuses, and grape hyacinths are examples.

Perennializing means that the bulbs will come back up for three years before they start to diminish. Many tulips and Dutch hyacinths (the big fragrant kind) are examples of this.

If you use these "repeat performers" as the basis of your outdoor collection, your planting chores will lessen over the years, and you can also indulge yourself with some additional special varieties which will provide a dazzling display for one year only.

There are two species of begonias in the bulb category, the hardy begonia and the spectacular tuberous begonia. Both species bloom in summer, require shade, and grow from tuberous roots.

The hardy begonia produces clusters of tiny pink flowers on 2-foot-tall plants. Plant the small tubers 1 to 2 inches deep. In the South, they may remain in the ground unprotected; in the middle states, they require a winter mulch; and in the North, they should be taken indoors in winter.

The tuberous begonia produces blossoms from 2 to 10 inches in diameter, and in every color except blue and green. Both upright and trailing varieties are available. The tubers may be started indoors or out, but in all parts of the country, they must be taken indoors for the winter. To start them indoors, set the tubers in flats or boxes of damp peat moss; press them down firmly but don't cover them. After the tubers sprout, transplant them to 6-inch pots; move them outdoors when the night temperatures stay above 50°F. Outdoors, set the tubers in soil to which manure and peat moss have been added. Apply a mild fertilizer every 2 or 3 weeks throughout the growing season.

Propagate begonias from seed in midwinter for blooms the following summer, or from stem or root cuttings in spring.

THE BEST OF THE BEGONIAS

The most popular types of tuberous begonias are the large-flowered begonias. These have double flowers, and come in many colors including rich yellow, dark red, orange, salmon, and white. Large-flowered begonias reach a height of 10 to 14 inches tall. They have extremely long flowering times, flowering continually from early June until far into September. Look for varieties that resemble other flowers. "Bouton de Rose" and "Bouton de Rose Jaune," for example, have blossoms that recall half-opened rosebuds. A stunning flower is "Marmorata," a full double begonia with red- and white-speckled flowers.

Canna

Cannas are becoming popular as bedding plants again. The modern hybrids range in height from 1-$\frac{1}{2}$ to 5 feet tall, and send up spikes of large blossoms from early summer until frost. The color range covers white, yellow, and pink to scarlet. The handsome, broad leaves may be green, bronze, or blue-green.

All cannas prefer moist, rich soil, full sun, and high temperatures. In the southern half of the country, cannas can remain in the ground all year; elsewhere, they must be dug up in fall after frost blackens the foliage. In the North, start cannas indoors in professional mix in late February; elsewhere, set them 15 to 18 inches apart in the garden after all threat of frost has passed, and cover with 1 or 2 inches of soil.

Canna

CANNA DO

Cannas tend to dry out during winter storage, so check them every 3 to 4 weeks, and lightly sprinkle any that start to shrivel with water.

Propagate by dividing the rhizomes in spring.

Chionodoxa
(Glory-of-the-Snow)

As its popular name implies, the tiny chionodoxa is one of the first bulbs to bloom in the spring. The most common species bears small, star-shaped, violet-blue flowers with white centers, 8 to 10 per stem. Other species bear lilac, white, pink, and porcelain-blue blossoms.

Plant the bulbs 2 inches deep in fertile, well-drained soil in early autumn. They do best in full sun or light shade. No further care is necessary.

Colchicum
(Autumn Crocus)

Colchicum blossoms spring out of the ground in fall, long after their foliage has died. The flowers look like crocus and occur in shades of pink and lavender as well as white.

Plant colchicums in late summer, covering them with 3 to 4 inches of soil. They prefer full sun or light shade, and should be situated so they can remain undisturbed for many years.

Propagate from cormels after the foliage dies back in early summer.

Colocasia
(Elephant's Ear)

Elephant's ears are grown for their large, spear-shaped leaves which often grow up to 2 feet long. The plants often reach 6 feet tall.

Only in the Deep South can elephant's ears remain outdoors over the winter. Elsewhere, they must be dug up after the first fall frost.

Plant them in a sunny or lightly shaded spot in moist soil that's been worked with peat moss, sand, and rotted manure. For container planting, use a mixture of **2 parts potting soil, 2 parts peat moss, 1 part rotted manure, and 1 part sand.** Move indoors before frost, and place in bright indirect sunlight.

Propagate by cutting the tubers into pieces each spring. Dust with a fungicide powder, and allow to dry for 2 or 3 days before planting.

Colocasia

Convallaria
(Lily of the Valley)

Delicate, fragrant lilies of the valley are indoor and outdoor favorites, blooming all summer long. They are good for indoor forcing, and for creating a neglectable ground cover in shady areas.

Lilies of the valley do not do well in warm climates. Elsewhere, in fall or spring, plant the pips one inch deep in moist, acidic soil.

Propagate in fall by dividing the pips after the foliage yellows.

TIMELY TONIC

Give your elephant's ears an earful by feeding them with the following tonic:

**1 can of beer,
1 cup of All Purpose Plant Food, and
1/4 cup of ammonia**

in a 20 gallon hose-end sprayer, filling the balance of the sprayer with water. Spray the plants every 3 weeks to the point of run-off.

Crocus

Crocuses are among the most popular of the spring-flowering bulbs. Less widely known species also bloom in fall and even in winter in mild climates. The small, cup-shaped blossoms are available in a wide range of colors, including lavender and purple, yellow, white, or striped.

Crocuses are hardy throughout the country, and do best in areas with low winter temperatures. Plant crocus corms 2 to 4 inches deep as early in the fall as they are available. Every fall, sprinkle a little bone meal or 5-10-5 fertilizer on the soil covering them. No other care is necessary.

For indoor forcing, plant corms in October in a mixture of equal parts potting soil, peat moss, and clean sand. Place the pots in a coldframe until February, then take them indoors to sprout.

Cyclamen

There are two types of cyclamen —the large-flowered florists' cyclamen *(C. persicum),* and the smaller, but more hardy species cyclamen. Florists' cyclamens are usually bought as pot plants, and may be grown outdoors in the Deep South. Species cyclamen can be grown outdoors in all but the Deep South and far North. The butterfly-shaped flowers of cyclamen may be pink, red, or white, and may appear at various times in the spring, summer, and fall, depending upon the species. The attractive, heart-shaped foliage may be either marbled or solid green.

CRAZY FOR CROCUS!

When crocuses pop up, suddenly "It's spring!" Their slender slips of color poke up through snow and bare ground. Their egg-shaped spots of color dot the ground—then open in the sun. Crocus come in many colors, some bright, some delicate, all charming: golds, purples, whites, blues, violets, bronze, and stripes.

Americans prefer, in this order: the giant "snow" crocus in yellow, blue, white, and striped; and the species crocus 'Cream Beauty' (pale creamy-yellow); 'Gypsy Girl' (outside striped and feathered purplish-brown, inside golden yellow); and 'Blue Bird' (outside rich violet blue with a white edging, inside pale cream).

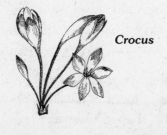

Crocus

Plant the tubers of the small-flowered species cyclamens 1 or 2 inches deep in midsummer in a lightly shaded location in soil that has been worked with compost. Compost also should be applied as a mulch every spring.

Propagate cyclamen from seed. Blooming plants can be expected in about eighteen months.

Dahlia

Dahlias will provide blossoms in every color but blue from midsummer until frost in all areas of this country. The flowers range in diameter from 1 inch to 1 foot, and the plants vary in height from 1 to 7 feet tall. Dahlias come in a wide variety of shapes, including ball-shaped, cactus-flowered, pompon, anemone-flowered, and single-flowered.

Dahlias may be bought in 3 forms—root divisions, plants grown from cuttings, and pot roots. In all but the Deep South, dahlias should be planted in spring, and dug up in the fall. They prefer full sun, but will tolerate light shade. Before planting, work compost, peat moss, and 5 pounds of 0-20-20 fertilizer per 100 square feet into the soil. Plant pot roots and plants the same as you would any other seedling. Lay root divisions on their sides in 7-inch-deep holes, and cover with 2 inches of soil; add more soil as the plants grow. When the plants are growing well, water with a light application of complete fertilizer. Tall plants may need to be pinched back to encourage bushiness, or staked to prevent them from toppling over.

In the fall, after the plants have stopped flowering, dig up the roots and place them in plastic-lined boxes of dry peat moss or vermiculite. Keep in a very cool place to prevent premature sprouting.

CYCLAMENS ARE GREAT FOR SHADY GARDENS

Dahlia

DAHLIA MARKERS

The best way of marking dahlias is to use tongue depressors marked with a wood-burning tool. Burn the name of the dahlia on one side, and the color and type on the other. Drill a small hole in the top of the stick, tie a string to it at planting time, then retie the stick to the tuber at storing time.

185

Dahlias may be propagated from root divisions, stem cuttings, or seeds, which will produce flowering plants the first year.

Eranthis
(Winter Aconite)

The honey-scented, yellow flowers of winter aconite are among the first to appear in spring. Winter aconites are hardy in all but the far North, and will flourish in virtually any soil. They do best in full sun or light shade, and should be planted in a location protected from the wind.

Plant the tubers as early as possible in late summer or fall. Soak them in weak tea water for twenty-four hours, then plant them 3 inches deep.

Propagate winter aconite by cutting the tubers. They also grow readily from seed, but will take two to three years to flower.

Eranthis

A CLASSIC SPRING IN YELLOW AND WHITE

For a crisp, sophisticated springtime look, white and yellow color combinations beat all. No colors have more "jump" in the landscape—the eye is drawn immediately when white or yellow appear against a backdrop of endless green.

Eranthis is little known by most gardeners. Yet this small wonder (also known as winter aconite) has both presence and staying power in the garden. Just 3 inches tall, with a yellow flower that looks like a fairy forest buttercup, the *eranthis* is one of the first flowers to bloom in the spring, often blooming right through the snow. Its short stems and bright sunny flowers, ringed by a green leafy collar, create a carpet effect when planted en masse. The flowers open wide in the sun, and close in the evening. Plant with beds of white flowers such as *galanthus* (also known as Snowdrop, petite pendant white flower), and crocus 'Joan of Arc' (white with orange stamen).

Freesia

Freesias are popular as winter-blooming house plants because of their bright blossoms and intense fragrance. They can be grown outdoors only in the Deep South (with the exception of corms specially treated to bloom in summer). Freesias come in pink, white, yellow, lilac, blue, purple, orange, and vermilion.

To grow as house plants, set the corms in a mix of equal parts peat moss, potting soil, and clean sand. Cover the corms very lightly. In the summer, set the pots outdoors in a cool, shaded place. Move them indoors to a sunny window before the first frost. Keep the soil moist, and apply a house plant fertilizer once a month until the buds begin to color.

Freesia

FREESIAS
CAN BE
GROWN AS
HOUSE
PLANTS

Propagate from cormels after the foliage dies back. Store both corms and cormels in a dry place until June, when they should be repotted. Plants grown from seed will flower in six months to a year.

Fritillaria
(Crown Imperial, Checkered Fritillary)

The striking flower clusters of crown imperiala *(F. imperialis)* appear atop 2 to 4-foot-tall stalks in early spring. The cluster of large, bell-shaped blossoms, which may be red, bronze, yellow, or orange, are crowned with a mass of narrow, pointed leaves. The smaller, checkered fritillary *(F. meleagris)*, also known as the guinea-hen flower, grows to thirteen feet tall, and bears pendant, bell-shaped flowers which may be purple- and white-checkered or all white.

The checkered fritillary is hardy throughout the country, and the crown imperial is hardy in all but the northernmost states. Plant the bulbs of both in summer in a lightly shaded location.

Plant crown imperials 6 inches deep, and checkered fritillaries 4 inches deep. When the plants appear in spring, apply a light application of 5-10-5 fertilizer.

COLD WON'T NIP THE BUDS

Can spring's drastic temperature swings hurt the emerging shoots of crocus, daffodils, and tulips that were planted last fall? Generally not, since healthy spring-flowering bulbs will usually withstand extreme cold, snow, or early warm spells.

When the weather turns, don't bother dashing outside to cover early-sprouting bulbs with extra "weather protection." Adding additional mulch or coverings will only cause more gardening work. A short freeze won't do lasting damage to young bulb shoots and buds, though it may "burn" already open blossoms. Many, such as snowdrops, crocuses, and early rock garden narcissi, are supposed to come up in very early spring, even peeking through the snow. Mother Nature has provided them with the means to survive. An unseasonably warm spell may cause some bulbs to bloom earlier than anticipated, but in most cases, this won't result in permanent damage.

Propagate them from offsets in early summer after the foliage has died back.

Galanthus
(Snowdrop)

Snowdrops are among the first flowers to bloom in spring. Their delicate blossoms are white, tipped with green, and the leaves are slender.

Snowdrops can be grown in all parts of the country, except the Deep South. They do best, however, in cool climates.

Plant the bulbs 2 or 3 inches deep in early fall, preferably in a shady location. No further care is necessary.

To grow snowdrops indoors, plant the bulbs in fall in a mixture of equal parts potting soil, peat moss, and sand. Leave the pots in a coldframe until after the first of the year, then place them in indirect sunlight in the coolest room in your house.

Snowdrops can be propagated from offsets after the first frost.

Gladiolus

The gladiolus is the best-selling bulb in the United States, primarily because of its popularity as a cut flower. Gladioli are available in many sizes (ranging from 1 to 5 feet in height) and in 28 different colors. A gladiolus plant has a bloom period lasting only a week to 10 days, but staggered plantings can provide blooms over a period of three months. Because its tall, stiff foliage is not very attractive, gladioli are usually planted in a special cutting garden.

In the South, gladiolus corms may remain in the garden all year long, elsewhere, they must be dug in the fall, and replanted in spring. Regardless of climate, gladioli do best when dug and replanted annually.

Prepare the gladiolus bed, which should be in full sun, by working compost, peat moss, and 5-10-5 fertilizer (at a rate of one cup per 25-foot row) into the soil. Plant the corms 5 inches deep in spring after the last frost. New plantings should be made every week to ten days up until two months before the first fall frost; this will ensure a prolonged period of continuous bloom.

When the spikes appear, apply 5-10-5 fertilizer at the same rate as above, watering it into the soil. When the spikes are about a foot tall, some sort of support will be necessary. Either stake them, or mound up 6 inches of soil around the stems.

About a month after the flowers fade, lift the corms with a spading fork, cut off the foliage, and dry in a dark place for two or three weeks. Remove the spent corm, divide the corms and cormels, and dust them with an

Gladiolus

GLAD REMINDER

To enjoy abundant blossoms from July through September, plant glads in "waves" that will bloom successively, one after another. Starting in May (or earlier in warm climates), plant a quantity of corms every two weeks until June.

Here's one precaution: to avoid soil/corm infections, rotate glad planting sites yearly. Avoid planting glads where beans have grown the year before because there is a bean mosaic virus that could stay in the soil and infect the flowers.

all-purpose insecticide-fungicide. Place in an old stocking or mesh bag, and store them in a very cool place over the winter.

Gloriosa
(Glory Lily)

Surprisingly, the glory lily is a climbing vine. The 3- to 4-inch flowers are composed of long, recurved petals which may be either yellow tipped with scarlet, or orange tipped with red. They are popular as house plants because they can be induced to bloom in any season, and they can when grown outdoors in the Deep South. When planted outdoors in colder areas, they bloom in summer.

For outdoor culture, plant the tubers 4 inches deep in manure-enriched soil, preferably in full sun. Apply 5-10-5 fertilizer once a month during the growing season. In the North, the tubers must be dug up in fall after the first frost.

To grow as house plants, pot glory lily tubers in a mixture of equal parts potting soil, peat moss, and clean sand. Keep the soil moist, and fertilize every 12 weeks during the growing season. The dormant period usually lasts from October through January; during this time, withhold both water and fertilizer.

Propagate from the tubers in early summer.

Gloriosa

CLIMBING BULBS

Plant a low, shallow-rooted evergreen on the sunny side of the bulb. The shade will help the vine get established. Then mulch well to keep both plants cool.

Hyacinthus
(Hyacinth)

The sweet spring fragrance of hyacinths makes them as popular for indoor forcing as they are for outdoor bedding. The most popular species, the large-flowered hyacinth, grows 8 to 12 inches tall, and bears tight, 6- to 10-inch clusters of tiny pink, blue, white, or yellow flowers. Almost as widely known are the smaller and more sparsely flowered French-Roman hyacinths.

Large-flowered hyacinths are hardy throughout this country, but French-Roman hyacinths are hardy only in the South. All hyacinths should be planted in the fall, and do best in full sun.

Plant large-flowered hyacinths 5 inches deep; French-Roman and other smaller hyacinths 3 inches deep. In the North, a winter mulch is beneficial. Although large-flowered hyacinths will survive if left outdoors over the winter, it is advisable to dig them up every fall, and replace the small bulbs (resulting from division of the parent bulb) with large, new ones. The small bulbs can be replanted in enriched soil in another bed, and left there until they reach the size necessary for good bloom development.

To grow hyacinths indoors, pot them in the fall in a mixture of equal parts peat moss, potting soil, and clean sand. Set the pots in your cellar or some other dark, cool place, and leave them there for 3 months, or until the sprout is about 2 inches tall. Move the plant into a very cool spot that receives indirect light. In about a week, move the plant into a sunny window. When the buds begin to color, move the plant into curtain-filtered sunlight. After the plants have bloomed and the foliage matured, allow the soil to dry out. Replant the bulbs in the garden in the fall.

GIVE YOUR HYACINTH ANOTHER CHANCE

Flowering bulbs, like hyacinths, are forced to bloom out of season in response to controlled environmental conditions in the greenhouse. To bloom again outdoors, they require a rest period, and natural outdoor environmental conditions.

To reflower your bulb plants, remove the faded blooms, and keep the plants watered in a cool, bright location until the foliage matures and dries out. Plant the bulbs outdoors after all danger of frost has passed, two to three times deeper than their diameter. They should bloom in a year or two during the normal spring season.

191

Hymenocallis
(Spider Lily)

Spider lilies, also known as Peruvian daffodils, bear fragrant, delicately exotic 4-inch blossoms in midsummer. The most popular species is white with green stripes; another species is yellow, and still another is white with very faint stripes. The flower stalks grow 18 to 24 inches tall, and the strap-like leaves are often 2 feet long.

BULB REPAIR

You can repair bulbs that have been damaged in a couple of ways. If the wound isn't deep, dust it with sand or ashes, and let it dry. If it's deep, store the bulb, cut side up, in a cool, dry place. Small bulbs will develop on the top of the piece, which can be planted in the fall.

In the Deep South, spider lilies may be left outdoors over the winter; elsewhere, they must be dug up before frost or grown as house plants. In spring, work well-rotted or dried cow manure into the soil, and plant the bulbs 4 inches deep. In the Deep South, bulbs may be planted in fall as well as spring.

In areas having cold winter temperatures, dig the bulbs up when the foliage dries out; cut off the foliage, and store the bulbs upside down in dry peat moss or vermiculite in a shady, airy place at 65-70°F.

Propagate from offsets.

Iris

Only 3 groups of irises are classified as bulbous plants; the rest are perennials. *Reticulata* irises grow only 4 to 8 inches tall, and bear small purple, blue, or yellow flowers in early spring. The *Xiphium* group includes the Spanish, Dutch, and English irises, all of which grow 1 to 2 feet tall, and are available in a wide variety of colors. Juno irises bear 5 to 7 blossoms on each 2-foot stalk; the blossoms may be one of several colors or bicolored.

Juno and *Reticulata* irises are hardy except in the northernmost states; *Xiphium* irises are hardy only in the southern half of the country.

Iris

All bulbous irises should be planted in late summer or early fall, and all do best in full sun. Cover *Reticulata* irises with 3 inches of soil; cover *Xiphium* and Juno irises with 5 inches of soil. When the plants appear in spring, make a light application of 5-10-5 fertilizer. Dig up and divide the bulbs during their midsummer dormancy once every four or five years.

Lilium
(Lily)

Lilies have been greatly improved in recent years. Modern hybrids are stronger, more adaptable, and more colorful than their old-fashioned ancestors. If you choose wisely, you can have a parade of different lilies beginning in June, and lasting through July. With the many sizes, shapes, and color combinations now available, you need never become bored. Lilies vary in height from 2 to 8 feet, and are available in every color but blue; they also come in striped and spotted color combinations.

According to the Royal Horticultural Society and the North American Lily Society, lilies can be divided into the following groups: Asiatic Hybrids, Martagon Hybrids, Candidum Hybrids, American Hybrids, Longiflorum Hybrids, Aurelian Hybrids, Oriental Hybrids, Unclassified Hybrids, and True Species of Lilies. There are also various sub-groups within each of theses 9 groups.

SUPER GROWING SECRET

Mix 4 parts bone meal and 6 parts hydrated lime, and sprinkle it around iris plants freely. Cultivate it into the ground when the soil is dry enough, and your iris will be off to a flying start!

Lilium

Most lilies are hardy in all areas of the country, and most need at least 5 or 6 hours of sun a day. The exceptions are tiger lilies and wood lilies, which will tolerate light shade.

No lily will do well in wet soil, so good drainage is a must. It is also important that the soil have adequate organic matter, so be sure to work in a large amount of compost, peat moss, or leaf mold before planting. As soon as possible after purchasing your bulbs, plant them 4 to 6 inches deep, except for Madonna lilies which should be planted only one inch deep.

All lilies benefit from mulching because it prevents their roots from drying out, and keeps them cool. In the Deep South or in any other area where frost is rare, dig up the bulbs in the fall, and refrigerate them for two months to simulate the period of dormancy. It may become necessary to stake lilies to protect them from rain and wind damage.

ARRANGING LILIES

❀ Lily flowers need gentle handling because they tend to bruise easily, which affects their appearance and vase life.

❀ Don't crowd lilies in an arrangement. Part of their appeal is their bold, individual appearance. For lily arrangements, simpler is more elegant!

❀ For longest life, lily arrangements should be placed in a shaded spot away from direct sunlight. Don't place lilies (or any bulb flowers) near bowls of fruit. Fruit, as it ripens, gives off ethylene gas which can damage cut flowers.

❀ As leaves yellow, remove them, plus any other foliage that has fallen into the water.

❀ Change the water frequently; every few days is ideal!

Lilies may be propagated in the fall from the scales that make up the bulb, from the bulbils that form in the leaf joints of some varieties, or from the small bulbs which form around the parent bulb. Plants propagated from any of the above methods will flower in 2 to 3 years; plants grown from seed usually take four years to flower.

CUT LILY CARE TIPS

Here are easy-to-follow tips on how to enjoy this most luxurious of flowers.

❋ Buy lilies when the lowest flowers on the stems have just opened; the upper flowers will open one by one.

❋ Handle the flowers carefully on the way home, protecting them from direct sunlight.

❋ Once home, cut the stem end with a sharp knife, and place the stems into a container with 6" of warm water.

❋ The best cutting technique: hold the stem underwater while cutting it to minimize air bubble uptake; cut at a 45° angle to increase water uptake.

❋ After selecting (and cleaning) a vase; remove any lower leaves that will stand below the vase's water line and cause bacteria growth.

❋ Add "cut flower food," but only use about half the recommended dosage.

❋ Cut lilies should be handled with care: the pollen on the stamens easily rubs off onto clothes, leaving a stain that's difficult to remove. Clipping off the small pollen-laden anthers is one way to avoid this problem. Any pollen that does get onto fabric should be removed by lightly dabbing at the spot with adhesive tape, or brushing the area carefully with a very small, soft brush.

Muscari
(Grape Hyacinth)

Grape hyacinths are among the most agreeable of bulbous plants. They can be grown anywhere in this country with a minimum of care, and their tiny, fragrant blossoms have long been spring favorites. They are charming when naturalized in grass, or scattered about in a rock garden. Grape hyacinths may also be grown indoors as house plants. The most common grape hyacinths have sky-blue flowers. Less well-known varieties come in white and purple, as well as in combinations of yellow and purple, and light and dark blue. A plumed mauve variety is also available.

Plant the bulbs 3 inches deep in early fall, preferably in a sunny location. No further care is necessary. Propagate from offsets on fall.

TOP OF THE CROP

Top selections for narcissi among U.S. gardeners are the yellow, large-trumpet King Alfred "types" (America's favorites: large-cupped **'Carlton'** and trumpet narcissus **'Dutch Master'**), followed by: **'Barrett Browning'** (small cup, white with bright orange cup); **'Ice Follies'** (large cup, white with canary yellow cup); **'Salome'** (large cup, white with salmon-colored cup); **'February Gold'** (cyclamineus or dwarf species, yellow-gold); **'Flower Drift'** (double flowered, creamy white with rumpled cup of white, yellow, orange); **'Mount Hood'** (trumpet narcissus, ivory white); **'Tete a Tete'** (cyclamineus, lemon-yellow); **'Geranium'** (tazetta, white with orange cup); and **'Cheerfulness'** (tazetta, either white or yellow).

Narcissus
(Daffodil)

Narcissi are on everyone's list of favorite springtime flowers—and for several good reasons. With a minimum of care, narcissi will produce great clumps of cheerful, fragrant flowers every spring. Basic narcissus colors are white and shades of orange, yellow, and red; however, they're available in many different combinations, and still more shadings and variations in size and shape.

Most narcissi are hardy in all parts of the country, the exceptions being the Tazetta types, the cyclamen-flowered narcissi, and some of the species narcissi.

Plant the bulbs in late summer to ensure good root development before the first fall frost. All types prefer full sun or light shade. Before setting the bulbs, work bone meal into the soil at a rate of 5 pounds per 100 square feet for bed plantings, or 1 teaspoon per hole for individual plantings. Set each bulb 3 times as deep as its diameter at the widest point. (Depth may vary from 3 to 6 inches.) In the spring, when the bulbs begin to sprout, sprinkle bone meal around the plants again.

Narcissus

Propagate from offsets in midsummer.

Nerine
(Nerine Lily)

Nerine lilies are very popular as potted plants because of their striking and long-lasting clusters of long-stemmed flowers. The flowers, which may be white or one of various shades of pink and red, appear atop 1- to 2-foot-tall stalks in early fall. Long, strap-like leaves appear at about the same time, and continue to grow long after the flowers have faded.

Nerine lilies can be grown outdoors in the Deep South, but because they flower more profusely when crowded, they are usually grown in containers even in mild climates. In midsummer, pot the bulbs in a mixture of equal parts potting soil, peat moss, and clean sand, setting only the bottom half of each bulb below the soil surface. Don't water until

WELCOME!

Use containers of flowers to create colorful focal points at your front door. Select pots of different styles and sizes for bulb flowers of different heights and bloom times—then mix and match. In larger containers, plant a mixture of many bulbs to achieve months of successive bloom. These can be planted in layers, like lasagna, with larger bulbs such as tulips, hyacinths, and narcissi about 8 inches deep, and smaller bulbs such as crocus, snowdrops, and grape hyacinths 5 inches down.

the flower stalks appear; then feed and water regularly throughout the winter and spring. Cut back the watering in summer. Let the foliage die back, then cut. Move the pots indoors to a cool, bright location before frost.

Propagate from offsets during repotting, which will be necessary only once in five years.

Oxalis

There are several different species of oxalis, but all produce small blossoms atop neat clumps of foliage, which vary from a few inches to a foot in diameter. The blossoms may be pink, red, yellow, or white, and appear at various times during spring and summer, depending on the species.

Plant the bulbs in spring 2 inches deep in a sunny location, and apply 5-10-5 fertilizer when growth appears. In the North, oxalises must be taken indoors in winter.

Propagate from offsets in the fall; they will flower in one year.

Polianthes Tuberosa
(Tuberose)

The extraordinarily fragrant white blossoms of tuberoses are borne on tall (1 to 4 feet) stalks in late summer and early fall. They make excellent cut flowers, but because of their intense fragrance should be used sparingly.

Once night temperatures remain above 60°F in spring, plant tuberose bulbs 3 inches deep in a sunny location. Fertilize them once a month from the time sprouts appear until the buds begin to color. After the foliage has been browned by frost, dig up the bulbs, remove the stems, and dry them for 2 weeks before storing them in a cool, dry place.

Polianthes

Propagate from offsets. These smaller bulbs often take 2 years to bloom. It's best to start out with less than full-sized bulbs to ensure 2 or more years of flowering before division occurs, which will result in smaller blossoms. If you prefer, you can, of course, buy new large bulbs every spring.

Ranunculus Asiaticus
(Persian Buttercup)

Persian buttercups bear large, lushly petaled blossoms in every color of the rainbow (except blue and green), as well as in various shades and combinations. A single plant may produce as many as 75 flowers in one blooming season.

Ranunculus

In the Deep South, Persian buttercups may be planted in late fall for early spring bloom; elsewhere, they should be planted in early spring for late spring bloom. To provide proper moisture conditions for the tubers (dry crowns and wet roots), knock the bottoms out of some clay pots, and set them so that their rims are 1-$\frac{1}{2}$ inches above the soil surface. Place the tubers in the pots, and cover them with 1-$\frac{1}{2}$ inches of soil. Water once, withhold any more water until growth begins, and then keep them evenly moist. Dig up, and store the tubers after the foliage withers. Tubers may be divided for propagation at this time. Spring-sown seed will reach flowering size the following year.

Scilla
(Squill)

The most well-known squill is blue, but pink, purple, lavender, red, and white varieties are available also. All send up 6- to 12-inch spikes of small, drooping blossoms early in spring.

SIZE 'EM UP

What is the minimum number of bulbs needed to make a good showing?

Ten to twelve tulips will look far better in a group than six or seven. For hyacinths, you need six to eight to make a good showing. With daffodils, you should also have ten to twelve. And when it comes to the tiny bulbs, you'll need to plant twenty to one hundred to get a beautiful carpet of color.

The most popular varieties of squill are hardy throughout the country. Others will grow only in the southern half of the country; still others won't grow in warm climates, so make sure you know the growing requirements of the species you buy. Most squills should be planted in fall, and all will flourish under any light conditions. Plant 3 to 4 inches deep.

Squills may be propagated from offsets, but the bulbs are so inexpensive, most people buy new ones rather than disturb the original planting.

Tigridia
(Tiger Flower)

Tigridia

The 6-inch blossoms of tigridias have one very distinctive feature—brightly-spotted inner petals. Tigridias come in white, yellow, pink, lavender, buff, and orange. A single plant often produces several 3- to 5-inch wide blooms with foliage collars over a period of 2 weeks.

Tigridias can remain outdoors through the winter only in the South; elsewhere, they must be dug up in the fall after their leaves turn yellow. Dry the bulbs thoroughly, and store them in dry peat moss or vermiculite in a place that is cool and dry.

In the spring, when the night temperatures stay above 60°F, plant the bulbs 4 inches deep in a sunny location. Apply 5-10-5 fertilizer twice a month, and keep the soil moist.

Propagate from offsets.

THUG BUSTER

Here's a neat trick to keep squirrels away from your bulbs: after planting new areas, lay old window screens in frames on the ground, and cover them with the newly-worked soil. The screen weighs just enough to foil the squirrel, but allows for air circulation and rainfall. Once the ground has settled, remove the screens and store for future use.

Tulipa
(Tulip)

Today, there are 15 classes of tulips, and over 4,000 named varieties. These include many different shapes, sizes, colors, and color combinations.

Tulips blossom at various times during the spring, from March through May, depending on the specific variety and the climate they are growing in. Early tulips, for example, may not bloom until mid-April in Pennsylvania or states further north.

TULIP TIPS

Don't let the soil around tulips dry out. Generally, they need about 1 inch of water per week. A soaker hose works best.

Large-flowered garden tulips do best in the northern half of the country, where they can remain in the ground all year long. Before planting, work bone meal into the soil at a rate of 5 pounds per 100 square feet. When sprouts appear in the spring, apply a light application of 5-10-5 fertilizer.

Tulip bulbs should be planted as early as possible in the fall after a good hard frost. If you are going to discard the bulbs after blooming (to avoid multiplying and the resultant decrease in flower size), plant them 5 inches apart and 5 inches deep. It is better, however, to plant the bulbs deeper because this slows their multiplying process, and results in good flower production for up to 8 years. For deep plantings, work up the soil to a depth of 18 inches, then set the bulbs 10 inches deep and 6 inches apart.

Tulipa

To grow large-flowered tulips in the South, refrigerate the bulbs for 2 months after purchasing, then plant 6 to 8 inches deep. Discard them after flowering.

Species tulips can be grown in all but the Deep South. In the fall, plant them 3 to 6 inches deep and leave them undisturbed.

Propagate from offsets in midsummer.

Zantedeschia
(Calla Lily)

In spring and summer, calla lilies produce large, upright goblet-shaped blossoms on tall (1-$\frac{1}{2}$ to 4 feet) stems. The broad, erect leaves are attractive in their own right. The various calla lily species and hybrids bear flowers in white, pink, red, and yellow.

The white calla lily flourishes in mucky soil that is frequently covered with water. All the species do best in light shade. If in full sun, midday shade is advisable.

In the North, calla lilies should be planted in spring, and dug up in the fall. Store in dry peat moss or vermiculite in a cool (40-50°F) place. In the South, they may be planted at any time of the year. Plant them 4 inches deep, and apply 5-10-5 fertilizer once a month.

To grow calla lilies as house plants, plant the rhizomes in fall, setting them 3 inches deep in equal parts peat moss, potting

Zantedeschia

MARIA! WHAT CALLAS?

The calla lily comes as close to perfection as one flower can. Its flower boasts a texture so smooth and velvety that one suspects that it's unreal! Officially known as the *Zantedeschia*, the calla has sheath-like flowers in pink, yellow, or white, or one of the newer shades of bronze, gold, or deep rose. When we think of callas, we can recall the 1937 movie "Stage Door" featuring the young Katherine Hepburn. "The calla lilies are in bloom again," she said in her play-within-the-film entrance. And so, the calla goes down in movie history. Plant sumptuous callas in full sun, sheltered from the wind.

soil, and clean sand. Water them lightly until a sprout appears; from then on, keep the soil moist and apply a good house-plant fertilizer once a month. In the summer, cut back on watering. When the leaves wither, stop watering altogether until fall. At that time, begin watering again, and growth will begin again.

Propagate by dividing the rhizomes in early fall.

Zephyranthes
(Zephyr Lily)

Zephyr lilies can be found blooming from spring to fall. The plants grow only 6 to 8 inches tall, and produce single, upright, lily-type flowers. The many colors available include white, yellow, pink, apricot, and salmon.

In the South, zephyr lilies can be planted in the fall, and left undisturbed for many years. In the North, the bulbs must be planted in spring 2 inches deep in a sunny location, and then dug up in the fall. When you do, wash them in a mild soapy water solution. Let them dry, and dust with medicated baby powder before storing in dry paper or sawdust. Repot them in February, and set them outside in May.

Propagate these plants from offsets.

Zephyranthes

❀4❀

ROSES
Everything Is Coming Up Roses!

Whenever I sit down to write about roses, I always find my mind going in a million different directions all at one time, looking for just the right introduction, just the right words, that will motivate all of you new gardeners to include as many roses as possible in your flower garden plan. I am also hoping to interest those of you who have heard how hard roses are to grow to try them for yourself, and see how wrong that warning is.

By far and away, roses are the most popular plant sold in garden centers year after year. It is true that many, many roses are lost each year, but in most cases, it is the rose grower's fault, and not that of the rose.

Like any other plant you select for your flowerscape, there are some basic rules you must follow to ensure growing success. The rose is no exception.

Here again, as with each of the other sections, I'm going to give you a rather broad overview of the plant group referred to as roses, including background material, information on their needs, and possible problem areas. I'm also going to explain the care and cultivation methods used by professional rose growers, amateur growers, and the U.S. experimental stations, along with my own tips, tricks, and tonics.

THEY'RE NOT ALL CALLED ROSE BUSHES

Roses are separated into two main classes—bush roses and climbing roses—according to their habits of growth. Full-growth bush roses grow from 1 to 6 feet tall, and require no support. Climbing roses, on the other hand, produce long canes, and must have some kind of support to grow.

TWO MAIN TYPES— BUSH ROSES AND CLIMBING ROSES

Bush Roses

The bush roses are subdivided according to their flowering habit, winter hardiness, and several other traits. The types of bush roses are hybrid tea, floribunda, grandiflora, polyantha, hybrid perpetual, shrub, old-fashioned, tree or standard, and miniature. All of them will require proper winter protection.

Hybrid Teas

Hybrid teas are the so-called monthly, or everblooming roses. They are grown more widely than all other types of roses combined. When the word "rose" is used, a hybrid tea variety is usually what is meant.

Mature hybrid tea rose bushes are 2 to 6 feet tall, with the height depending on the variety and pruning frequency. The flowers vary from singles, which have but one row of petals, to doubles, with many rows. In general, the buds are pointed and long, and the flowers are borne one to a stem or in clusters of 3 to 5 from July until fall. Hybrid tea varieties are available in a wide range of colors, including pure white and many shades of red, yellow, pink, and orange. All varieties are good for cutting.

HOME REMEDY

A little dose of sugar opens buds. So, to force rosebuds to open indoors, put a lump of sugar in the water of the vase.

Most hybrid teas have some fragrance. This characteristic, however, is variable. When fragrance is present, it is usually most intense in the early morning before the fragrant oil has evaporated from the base of the petals.

Most hybrid teas are winter-hardy in areas where the winter temperatures do not often go below zero, but varieties differ in cold resistance.

Floribundas

Floribunda roses bear their flowers in clusters from late June until fall, and the individual blooms of many of them closely resemble those of hybrid teas. They are increasing in popularity, especially for bed plantings, where large numbers of flowers are wanted. Floribundas will tolerate more neglect than any other type of rose, with the possible exception of some of the shrub species.

SUPER GROWING SECRET

To keep your everblooming roses flowering through the summer, dissolve 3 tbsp. of brewer's yeast in 2 gallons of water, and soak the roots of each bush after their first blooming.

Grandifloras

Grandiflora roses resemble hybrid teas in bloom—single on long stems—and in hardiness. Though the flowers are somewhat smaller than those of hybrid teas, grandifloras bloom more abundantly. The flowers are good for cutting.

Polyanthas

Flowers of polyantha roses are smaller than those of the grandifloras, and are borne in rather large clusters. The clusters are similar in form and in size of the individual flowers to many of the climbing roses, to which the polyanthas are closely related. The polyanthas are hardy, and may be grown in many areas where hybrid teas are difficult to grow. Their chief use is in bed plantings or in borders with perennials. They are excellent for mass plantings. They tend to flower only once a year in early summer.

Hybrid Perpetuals

Hybrid perpetuals are the June roses of yesterday's garden. Their flowers are large. Generally, they lack the form of hybrid teas; an exception is the white-flowered variety 'Frau Karl Druschk,' which many consider the finest white rose in existence.

Before the development of modern hybrid teas, hybrid perpetual roses were very popular. As their name indicates, they are considered everblooming types, although most of them do not bear continuously through the growing season as hybrid teas do. They usually develop into large, vigorous bushes if provided with good care and proper pruning. They are very hardy, and can stand low winter temperatures without protection.

Shrub Roses

Shrub roses are actually a miscellaneous group of wild species, hybrids, and varieties that develop a large, dense type of growth that is useful in general landscape work. They are hardy in all sections of the country, blooming from June till the end of the season. While their flowers are equal in size or form to the other types of roses, many bear very attractive seedpods in the fall. They have fine-textured foliage, and some are quite useful for hedges or screen plantings.

ROSES ON THE WEB

Web enthusiasts who enjoy their gardens as much as their computers should stroll through "The Rose Resource" at

http://www.rose.org

The 60-plus page site is the first to offer a complete guide to gardening with roses.

The photo-filled site shows everything from gardening tips to landscape design ideas to purchasing information. The site was created by All-American Rose Selections (AARS), and includes a catalog of 57 years of AARS award-winning roses. A specially-designed search engine indexes all 137 AARS public gardens by state, so you can find the nearest AARS accredited public rose garden.

Old-Fashioned Roses

Old-fashioned roses include the varieties and species that were popular in Colonial gardens. Though the flowers of old-fashioned roses are not as attractive as those of the newer varieties, they usually are much more fragrant. These roses are all very hardy, require little care, and furnish an abundance of flowers in June.

Among the varieties occasionally found in gardens are:

TYPE	COLOR
Rosa centifolia (cabbage rose)	Light pink
Moss roses	Pink
'Cardinal de Richelieu'	Purplish red
Rosa mundi	Striped white and red
'York' and 'Lancaster'	Pink and white and variegated

Tree, Or Standard, Roses

Tree, or standard, roses are distinctive because of the form of the plant rather than the type of flower. They are made by grafting any of the bush-type roses onto upright trunks. Many of the better-known varieties of bush roses are available as tree roses. Tree roses are used in formal plantings or to accent a particular part of the garden. In areas where winters are severe, these plants need special protection.

GREEN THUMB TIP

Parsley increases roses' fragrance, so plant some around your favorite bushes to enhance their sweet smell of success!

Miniature Roses

Miniature rose plants, including their leaves and flowers, are very small; for some varieties, the maximum height is about

6 inches tall. They are available in all colors, forms, and fragrances of the large-flowered plants. Miniatures are used mostly for rock gardens, edging beds, and borders. They also may be grown in containers in a window, or inside under fluorescent lights. Miniature roses should be brought in for the winter; if you do, they will oblige you by blooming year 'round.

Flower Carpet Roses

THE MOST

HARDY,

DISEASE-

RESISTANT

ROSES

AVAILABLE

These landscape roses are long-blooming, easy-care ground-cover roses that are now available at garden centers everywhere. These roses currently come in pink and white, and are prolific bloomers with large camellia-like, fragrant flowers and lush foliage. They have won numerous prestigious international gold medals for performance and natural disease resistance.

These roses are considered by many to be the most disease-resistant roses available on the market today, which make them ideal for the novice rose grower.

One of the primary attributes of this rose is its habit of cleanly dropping its spent petals for a constantly fresh look, uncluttered with dried blossoms. Unlike most roses, Flower Carpet petals do not "brown" on the bush, even after rain. They remain "clean" for the life of the flower, and flutter to the ground when spent where they create a pleasing "fresh snowfall effect" beneath the bush.

These roses are very hardy, so you need to do little in the way of winter preparation.

Climbing Roses

Climbing roses include all varieties that produce long canes and require some sort of support to hold the plants up off the ground. They are often trained onto fences or trellises, and some are used without support to cover banks and aid in holding the soil in place. Climbing roses are hardy. They are becoming more popular with the development of finer varieties.

Climbing roses, like bush roses, are grouped into several types. There is an overlap among types, and some varieties could qualify under several. Most rose catalogs list the following types: ramblers, large-flowered climbers, everblooming climbers, climbing hybrid teas, climbing polyanthas, climbing floribundas, and trailing roses.

Ramblers

Rambler roses are very rapid growers. They sometimes develop canes as long as 20 feet in one season. The flowers are small—less than 2 inches across—and are borne in dense clusters. The plants flower only once a season, in June, and on wood that has produced the preceding year. The foliage is glossy and the plants are very hardy; unfortunately, many varieties are very susceptible to mildew. They are being replaced by other climbing types that bear larger flowers during a longer growing season and are less subject to mildew.

Large-Flowered Climbers

Large-flowered climbers grow slowly in comparison with ramblers. They are often trained on posts or some other type of support, and may require rather heavy pruning to keep them in bounds. These roses are well adapted to small gardens, where they may be trained against a wall, fence, or small trellis. When the plants are grown well, the flowers are rather large, and are useful for cutting.

RAMBLERS ARE THE FASTEST GROWERS

DID YOU KNOW?

Despite their name, climbing roses need to be tied to a support to grow properly. They flower better if you tie them to a horizontal support on a trellis while the canes are still young and flexible. And to encourage even more blooms, train them in the shape of an arch.

CLIMBING

HYBRID

TEAS

DON'T

BLOOM

AS WELL AS

THE BUSH

VARIETIES

Everblooming Climbers

Everblooming climbers usually bear an abundance of flowers in early summer. After this period of heavy bloom, the plants continue to produce a few scattered flowers until fall. If growing conditions are favorable, the plants may then bear heavily again.

Plant breeders are rapidly improving this type of rose. Some everblooming climbers are available that bloom continuously as hybrid teas, and are more winter-hardy.

Climbing Hybrid Teas

Climbing hybrid tea roses have originated as seedlings and as chance sports (mutations) of bush varieties.

When a bush hybrid tea produces a cane that has climbing characteristics, the new type of plant is usually given the same name as the bush variety from which it originated—for example, 'Climbing Crimson Glory' from a 'Crimson Glory.'

The climbing forms of hybrid teas, in general, do not bloom as continuously as their bush parents. The flowers, foliage, and other characteristics, however, are usually identical. The climbing hybrid teas are just as susceptible to winter injury as the bush forms.

Climbing Polyanthas And Floribundas

These types, like the climbing hybrid teas, originated as sports (or mutations) and seedlings from polyanthas and floribundas. The flowers of these sports are generally identical with the bush form from which they originated, and they are also fairly continuous in blooming. They are hardier than the climbing hybrid teas, but not hardy enough to withstand severe winter climates unless they are properly protected.

Trailing roses are climbers adapted to planting on banks or walls. They produce long canes that creep along the ground, making a pleasing ground cover. Their flowers are not as attractive as those of the other types, but they are hardy and have a place in some gardens.

Rose Buyers, Beware!

Buy your rose plants from reputable sources. Generally, local nurseries and garden centers are good sources of planting material. Retail stores—drug stores, supermarkets, and department stores—are also good sources if their stock has been kept dormant, and has been protected from drying out.

You can also get a good selection of high-quality plants from mail-order nurseries and nursery departments of mail-order houses. Reputable mail-order organizations will send you catalogs listing the plants that they sell. They will guarantee their plants to grow and bloom if given normal care.

For help in deciding which of the many varieties of roses to buy, get catalogs from several of the large nurseries. The varieties listed in these catalogs generally are favorites with rose growers, and you are likely to be satisfied with any of them.

Members of local garden clubs and rose societies are great sources of specific information on the varieties that do well in your area. So don't be afraid to contact them.

BE PARTICULAR WHEN BUYING ROSES— BUY ONLY FRESH, FLEXIBLE STOCK

PLANTING: HOME SWEET HOME

There Is A Right Time And A Wrong Time To Plant

DO NOT DISTURB!

When planting roses, you want to disturb the root ball as little as possible. So, if you're planting container-grown roses, cut out the bottom of the container before planting. Then set the container in the hole, cut away the sides, and ease the container out of the hole before backfilling with soil. This will help the rose become adjusted to her new home better.

The proper time to plant packaged roses depends on the severity of winter temperatures in your area. Use the following as your rule of thumb:

*If winter temperatures do not go below 10°F, plant any time the bushes are fully dormant.

*If winter temperatures do not go below -10°F, plant in the fall or spring.

*If winter temperatures regularly go below -10°F, plant in spring only.

Some nurseries and garden centers sell roses that are planted in containers. These container-grown roses can be planted any time from spring to fall.

They've Got To Like Where You Plant Them

Roses grow best where they have full sunshine all day. They will grow satisfactorily, however, if they have at least six hours of sun a day.

If you must plant roses where they are shaded part of the day and you have a choice as to morning sun or afternoon sun, plant them where they have morning sun. If plants are shaded in the morning, their leaves will remain wet with dew a few hours longer than if they were in morning sun. Moisture on the leaves is favorable for the development of several leaf diseases.

They All Need Room To Grow

When planting hybrid teas, grandifloras, polyanthas, and floribundas, space them about 2 feet apart where winter temperatures are very cold (-10°F or below), about 2-$\frac{1}{2}$ feet apart where winter temperatures are moderate (10° to -10°F), and at least 3 feet apart where winter temperatures are mild (above 10°F). In all areas, space hybrid perpetuals, tree roses, shrub roses, and old-fashioned roses 3 to 5 feet apart. Climbers should be planted 8 to 10 feet apart; with miniatures the spacing is up to you.

SUNLIGHT SECRETS

How much sun does a rose bush need to bloom like crazy? Five hours is the minimum, six is even better, and lucky seven is best!

You Don't Need Kid Gloves To Handle Roses

Unless your rose plants are frozen when they are delivered, unpack them at once. If they are frozen, store them where they can thaw out gradually; do not unpack them until they are completely thawed.

Inspect the roots for drying. If they are dry, soak them in warm (100°F) water for an hour or two.

The plants are best planted as soon as they are received. If you cannot plant them immediately, moisten the packing material and repack the plants. They can be kept this way safely for two or three days.

If you must hold the plants for more than two or three days before planting, heel them in a protected spot in the garden. That is, place them in a trench, and cover the roots with moist soil. If the canes are dry, cover them with soil also.

215

When you are ready to set out the plants, examine their roots. Cut off all dead or injured growth. Remove broken and dead canes and, if necessary, cut the canes back to about 12 inches in length. Nurseries usually cut the tops back to about 12 inches before shipping the plants. If the tops have been cut back, do not cut them further; flowering usually is delayed if canes are cut back to less than 10 inches.

Protect the roots from drying at all times. Never expose them to sun or drying winds. Move the plants to the garden with their roots in a bucket of water or coat the roots with a thin clay mud, and keep them covered with wet burlap or some other protection until planted.

Any Old Dirt Won't Do

If you are planting only a few roses, dig individual planting holes for them. Make the holes 12 inches deep and at least 18 inches wide. If you are planting a large number of roses in one bed, prepare the bed by spading the soil to a depth of about 12 inches. Then, dig planting holes in the prepared bed.

Any good garden soil will produce good roses. If you can grow good grass, shrubs, and other plants, your soil probably needs no special preparation for roses. If your soil is very heavy, or if it is light and lacking in fertility, or if the builder of your house has used subsoil from the basement excavation to level your lot, you can improve your soil by adding organic matter, like peat moss, leaf mold, or manure. Most gardeners prefer to use manure. But remember, never add fresh manure to the soil—you'll burn your plants' roots. Dehydrated cow manure is available

TIMELY TONIC

Before planting bare root rose bushes, soak them in the following mixture:

**1 tbsp. of Vegetable &
Flower Food (5-8-5),
1 tbsp. of Shampoo, and
1 tbsp. of corn syrup
in 1 gallon of warm water
to wake them up.**

When you're done, sprinkle this mixture on all of your other rose bushes, too—they'll love you for it!

from garden supply stores. If you use it, add about one-half pound of superphosphate (it increases root growth) to each bushel.

Spread a layer of organic matter 2 to 4 inches deep over the spaded bed. Work the organic matter into the soil to spade depth.

If you are digging planting holes in unprepared soil, mix soil from the holes with organic matter. **Use 1 part peat moss or leaf mold to 4 parts soil, or 1 part manure to 6 parts soil.** Mix thoroughly.

After the planting holes are dug, either in beds or unprepared soil, loosen the soil at the bottom of the hole and work in about half a spadeful of well-rotted manure.

Prepare the beds and dig the planting holes well in advance of planting so that the plants can be set out as soon as you get them. It's best to prepare the soil in fall, whether for a fall or spring planting. If the soil has to be completely reworked, do it at least four weeks before planting.

If Planted Right, They Grow Right

Place a small, cone-shaped pile of soil in the center of each planting hole. Set the plant on top of the cone, and spread the roots down the slope

If winter temperatures in your area regularly go below -10°F, make the top of the cone low enough so the bud union of the plant is about 2 inches below ground level. If the temperatures go below 10°F but not lower than -10°F, set the bud union at ground level. If winter temperatures are warmer than 10°F, set the bud union at ground level or just slightly below it.

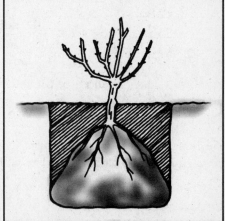

Carefully work the soil about the roots so that all of the roots are in contact with it. When the roots are covered, add water to help settle the soil about the roots. Then fill in the hole. After that's done, give each plant a dose of my Start-Up Meal.

Mound the soil 8 to 10 inches high around the canes of bush and climbing roses, and 3 to 4 inches high around the canes of miniature roses. Remove the soil mound when all danger of frost is past.

After planting tree roses, drive a sturdy pole into the soil beside the trunk, and tie the trunk to the pole. This prevents the trunk from whipping about in the wind, and loosening the roots.

START-UP MEAL

Here's the perfect meal to get your roses off to a flying start:

1 tbsp. of liquid dish soap,
1 tbsp. of hydrogen peroxide,
1 tsp. of whiskey, and
1 tsp. of Vitamin B-1 Plant Starter

in a half gallon of warm tea water.

EAT, DRINK, AND BE MERRY!

They're Big Drinkers

Roses need large amounts of water. Even where rainfall is plentiful, occasional waterings are beneficial. Roses should receive the equivalent of one inch of water every seven to ten days throughout the growing season.

Soak the soil thoroughly to a depth of 8 to 10 inches. Direct a small, slow-moving stream of water from a garden hose around the bases of the plants. A heavy stream usually is wasteful; most of the water runs off and fails to penetrate the soil more than a few inches.

Feed Me—Please!

Roses are the hardest-working flowering plants in your garden. No, I'm not kidding! Roses bloom only for the sake of showing off, as much as they can, for as long as they can. And let me tell you, folks, it takes a whole lot of work and work builds up an appetite. That's where you come in—you are the food provider.

If you follow these two steps, your roses will be well-fed and satisfied.

Step 1—Roses should be fed first in the early part of the growing season when the new growth is well-established, and the danger of freezing is past. I make a mixture of:

> **4 cups of bone meal,**
> **1 cup of dry fertilizer, and**
> **1 cup of Epsom salts.**

I give each bush one generous tablespoon, or work in 4 pounds per 100 square feet of rose bed.

Step 2—Then I feed my roses one pint of the following mix every three weeks, in the morning, after I've watered.

> **1 cup of beer,**
> **2 tsp. of instant tea,**
> **1 tsp. Rose/Flower Food,**
> **1 tsp. of Fish Fertilizer +,**
> **1 tsp. of hydrogen peroxide,**
> **and 1 tsp. of liquid soap**
> **mixed in 2 gallons of**
> **warm water.**

Roses should never be fed after July 15 in the North, or August 15 in the South.

BETTER ROSES WITH LESS WATER

Here's my advice for anyone who wants great roses with a minimum amount of water:

A low-pressure soaker hose is one of the most cost-effective and efficient ways to water. The soaker hose uses less water than traditional hoses, and provides for deep penetration. Light, frequent surface watering can cause rose roots to grow upward near the soil surface, which makes the roots vulnerable to damage during hot days or when weeding.

Five to six hours of watering with the soaker hose two or three times a week is ideal. Sandy or loamy soil may need soaking more often, while clay soil may require less. Early morning is the best time to water because less wind and lower temperatures keep evaporation to a minimum.

If the foliage turns a yellowish-white (a sure sign of iron deficiency), apply Liquid Iron as directed on the package.

SUPER GROWING SECRET

Give your roses a midsummer pick-me-up by placing any left-over tea bags on the soil underneath each bush. The tannic acid in the tea bag will make the soil slightly acidic, which roses just love!

Weeds Don't Need To Be A Worry

Cultivate roses carefully; their roots may grow close to the surface, and can be injured by deep cultivation. The main purpose of cultivation is to remove weeds. This can also be accomplished by hand-pulling weeds or cutting them at the soil's surface.

Use mulch to aid in controlling weeds, conserve moisture, and provide additional fertility. Peat, ground corn-cobs, ground tobacco stems, buckwheat and cottonseed hulls, spent mushroom manure, and well-rotted, strawy manure are all effective mulching materials.

Apply mulch about a month before the roses bloom. Remove all weeds, and rake the soil lightly before applying it. Then spread the mulching material evenly around the plants to a depth of 2 or 3 inches.

Keep the mulch on the soil throughout the year. The mulching material decays and becomes incorporated in the soil. Add new material as the mulch settles and becomes thin about the plants.

Enjoy Your Beauties

Cutting roses is an important part of growing them. Improper cutting can injure the plant and decrease its vigor.

Use only clean, sharp tools to cut flowers. Breaking or twisting off flowers injures the remaining wood.

It probably is best if you do not cut any flowers during a plant's first season of bloom. If early flowers are not cut, the plants usually develop into large bushes by fall. You may cut some of the flowers at that time.

If you do cut flowers during the first season, cut them with very short stems—snip off only the flowers. Removal of foliage with long-stemmed flowers robs the plant of its food-manufacturing capacity and cuts down on its growth and subsequent flower yield and its chances for survival the following winter.

Even when the plants are well-established, it is unwise to cut stems any longer than is actually needed. At least 2 leaves should remain between the cut and the main stem.

Hybrid tea roses usually have 3 leaflets at the top of the rose stem, and below that a spray of 5 leaflets. If the stem is weak, make a cut just above the topmost spray of 5 leaflets. If the stem is strong—as thick as a pencil—the cut may be made above a higher 3 leaflet spray.

GREEN THUMB TIP

For larger, single blossoms or single-stemmed roses, disbud the plants when the buds are very small. Remove all but the terminal bud on each stem. The terminal bud then develops into a much larger flower.

The flower clusters of polyanthas and other roses bearing many flowers per stem also will be improved by disbudding. Remove some of the buds from each stem—the more buds you remove, the larger the remaining flowers will be. It's that simple!

If you do not cut the flowers, remove them when their petals fall. Cut them off with sharp shears or a knife just above the topmost leaf. A withered individual flower in a cluster should be removed to give the remaining flowers more room to develop. After all flowers of a cluster have withered, cut off the entire stem just above the top leaf. This ensures that the new side shoots will begin to develop.

Roses that are cut just before the petals start to unfold will continue to open normally and will remain in good condition

221

longer than if they are cut after they are fully open. Roses will keep best if they are cut in late afternoon.

PRUNING: BE A CONTROLLED CUT-UP!

You must prune roses annually to improve their appearance, to remove dead wood, and to control the quantity and quality of flowers produced by the plants. If roses are not pruned, they soon grow into a bramble patch with small flowers of poor quality.

Sometimes undesired shoots (suckers) develop from the understock (usually the shoot has many small, dark green leaves). These should be removed as soon as they appear (cut them right off at the ground), or they are liable to eventually choke out the parent plant.

Rose pruning is not difficult. As when cutting flowers, use only sharp tools. A fine-toothed saw is useful for cutting dead canes. All other pruning can be performed with pruning shears.

Do not leave bare stubs when pruning! Make all cuts even with a cane, to the point on the crown from which the pruned member originated, or to a strong, outward-facing bud.

Rose bush before pruning...   after pruning

Bush Roses

Prune bush roses in early spring, just before growth starts. First, remove the dead wood; be careful to cut an inch or so below the dark-colored areas. If no buds are left, remove the entire branch or cane.

Next, cut out all weak growth and any canes or branches growing toward the center of the bush. If two branches cross, remove the weaker.

Finally, shape the plant by cutting the strong canes to a uniform height. In mild climates, strong plants can be pruned to a height of 24 to 30 inches.

In some areas, the winters are so severe that much of the top of the plant is killed. Under these conditions, it is not possible to do much toward shaping the plants. Just cut out the dead wood, saving all the live wood you can.

CUT OUT SUCKERS!

Most roses are budded or grafted, and only the top part of the plant produces the kind of flowers we want. The roots are of a different and (from the point of view of floral display) inferior kind. Shoots that arise directly from the root, which are of a distinctly different appearance from the stem shoots, should be cut out as soon as possible, or they'll end up dominating the plant.

Tree Roses

Tree roses require heavy pruning in spring, and some pruning during the growing season to keep the tops from becoming too large for the stem. After removing the dead wood, cut back the live canes so that they're 8 to 12 inches long, and shape the overall structure of the plant.

Most of the shrub roses should be pruned after they have bloomed. As a general rule, these plants are very hardy, so pruning is needed primarily to thin out and remove old canes. They do not require shaping; in almost all instances, shrub roses are most attractive when they are allowed to develop their natural shape.

Climbing Roses

Remove all dead canes and weak branches in spring, but don't prune hardy ramblers until after they have flowered; otherwise, you will reduce the production of flowers. This pruning stimulates new cane growth and the development of new laterals on which the next year's flowers will be borne.

Where ramblers are trained to a trellis or support so high that one season's growth will not cover it, cut off some of the older shoots, and shorten the strong, vigorous canes. This pruning will stimulate laterals to develop, and continue to elongate and eventually cover the trellis.

Many of the large-flowered climbers, especially the everblooming types, do not produce as much growth each year as the hardier climbers. As a result, your pruning should be less severe.

WRAP THEM UP FOR THE WINTER

Roses must be protected not only against low winter temperatures, but also against fluctuating temperatures. Occasionally, rose varieties that are hardy in the North, where winter temperatures are constantly low, are injured during the winter in areas farther south, where the temperature fluctuates considerably.

As the first step in avoiding winter injury, keep your roses healthy during the growing season. Roses that have been sprayed to control diseases and have been properly nourished are more likely to escape winter injury than plants that have lost their leaves because of diseases or nutrient deficiencies.

TIMELY TONIC

It is very important to remove all fallen rose leaves and petals from underneath the bushes before you cover them. After removing the debris, spray the bushes with this tonic:

**1 cup of Shampoo
1 cup of antiseptic mouthwash, and
1 cup of chewing tobacco juice
in your 20 gallon hose-end sprayer.**

Apply this tonic thoroughly to the point of run-off.

Bush Roses

Immediately after the first killing frost, while the soil can still be easily worked, pile soil 8 to 10 inches high around the canes. It is best to bring in soil from another part of the garden for this; if you dig it from the rose beds, you may injure the roots of the rose plants.

After mounding the soil about the canes, tie all the canes together to keep them from being blown about, and loosening the soil around the root system.

Inspect the plants frequently to be sure the soil is not washed away before the ground freezes.

Protection by mounding usually is effective if the temperature does not drop below zero.

Where the temperature regularly goes below zero, further protection is necessary. Pile hay, straw, or well-rotted, strawy manure over the mounded canes. Hold it in place by throwing on a few shovelfuls of soil on it.

Remove covering materials—straw and soil—in spring as soon as danger of severe frost has passed. Remove the soil mound carefully to avoid breaking off any shoots that may have started to grow beneath the mound.

WINTER PREP

There is nothing more beautiful than a brightly blossoming rose garden. On the other hand, there is nothing more depressing than the black canes of death on unprotected roses in the middle of winter. Setting up fall protection for most types of roses is a simple task, and takes very little time.

Insects, as a rule, tend to spend the winter snuggled up in the soil. In the early spring, they wake up to feast on the new roots of your rose bushes. So in mid-September or early October, spray the soil around your roses with a warm soapy water solution of one cup of Shampoo to 20 gallons of water. Wait one-half hour, and apply Dursban® at the recommended rate. When it's time to mulch your roses with leaves, straw and soil, or cover them with styrofoam cones, add a half cup of crushed mothballs per bushel of mulch, and mix well.

Tree Roses

In areas where the temperature does not often go below zero, you can simply wrap the heads of the plants in straw, and cover them with burlap.

Where the temperature goes to 10-15 degrees below zero, protect your tree roses by covering the plants with soil. Do this by digging carefully under the roots on one side of the plant until the plant can be pulled over to the ground without breaking all root connections with the soil. Then cover the entire plant with several inches of soil.

In spring, after the soil thaws and danger of severe frost is past, remove the soil cover, and set the plants upright again.

TREE ROSES

SHOULD BE

TIPPED ON

THEIR SIDES

FOR WINTER

Climbing Roses

Climbing roses need protection in areas where the temperatures regularly drop below zero. Lay the canes on the ground, hold them down with wire pins or notch stakes, and cover them with several inches of soil. Remove the soil in spring after danger of severe frost is past.

PROPAGATION: START YOUR OWN ROSE FAMILY

Most varieties of roses can be propagated from cuttings taken during the summer or fall.

Take 6- to 8-inch cuttings from the stems after the flowers have fallen in summer. Remove all of the leaves except one or two at the top. For easy rooting, stick the cut end into a potato. Then plant the cuttings, potato and all, with half of their length below the ground. Water them, then invert a fruit jar over them. Remove the fruit jar the following spring.

Take fall cuttings after the wood has ripened well. Cut the stems into 8- to 10-inch lengths, remove all of the leaves, and plant the cuttings in a well-protected sunny place with only the top bud above the ground. When freezing weather approaches, cover cuttings with a mulch of vermiculite several inches deep to keep the ground from freezing.

FACE TROUBLE HEAD-ON

I have never known any rose grower who has never had to face a bug or blotch in his/her growing career. If you take your roses seriously, then you must be ready to act or react to a problem as soon as you notice it.

What follows are descriptions of just about all of the known insects and diseases that the average home yardener might come into contact with, and the chemical controls of the U.S.D.A. Keep in mind, however, that if you give your roses a bath with my All Season Clean-Up Tonic every other week, odds are you won't need any chemical controls!

Many different diseases and insects attack roses. These pests vary in type and severity from area to area. You can control most of them effectively—no matter where you live—if you follow these general recommendations:

* Buy plants that are free of insects and diseases.

* Keep your rose garden cleaned of weeds, fallen rose leaves and petals, and diseased or insect-infested canes.

STARTING ROSES FROM SEED

To grow roses from seed, let rose hips mature on the plant until they begin to crack open. Snip them off, and remove the seeds. Plant in a prepared seedbed, cover lightly with sifted peat or sand, water them, and cover with clear plastic. Seeds should sprout before frost.

Once sprouted, cover the young plants with jars, and mulch heavily at the bases to protect them during the winter. Remove jars in spring, after all danger of frost has past. Plants grown from seed may produce a few flowers the second summer after planting, but generally, do not blossom until the third year.

227

* Apply pesticide sprays or dusts as needed at the recommended rate.

Three types of pesticides are used on roses: **fungicides** for diseases; **miticides** for spider mites; and **insecticides** for insects. You can use any of them in dust or spray forms. Ready-to-use dusts are available from pesticide dealers. Few sprays come ready-to-use on roses. It is usually necessary to prepare them by mixing wettable powders or emulsifiable concentrates with water.

Select the proper pesticide by studying this section and the pesticide container labels. Be sure to follow label directions for dilution and care in handling.

GREEN THUMB TIP

To prevent the spread of disease, sterilize all cut branches with a mixture of 2 tbsp. of ammonia and 2 tbsp. of Shampoo per quart of water. Then seal the cuts with a mixture of 2 tbsp. of antiseptic mouthwash in 8 oz. of interior latex paint which has had 3 drops of liquid Sevin® added to it.

Diseases

Of the many diseases that can attack roses, black spot, powdery mildew, rust, crown gall, and the cankers are the most serious.

Black Spot

Circular black spots, frequently surrounded by a yellow halo, appear on the leaves. Infected leaves turn yellow and fall prematurely. Severely attacked plants may be almost completely defoliated by midsummer. The plant is weakened, becomes subject to winter injury, die back, and stem cankers.

Black spot is spread by water, which must remain on the leaves for at least six hours before the infection can take place.

ROSE DISEASES

Black Spot

Powdery Mildew

Rust

Virus

Cankers

Crown Gall

229

Severe pruning in spring eliminates some infected canes on which the disease overwinters. Begin spraying or dusting when leaves are half grown. Spray or dust weekly throughout the growing season.

Maneb, zineb, and Daconil are effective for black spot control. Follow the label directions.

TIMELY TONIC

To control black spot on roses, mix:

1 tbsp. of baking soda,
1 tbsp. of vegetable oil, and
1 tbsp. of liquid dish soap
in a gallon of warm water.

Shake well, and then apply with a pump type sprayer every 7 to 10 days, or at the first sign of any disease.

Powdery Mildew

White powdery masses of spores appear on young leaves, shoots, and buds. Young shoots become swollen or distorted. Foliage may be stunted.

This disease is spread by the wind. It overwinters on fallen leaves and in infected bud scales, and flower stems.

For control during the growing season, apply Daconil or Dinocap at the recommended rates. Do not apply Dinocap when the temperature is above 85°F.

Rust

Yellow or orange pustules appear on leaves, and the plant may lose its leaves. The disease may also attack young stems. Spread by the wind, rust overwinters in fallen leaves. Cool, humid summers and mild winters are conducive to the development of rust. It is particularly prevalent along the Pacific coast.

For control, apply Zineb or Maneb (registered for use on rust in California only).

Cankers commonly occur in plants that have been weakened by black spot, winter injury, or lack of nutrients. They first appear as small reddish spots on the stem. They enlarge, and eventually encircle the stem, causing the cane to die.

For control, keep the bushes free of black spot, and provide them with proper winter protection. When pruning, make clean cuts near a bud. Prune out all cankered canes. Disinfect pruning tools with alcohol after taking out a canker shoot.

Crown Gall

Galls begin as small swellings, usually at ground level, but sometimes on the upper part of the stem or on the roots. They slowly increase in size. Infected plants become stunted and may die.

Control is a matter of prevention; buy plants free of crown gall, and plant them in soil that has been free of crown gall-infected plants for at least two years. If crown gall appears, remove the infected plants and burn them.

Virus Diseases

Rose viruses are spread by the propagation of infected plants. The diseases do not seem to be spread by insects or by handling.

DUSTING ROSES

The best time of day for dusting your roses is late evening when the air is still, and the fresh dew on the foliage catches and holds the dust. Hold the duster low, and shoot the dust up under the bushes without actually walking among them. Allow the protective cloud to settle gently over the whole bed. The second best time to dust is pre-dawn. If it rains, repeat the process immediately thereafter; in times of heavy dews, twice a week is recommended. With light dews and the hotter, drier weather of summer, once a week is enough.

Special Note: Less than four hours in a droplet of water (dew) will start diseases on unprotected bushes. Excessive use of some dusts may be caustic in temperatures above 85°F, with foliar burn resulting. So be careful.

Viruses cause small, angular, colorless spots on the foliage. Ring, oakleaf, and water-mark patterns also may occur. Infected plants may be otherwise unaffected, or they may be slightly to severely dwarfed.

The only control for viruses is prevention; buy plants that are free of the symptoms of virus diseases.

SPRAYING TIPS

Never spray or dust when the wind is blowing hard, or when the plants are wet. All the foliage should be thoroughly covered with the spray to the point of run-off! All insect controls should be applied after 7:00 p.m., when the bugs are less active and more likely to be home.

Insects

Roses are the favorite food for a large number of insects. The most common ones are the Japanese beetle, rose chafer, rose leaf beetle, rose leafhopper, flower thrips, rose aphid, rose scale, rose mite, rose stem girdler, mossy rose gall, and rose root gall.

When preparing blooms for exhibition, it may be desirable to protect prized plants and flowers from insect attacks by covering them with cheesecloth or other coarsely-woven cloth on a light framework. This is known in the biz as hauling out the heavy artillery.

Japanese Beetle

The Japanese beetle attacks rose flowers and foliage during July and August. This beetle is about $3/8$-inch long and metallic green with coppery-brown wing covers. In areas of moderate infestation, plants can be protected by planting garlic in and among your roses—they just love it! The next step up is frequent applications of Carbaryl or Malathion.

In heavily-infested areas you may have to cover the flowers with cheesecloth cages or bags to protect them from injury.

Rose Chafer

Yellowish-brown beetles, known as rose chafers, are often abundant in the North during June and early July, especially in areas of light, sandy soil. They are about $1/2$-inch long and have long, spiny legs. They appear on the rose petals on which they feed. They may destroy the entire flower. Rose chafers may be collected by hand, and disposed of. For control, apply Methoxychlor to newly opened flowers as needed.

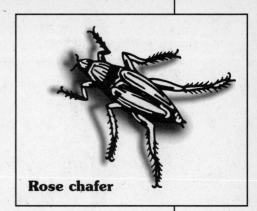

Rose chafer

Rose leaf beetle

Rose Leaf Beetle

The rose leaf beetle is a small, metallic-green beetle that feeds in the buds and on the flowers of roses, often riddling them with holes. The insects are most numerous in suburban gardens near uncultivated fields. There are no pesticides registered for use against this pest.

Rose Leafhopper

The rose leafhopper, a tiny greenish-yellow jumping insect, is frequently found on the underside of rose leaves. It sucks out the contents of the leaf cells, causing a stippling of the leaves that resembles the injury inflicted by spider mites. For control, apply Carbaryl, Malathion, or Diazinon to the underside of the foliage.

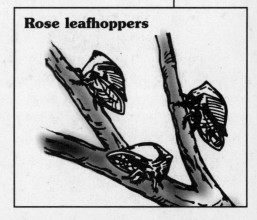

Rose leafhoppers

⌗

Rose Slugs

Rose slugs, the larvae of three species of sawflies, feed on the leaves of roses. Their injury is recognized by the skeletonized effect on the leaves. For control, use Carbaryl. Treatments must be applied promptly; the insects appear suddenly, and do their damage quickly.

Flower Thrips

USE

CHEESECLOTH

TO PROTECT

AGAINST

THRIPS

For several weeks each summer, the petals of garden roses, especially white varieties, may turn brown. This injury is caused by the flower thrips and related species that enter the opening flower. These tiny yellow or brown insects can be seen if an infested flower is shaken over a sheet of white paper.

No fully satisfactory control is available because of the daily influx of thrips to the rapidly expanding varieties of flowers, which cannot be kept adequately covered with an insecticide. Carbaryl, Diazinon, Acephate, or Malathion spray applied to flowers and buds every two to three days will destroy many thrips as they alight on flowers. Cheesecloth cages or bags around prized blooms may help to protect them from damage.

HOME REMEDY

Onions will discourage aphids from dining on your roses and evergreens. Emulsify a medium-sized onion in a quart of water. To make a larger portion of spray, strain off the clear juice, and pour 2 tbsps. of it per gallon of water together with 1 tbsp. of liquid dish soap. This will discourage most bugs from dining on your pride and joy.

Aphids

Several species of aphids may infest the stems, leaves, and buds of roses. By sucking its juices, they stunt the plants. They often occur in large numbers on rosebuds. The insects also secrete a sticky honeydew, which accumulates on foliage.

For control, apply the home remedy at left, or Acephate, Diazinon, or Malathion spray as needed.

**Damage caused
by rose scale**

Old rose stems sometimes become encrusted with white insects known as rose scale. These insects suck sap from the plants.

Acephate or Carbaryl spray applied at least once every two weeks during the summer will reduce the number of scales by killing the young rose scale crawlers. If scales persist until fall, prune out the stems that are most severely infested. During the dormant season, spray the remaining stems with an All Seasons Horticultural or Dormant Spray; this should kill the scale.

DORMANT

SPRAY TO

CONTROL

SCALE

Rose Midge

The rose midge can sometimes be a serious pest of roses. This tiny yellowish fly lays its eggs in the growing tips of the rose stems. The maggots that hatch from the eggs destroy the tender tissue, killing the tips and deforming the buds.

Cut and destroy the infested tips daily for one month to eliminate the maggots before they complete their growth and drop to the ground. Nicotine sulfate applied to the soil surface will control adult midges as they emerge from their pupation sites in the soil. Soak the ground thoroughly with it. Apply in mid-May, and again seven to ten days later!

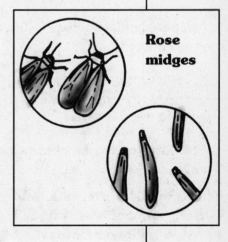

**Rose
midges**

Leaf-Cutter Bees

Leaf-cutter bees cut circular pieces from rose leaves and other plants, and store them as food for their young in burrows dug in the pith of rose stems, broken branches, or in plant crevices. The tunneled stems usually die back for several inches.

Leaf-Cutter Bees

No satisfactory insecticide control is available for these bees, which are valuable as pollinators of alfalfa and other plants. A carpet tack pushed into the end of the cut stem at pruning time will prevent the bees from entering and tunneling the stems. A mixture of **2 drops of antiseptic mouthwash, and 3 drops of Sevin® in 8 oz. of interior latex paint** can also be applied to the ends of the cut stem as a deterrent.

MITE REMEDIES

✓ Natural predators like ladybugs or green lacewings.

✓ Eliminate hot, dusty condtions— mist spray the plants early in the morning every 3 days.

✓ Mix up a batch of the following tonic:

¹/₂ cup of buttermilk, and 3- ¹/₂ cups of wheat flour in 5 gallons of water.

Spray to the point of run-off.

Spider Mites

The two-spotted spider mite and related species suck the juices from rose leaves, which soon become stippled. As the injury progresses, the leaves turn brown, curl, and drop off. When the mites are abundant, they spin a web over the leaf surface. Infested plants are unthrifty.

These spider mites are greenish-colored with two brown spots, although some are dark red. They are almost too small to be seen without a magnifying glass. The mites overwinter as adults on leaves of living weeds or perennial garden plants. They quickly multiply during hot, dry weather.

Spider mites and the damage they cause to a leaf.

When Carbaryl is used to control other pests, it destroys the insect enemies of spider mites, and the mites tend to become more numerous. To control spider mites, clean up trash and weeds in early spring, and make weekly applications of a spray containing either Diazinon, Dicofol, or Hexakis.

Rose Stem Borers

The stems of garden roses are occasionally infested with one of several kinds of borers. These stems usually die back, and those infested with the stem girdler develop a marked swelling at the point of injury.

Cut and destroy infested stems.

Rose Galls

Several species of wasp-like insects lay their eggs in the stems of roses and their larvae cause large swellings or galls. One species makes a gall on the stem resembling fibrous moss. Another causes a large wart-like gall near the ground surface. These galls may be confused with crown galls, which are caused by bacteria. However, if insect galls are cut open, numerous larvae—or the cells in which they develop—will be visible.

Rose gall on a stem, and the wasp-like insect that causes them.

No insecticide known will control the insects that produce these galls. The best control is to prune out the infested stems, removing the galls, and then bury them promptly, destroying the larvae in the galls before they emerge.

One Final Note...

For those of you who insist that the only effective control of insects and disease is rose dust, then by all means continue to use it. I have always found this to be an unsightly solution, especially when you have lots of visitors in your garden.

When I do use it, I mix my rose dust with a little water, making it into a paste, then add that along with 3 tsp. of Shampoo to 6 gallons of water. I apply it in the evening, thoroughly drenching the plants to the point of run-off.

Lastly, and certainly not leastly, an early application of any of the Systemic Rose and Flower Food is a good insurance policy against aphids and other sucking insects. These fantastic products contain insect controls <u>and</u> plant food that are actually taken up into the plants themselves, so they don't wash off, and keep on working all season long. That should about do it.

FLOWERING TREES
A Splash of Color

Most North American home gardeners, unlike their European, Asian, and Oriental counterparts, are not used to reading about trees in their flower gardening books. Yet they are, as a rule, the first plants to be placed in a new landscape planting. And for good reason, too—when properly selected and sited, flowering trees contribute beauty, balance, and stability to any garden for many years to come.

BEFORE YOU BUY YOUR TREE

It Pays To Be Choosy

After you have decided to include a flowering tree in your landscape plan, you must take several factors into consideration when making your selection:

(1) the size of the tree's root system—how much garden space you are willing to give up to a large root ball that must be covered with shredded bark for two years, preventing you from planting flowers in that area;

(2) the density of the tree's foliage when mature—this will effect what or whether you can plant under it;

(3) the tree's height and width when mature—you need to make sure your tree doesn't overshadow your flower garden, your living room window, or your house, for that matter; and

(4) the tree's hardiness—there's nothing worse than planting a tree that doesn't survive the winter, unless it's a tree that takes five years to die miserably and slowly.

DON'T PLANT TREES TOO CLOSE TO YOUR HOUSE!

The height and width of a tree will dictate how close it can be safely planted next to your home. Trees generally should not be allowed to get more than 50 percent taller than the highest part of the house—unless it is planted as far away as its ultimate height.

A tree that will reach 100 feet should be planted at least 75 feet away from the house. A tree that will be 20 feet tall should be planted at least 15 feet away. Planting your tree in the proper place ensures that it will provide beauty and value for many years to come.

Size Of The Tree's Root System

Remember, all plant roots are competing for the same food source, and tree roots have a distinct advantage over those of annuals, perennials, or bulbs. Some trees are compatible with flowers, but others have a very dense and vigorous root growth that will crowd out other plants within a certain radius—so, check with your nurseryperson before making a final selection!

Density Of The Tree's Foliage

All flowering plants need varying amounts of light. The future density of the foliage, and the height and circumference of your flowering tree will have a direct bearing on the flowers you will be able to plant beneath it. Remember, your tree will be throwing shade in several directions.

If I sound like I'm trying to discourage you from planting trees, you're wrong—it's just the opposite. I want you to have a well-balanced and integrated flowerscape that enhances and flatters your home. Also, a balanced landscape is seldom plagued with disease, insects, or discontented plants or garden tenders (that's you)!

The Tree's Height and Width

When you select a flowering tree for your landscape, you must think ahead. Look at pictures of mature examples of the variety you are considering, and check the accompanying plant tag for final height and width information while you're at the garden center. Remember, the tree that is the perfect size right now may overwhelm your garden in five years. And moving a tree, shrub, or evergreen because it has outgrown its space after it has been in the ground for only a year or two can cause severe damage, not only to the plant you are moving, but also to the dozens of others that have become quite comfortable growing around it.

The Tree's Hardiness

MOVING

A TREE

CAUSES

PROBLEMS

FOR ITS

NEIGHBORS

Finally, please heed this last bit of advice when selecting a flowering tree or, for that matter, any tree for your home landscape. Many of you have a habit of looking through mail-order catalogs, seeing an attractive picture, and then ordering that plant to be delivered at planting time to your home, without checking its hardiness zone to make sure it can survive in your yarden. Removing a tree for any reason causes problems for the surrounding plants, but when a tree or shrub dies and its decayed trunk and roots remain in the ground for a period of time, insects and diseases tend to move in and call it home, attacking and infecting neighboring plants, trees, shrubs, and flowers.

Tree Forms

Trees can generally be classified into one of three forms:

Freestanding—the tree is growing as it normally would in its natural habitat, with some pruning to control its growth.

Espalier—this is accomplished by severely pruning, bending, and binding the branches of a tree to grow flat against a surface, usually a garden wall. Many flowering trees, as well as fruit trees, are espaliered. They look terrific and produce well

241

when fruit-bearing, but also take more of your time than you may wish to invest, which brings up another point. As a rule, the initial cost of an espalier tree is 3 to 4 times that of a standard variety of the same species and, I must add, worth every penny of it! Having an espalier tree in your flowerscape will make it special, but also be aware of its special demands.

Dwarf—Many flowering and fruit trees are grafted onto a low-growing root stock, which inhibits their height but not head size. Dwarf trees are great where your vertical growing space is limited by overhead wires, a roof overhang, patio cover, or the like.

Freestanding

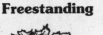

Dwarf

Espalier

Types Of Planting Containers

You can purchase flowering trees in any number of ways— either bare root from a mail source, pre-potted, field grown, field potted, balled and burlapped, or machine-dug and planted. Here's the lowdown on each:

Bare Root—This is the most chancy way of purchasing and planting trees because the roots can dry out if you miss even one day of watering. If you have a choice, pass this one up.

Pre-Potted—Bare-root stock that has been planted in permanent growing media in a plastic container or a corrugated container, both of which will rot in the ground. This type of packaging is reasonably safe.

Field Grown—Young whips are planted directly into a plastic, metal, or papier-mâché container, and grown above ground for one to three years before you buy them. These are about the safest and best trees you can buy.

Field Potted—This is chancy, since the young tree is dug up by machine or hand and placed into a container, watered, put on a truck, and shipped to you. I avoid this type of tree stock if I can.

Balled and Burlapped—Up until a few years ago, this was the popular way to buy trees, but the cost of labor and freight has just about done away with this practice. A freshly dug and balled tree in early spring or late fall (when the tree is dormant), especially if the ball is large, is pretty safe; if the tree's had a year in the ball and then been allowed to heal above ground, it's even better. If the tree is summer-dug, balled, and delivered, <u>don't buy it!</u>

Machine-Dug and Planted—This is the most expensive, but best way to buy a tree if you need, want, or can afford a mature tree. The tree is dug up and replanted the same day with a huge root ball; if done properly, the tree may never even know it's been moved.

If you dedicate yourself to your trees' safety and comfort, you can use any of these methods with great success. But if you don't plan to participate in your yard's care and comfort, don't take a chance—go with machine-dug and planted.

FAVORITE FLOWERING TREES

Here are my picks for the most beautiful flowering trees that can be used in your flowerscape. I've included their zone hardiness as well as their blossom color. I'm also giving you the botanical names of these trees—this is how they are known to professional nurserypeople. Asking for your tree by its botanical name will, in most cases, ensure that you get exactly what you want. Why? Because many trees have several common names or two different trees may be known by the same common name.

GREEN THUMB TIP

On bare root trees, soak them in a Vitamin B-1 Plant Starter solution for at least 24 hours before planting.

If you're planting pre-potted trees in plastic pots, cut the pot with a knife instead of yanking the sapling out of its container.

For balled and burlapped trees, you can either remove the burlap or just cut away the sides.

FLOWERING TREE FAVORITES

PROFESSIONAL NAME (BOTANICAL)	HOMEOWNER NAME	FLOWER COLOR	ZONE
Acacia baileyana	Cootamundra wattle	yellow	10
Acacia decurrens dealbata	Silver wattle	yellow	9
Acer platanoides columnare	Columnar Norway maple	yellow	3
Acer platanoides 'Crimson King'	Crimson King maple	yellow	4
Acer platanoides 'Emerald Queen'	Emerald Queen maple	yellow	3
Acer platanoides schwedleri	Schwedler maple	yellow	3
Acer platanoides 'Summershade'	Summershade maple	yellow	3
Albizia julibrissin	Silk Tree	purple	6
Albizia julibrissin 'Charlotte'	Charlotte silk tree	purple	6
Albizia julibrissin rosea	Hardy silk tree	purple	5
Albizia julibrissin 'Tryon'	Tryon silk tree	purple	6
Amelanchier canadensis	Shadblow serviceberry	white	4
Amelanchier grandiflora	Apple serviceberry	white	4
Arbutus unedo	Strawberry tree	white	8
Bauhinia variegata	Purple orchid tree	lavender	10
Bauhinia variegata 'Candida'	White orchid tree	white	10
Castanea mollissima	Chinese chestnut	white	5
Ceratonia siliqua	Carob	red	10
Cercis canadensis alba	Whitebud	white	5
Cercis canadensis 'Withers Pink Charm'	Withers Pink Charm redbud	purple	5
Citrus species	Citrus fruits	white	9
Cladrastis lutea	Yellowwood	white	4
Cornus florida	Flowering dogwood	white	4
Cornus kousa	Kousa dogwood	white	5
Cornus nuttalii	Pacific dogwood	white	7
Crataegus mollis	Downy hawthorn	white	4
Crataegus phaenopyrum	Washington hawthorn	white	4
Eucalyptus ficifolia	Crimson eucalyptus	red	9
Halesia carolina	Carolina silver bell	white	4
Heteromeles arbutifolia	Toyon	white	7
Jacaranda acutifolia	Sharp-leaved jacaranda	lavender	10

FLOWERING TREE FAVORITES

PROFESSIONAL NAME (BOTANICAL)	HOMEOWNER NAME	FLOWER COLOR	ZONE
Koelreuteria paniculata	Goldenrain tree	yellow	5
Laburnum x watereri 'Vossii'	Golden chain tree	yellow	5
Lagerstroemia indica 'Ingleside Pink'	Ingleside Pink crape myrtle	purple	7
Lagerstroemia indica 'Wm. Toovey'	Wm. Toovey red crape myrtle	red	7
Ligustrum lucidum	Glossy privet	white	7
Liriodendron tulipifera	Tulip tree	yellow	4
Magnolia denudata	Yulan magnolia	white	5
Magnolia grandiflora	Southern magnolia	white	7
Magnolia stellata	Star magnolia	white	5
Magnolia virginiana	Sweet bay	white	5
Malus 'Almey'	Almey crab apple	red	4
Malus x arnoldiana	Arnold crab apple	white	4
Malus x *astrosanguinea*	Carmine crab apple	red	4
Malus baccata	Siberian crab apple	white	2
Malus floribunda	Japanese flowering crab apple	white	4
Malus 'Hopa'	Hopa crab apple	red	4
Malus hupehensis	Tea crab apple	white	4
Malus 'Katherine'	Katherine crab apple	purple	4
Malus 'Prince George'	Prince George crab apple	purple	4
Malus pumila	Common apple	white	3
Malus sargentii	Sargent crab apple	white	5
Oxydendrum arboreum	Sorrel tree	white	4
Photinia serrulata	Hardy orange	white	5
Prunus cerasifera nigra 'Thundercloud'	Thundercloud plum	white	4
Prunus persica	Peach	purple	5
Prunus sargentii	Sargent cherry	purple	4
Prunus serrulata 'Amanogawa'	Amanogawa cherry	purple	6
Prunus serrulata 'Kwanzan'	Kwanzan cherry	purple	5
Prunus serrulata 'Shirofugen'	Shirofugen cherry	white	6
Prunus serrulata 'Shirotae'	Mount Fuji cherry	white	6
Prunus subhirtella 'Autumnalis'	Autumn flowering cherry	purple	5
Prunus subhirtella 'Pendula'	Weeping Japanese Higan cherry	purple	5
Prunus yedoensis	Yoshino cherry	white	5

FLOWERING TREE FAVORITES

PROFESSIONAL NAME (BOTANICAL)	HOMEOWNER NAME	FLOWER COLOR	ZONE
Pyrus calleryana 'Bradford'	Bradford Callery pear	white	5
Pyrus communis	Common pear	white	5
Sophora japonica	Japanese pagoda tree	white	4
Sorbus alnifolia	Korean mountain ash	white	5
Sorbus americana	American mountain ash	white	2
Sorbus aucuparia	European mountain ash	white	3
Sorbus decora	Showy mountain ash	white	2
Stewartia pseudocamellia	Japanese stewartia	white	5
Styrax japonica	Japanese snowbell	white	5
Syringa amurensis japonica	Japanese tree lilac	white	4
Tilia cordata	Littleleaf linden	yellow	3
Tilia cordata 'Greenspire'	Greenspire linden	yellow	3
Tilia euchlora	Crimean linden	yellow	5
Tilia tomentosa	Silver linden	yellow	4
Tilia tomentosa 'Princeton'	Princeton silver linden	yellow	4

SAVE MONEY *AND* HELP THE ENVIRONMENT!

You *can* make a difference! The planting of just one tree can help to cool the atmosphere and reverse the alarming trend toward global warming and the much publicized "Greenhouse Effect." The Garden Council estimates that one properly watered tree can "produce a cooling effect in its lifetime equal to ten room-size air conditioners operating 20 hours a day." And that's just for starters. If you plant shade trees on the south and west sides of your home, you can help to regulate your environment. Trees planted in these locations protect your home from the summer sun, and allow the sun to shine through in the winter after the leaves have fallen. This will dramatically save fuel consumption for heat in the winter, and reduce the need for cooling in the summer—saving you money on your utility bill and adding value to your home and property.

THE SCOOP ON PLANTING

When To Plant

The offhand advice given by most folks who sell landscape plants is that you can plant a tree any time you can get a shovel into the ground. Unfortunately, they forget to add, "That doesn't mean it will live."

The Best Time To Plant

In most parts of the country, early fall, after the dry hot weather has passed, is the very best time to plant trees. When the evenings are cool, but the days remain warm, most newly planted trees quickly acclimate themselves and begin to develop the needed root mass for winter survival. This is even more important if your flowering tree has a root ball that is wrapped in burlap.

Flowering Ash

The Second Best Time

As early in the spring as you can get a spade into the ground and not have the soil stick to it in a muddy mess is the second best time to plant. An early spring planting allows the tree to get its root source started and get a good supply of drinking water before the really hot weather comes along.

The Worst Time

The beginning of or during the hottest part of the year, unless you have professional training or are willing to take the precautions of wrapping the trunks and spraying the foliage with an anti-desiccant, a spray designed to keep moisture in the plant by coating it with a polymer-type material. (Read further in this

247

chapter for more information on both.) But ultimately, it is better to *wait* for the cooler weather than to *worry*.

One Last Thing

One last thing—ask the person who is selling you the tree what his or her replacement policy is, and then get a copy of it in writing; also—keep your receipt! You will seldom find a professional nurseryperson recommending an improper planting time, so check out the person's credentials to see if he or she is a member of the Nurserymen's Association.

DIG A $10

HOLE FOR

A $5 TREE

How To Plant

Labu

Digging The Hole

When digging the hole for a new tree, it should be at least a foot wider than the tree's root system, and 6 to 8 inches deeper. Remember, as strange as this may seem, the best time to plant or transplant is in the evening, after 6:00 p.m. It is more comfortable for you, the tree, the surrounding plants, and it gives them a chance to get settled before the sun comes up and they must crank up the food factory.

Sub-surface Drainage

After you dig the hole, partially fill it with water. Check closely on the time it takes the water to be absorbed into the soil. If it takes more than a few hours, then the sub-surface drainage is inadequate and should be improved. If you don't improve it, the soil will become waterlogged, resulting in unsatisfactory growth and the possible death of the tree.

There are a number of ways to improve the sub-surface drainage, including **percolation** and **drain tiles.**

Percolation

This condition is a result of compaction of the soil, generally caused by construction in your yard. Deep digging and backfilling with a lighter, sandier soil may restore the drainage.

Installing Drain Tiles

If the lack of sub-surface drainage is due to some other condition, consider installing drain tiles. To install a drain tile, dig a ditch 12 to 14 inches deep and 12 inches wide leading from the wet spot to a drier area where the water can drain. (Make sure that you pitch the ditch so that it is deeper on the drier end. This will facilitate the flow of water through the drain.) Lay down a 2-inch layer of gravel about the size of golf balls in the bottom of the ditch, then set down the drain tile, making sure the holes are facing down. Fill in with more of the gravel on either side of the tile, and then cover the top of it with 4 inches of the golf-ball-sized stones. Finally, cover the gravel with a sheet of building paper (this will prevent earth from filtering down and clogging up the drain), and then refill the remainder of the ditch with the excavated earth. Be sure to overfill the hole completely because rain and the elements will eventually pack it down to normal ground level.

Remember, simply throwing a layer of rocks or gravel in the bottom of the hole does nothing to improve sub-surface drainage.

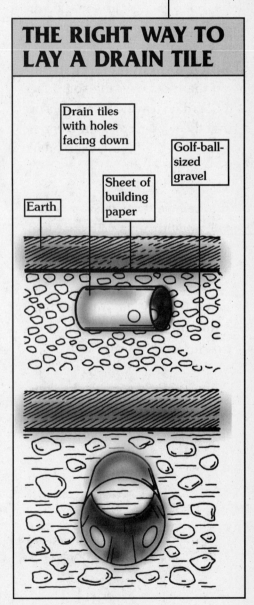

THE RIGHT WAY TO LAY A DRAIN TILE

Drain tiles with holes facing down

Golf-ball-sized gravel

Sheet of building paper

Earth

STEP-BY-STEP PLANTING

Place a rock in the bottom of the hole which the central root mass can rest upon. Mix 50% mulch with 50% soil from the hole, then pour some of the mix in the hole and firm it up.

Set the plant in the hole, spreading the roots over the soil. Place a board across the hole to ensure that the lighter part of the bark is level with the board; then adjust the soil level.

Fill the hole three-quarters full of soil, and firm it up with your foot. Fill the hole with water, and then let it drain.

Add the rest of the soil, and build a ring of soil 3" wide around the tree to act as a water well.

Prune branches back by one-third (not all to the same height) to help compensate for any damage to the roots.

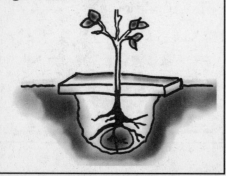

Planting In A Raised Bed

Another method of overcoming inadequate drainage is to build a raised bed. Simply dig a very shallow hole in the existing ground, and then pile soil in a large mound over the top of it. Pack the soil down, and then dig the planting hole. The raised bed of soil should be high enough above ground level to permit normal root functioning. You can leave it simply as a raised mound or build a retaining wall around it.

If a raised bed is impractical, trees may still be planted in poor soil as long as nothing is done to increase water contact in the root area. The addition of peat moss or compost increases the moisture retentiveness of soil and improves its structure, but if drainage is poor, using these materials as backfill will tend to make the planting hole a reservoir or pool. If such materials are not added to the planting hole, the likelihood of water-logged conditions is reduced. Conversely, the addition of vermiculite, perlite, sand, or cinders to the backfill soil could help improve drainage.

Preparing The Soil

The soil used to fill in the hole around the roots should be well prepared. Except where drainage is poor, you can add peat moss, compost, or other forms of humus. A third by volume of these materials should be added and thoroughly mixed into the soil so that when the tree is in place, the hole may be quickly filled. I also add a liberal amount of bone meal mixed with Epsom salts to stimulate root and leaf growth. Sprinkle this mixture into the hole and on top of the soil after the hole has been filled.

Fast & Easy Composting

There are many methods of composting. Magazines and newspapers frequently carry articles on the subject, and one book devoted exclusively to composting explains at least a dozen methods in its 800 pages. This vast body of information confuses many gardeners, particularly new ones. I would suggest that you adopt one method, and try it for a season. Then, if you're not satisfied, you can read up on other methods and do some experimenting. My method is a simple one. Because it has worked well for me, I have found no reason to try other ones.

SUPER GROWING SECRET

When planting your trees, make a mix of 4 parts bone meal and 1 part Epsom salts, and add a handful to the planting hole. This will energize the soil and give the tree something to snack on as it gets growing.

Crab Apple

Leave It Alone!

My compost pile consists entirely of leaves. My kitchen waste—*vegetables only*—is buried in a bare spot that will be planted the following year. My grass clippings—*dried on the driveway*—are used as mulch about the yard. The use of leaves exclusively eliminates the possibility of picking up any weed seeds and results in a compost pile that breaks down fast, efficiently, and at a fairly even rate.

Bins Are Best

Before leaves are collected, compost bins must be built. My lot is 50' x 160'. To screen my bins from the neighbors, I put them behind the garage. The first bin is about 4' x 6' x 4'. I use chain-link fencing for the sides, but you can use boards, or even concrete blocks. Whatever you use, air spaces <u>must</u> be provided— air is an absolute necessity for breaking down the leaves. You will also need a cover for your bins. A sheet of exterior plywood, painted or wrapped in plastic, will last three or four years.

My second bin is approximately 3' x 4' x 4'. The sides of this bin are solid, except for a drilled row of one-inch holes on all 4 sides to provide air. These two bins provide enough compost for my size yard. If you have a larger yard, you may need more than two bins, or bigger bins. You may also want to set aside a corner of your lot for compost bins, and screen the area with evergreens.

PALLET COMPOSTER

Discarded shipping pallets make great compost bins. Place one pallet on the ground, and drive 2 metal support poles per side into the ground. Then slip the pallet sides over top of the poles, and your bin is complete.

Fall Is The Time

My compost program begins in the fall. I rake several times during the fall so that my compost pile builds gradually. Discard any twigs you may encounter.

The raked leaves are collected and placed in the 4' x 6' x 4' bin. The pile should never be tightly packed. If the leaves are dry, I water them with a mixture of **½ cup of Thatch Buster™ and 1 can of cola in 2 gallons of water** because moisture is necessary for the breakdown. Avoid overwatering—soggy leaves will not decompose. I keep adding leaves throughout the fall. With the last raking my compost pile is done for the year.

One caution—a large number of oak leaves should be composted separately. They are acidic, and the compost made from them should be used only on acid-loving plants like rhododendrons and azaleas. The only leaves I throw away are the oak because I have few acid-loving plants.

In early spring—late March or early April—I use a spading fork or EZ Compost Turner™ to work the pile. If the pile is dry, I add more of the above mixture and replace the cover.

After I spade the pile in spring, I turn it every three or four weeks, adding the Thatch Buster Tonic as needed. By the end of August, my pile is fairly well decomposed, and I transfer the leaves to my 4' x 4' x 4' bin.

When fall comes and I start filling the larger bin again, the leaves in the small bin are reduced to the consistency of coffee grounds, and are ready for spring use. The only chore I have in the spring is to screen the material to remove any stones, twigs, or scraps.

Remember, the more times the compost pile is turned, the quicker it will decompose. I don't hurry the process because the leaves I collect in the fall of 1997 will not be used until the spring of 1999. For those of you who need immediate compost, how-ever, turning the pile weekly should result in usable compost in a month or two.

I want to emphasize that my compost method is not the only one, but it has done a good job for me. Try it or any of the others that you come across until you find one that works for you.

GREEN THUMB TIP

To save hours of your valuable time, use an electric Leaf Eater. The Leaf Eater weighs about 25 pounds, and can be placed over a 30-gallon trash can. Instead of steel blades, the unit uses inexpensive nylon line, the stuff used in weed trimmers. By using a Leaf Eater, I get lots more leaves into my bin, and because more surface area is exposed, the leaves decompose more rapidly.

If my leaves are dry or just a little moist, I shred them at the curb, and then dump them into my larger bin. Soggy leaves, however, do not shred easily, so if we're having an extremely wet fall, I put them into the large bin unground, and shred them late in the summer of the next year before putting them into the small bin.

Planting Depth—A Deep Subject

On nearly every tree trunk there is a soil line marking the depth at which it grew in the nursery. You can tell by the discoloration on the bark. Whether the tree is bare root (B.R.) or balled and burlapped (B & B), it should be placed so that allowing for settling, the soil line will be the same as it was when the tree was growing in the nursery and no deeper.

Your allowance for settling will vary according to the depth of the planting hole and the materials mixed into the soil. The deeper the hole, the greater the amount of settling to be expected. This may be reduced somewhat by thoroughly tamping the soil below the roots or root ball. However, even if you do that, still allow at least one inch for settling. If generous quantities of peat moss or other compacting materials are mixed into the soil, a 2-inch allowance for settling may be safer.

PLANTING HELPER

To keep a tree straight and steady when planting, tie the trunk to a long 2 x 4 that is setting at ground level. Remove the board after back-filling the hole.

Air Pockets—Fill 'Em Up!

For bare-rooted trees, the soil should be worked in and among the roots to avoid any air pockets. You can do this with your hands, but a better way is to shovel a quantity of soil into the hole, and then lift the tree up and down several times so that the soil filters in and among the roots. The soil should be firmed by tamping, but don't damage the roots in the process!

When the hole is refilled three-quarters of the way, and the soil is firmed, fill up the hole with water. This will help to eliminate air pockets and settle the soil, and thoroughly moisten the roots. After the water has percolated into the ground, finish filling the hole with soil. This soil should NOT be packed or tamped down. Excess soil can be used to form a slight ridge around the edge of the planting hole to facilitate future watering.

One final note—you should not completely remove the burlap from trees with balled and burlapped roots; the burlap will disintegrate in time. Simply cut back the sides, and let Mother Nature do the rest.

Staking And Guying—
Give Your Trees Some Support

Newly planted trees usually need some support to prevent their being whipped about by the wind. They need this support until their roots have had at least one year to become firmly established. Unsupported or unprotected trees frequently are unable to develop an effective root system.

PROPER SUPPORT

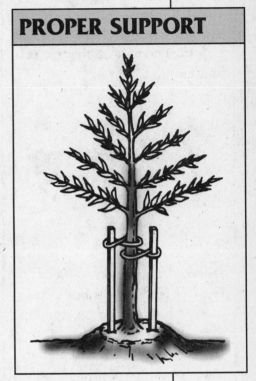

Pegs and guy lines, stakes, or posts may be used; they should hold the tree firmly in place without injuring the bark. Lengths of old rubber hose are perfect for slipping over the wire where it comes in contact with the tree's bark.

Upright, stout stakes positioned right next to the tree's trunk are the best for the average homeowner, since ground stakes and guy wires interfere with mowing and constitute a hazard.

Give Your Tree A Security Blanket

I always recommend a good, thick mulch for newly planted trees. This not only prevents moisture loss and controls weeds, but it also prevents a crust from forming on the soil over the root area that might exclude air and moisture. Mulch also acts as an insulator and provides nutrients to shallow-rooted trees.

255

Sick trees—Wrap any sick tree with 4" wide strips of burlap from the ground up to the first branch. Leave the tree wrapped through the hot weather. This wrap acts as insulation to keep the tree cool and moist.

Decorative stone—Place a layer of landscape fabric around trees, shrubs, and evergreens. Cover with 2" of dried, brown grass clippings or shredded bark. Then place decorative stone on top of grass clippings. The grass clippings/bark absorb the heat from the stones, and landscape fabric helps prevent weeds.

Peat moss, sawdust, and shredded bark are the three most commonly available mulching materials, but you must watch them because they will crust under certain conditions. Pine needles, straw, slat grass, peanut hulls, coco bean hulls and many other materials may be used. Coarse gravel works very well, if applied thickly, about 4 inches deep, over a layer of shredded bark. Vegetation, however, is preferred because it helps maintain the humus content of the soil.

The depth of the mulch will vary according to the material used. An inch of sphagnum moss will normally be adequate. A 4- to 6-inch layer of rotted compost, straw, or woodchips should be equally effective.

The First Haircut

Most newly planted trees should be pruned at planting time. The reason for this haircut is to compensate for loss of roots in transplanting—its decreased root system will not be able to support the same amount of foliage it did before transplanting. Since you generally don't know the extent of root loss, it is better to err on the side of heavy pruning rather than light pruning.

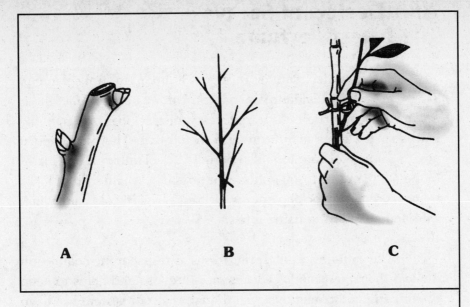

A   B   C

  The first step should be to remove all damaged branches by cutting them back to a fork or bud (A and B above). The cut should be made just beyond a bud or twig, pointing in the direction you want the new growth to go. That way, you can help to shape the growth of your tree. The bud immediately below the cut will develop and grow. Next, remove any and all branches that contribute to weak forks, or those that cross over one another.

  Injury to the leader or top stem of the tree may require it to be shortened. This need not be a cause for alarm. Make the cut above a twig or bud. A new leader will grow; once the new shoot has reached a foot or more in length, tie it in a vertical position to a bamboo stake that has been fastened securely to the trunk below the shoot with a strip of nylon pantyhose (C above).

Peach

HOME REMEDIES

To seal pruning cuts: mix antiseptic mouthwash with latex paint, and apply to seal wounds after pruning.

Use an old garden hose to cushion wire/rope when staking/tieing up trees, as a guard on your sharp tools, and as a soaker hose.

257

Anti-Desiccant Sprays—
The Latest Perfume

WEATHER-

PROOF YOUR

TREES TO

PROTECT

AGAINST THE

ELEMENTS

The anti-desiccant sprays are a boon to transplanting. They can be found under many names, but my personal favorite is my own WeatherProof™. It reduces moisture loss through the leaves so the trees may be moved in full leaf. The protection it gives against moisture loss also permits the planting of trees later in the fall than was formerly thought possible. WeatherProof locks in moisture, while locking out the elements—heat, cold, sun, wind, salt, and pollution to name a few.

The anti-desiccant spray forms a transparent coating on the leaf that significantly reduces moisture loss and helps to keep the tree in good condition, even though the root system has been reduced. The coating eventually sloughs off. The sprays have not only proved useful for transplanting, but they can be applied to trees and evergreens in exposed situations, substantially reducing desiccation from drying winds.

Cover Up To Prevent Sunburn

Wrapping the tree trunk to prevent sunscald is frequently overlooked when planting new trees. But you should know that many trees suffer irreparable damage from this type of injury. It is especially severe on trees transplanted from a secluded, woody area to a sunny situation.

*Carolina
Silver Bell*

You can reduce the need to wrap by selecting trees that have been growing at the edge of woods or in an open field. Also, if you mark the north side of the tree and then maintain the same orientation when you replant it, you can lessen the likelihood of injury.

If you must wrap a tree, you can use cheesecloth, old silk stockings, or the commercial tree wraps available in any garden center. The wrap should be left on for a year—the cheesecloth and old silk stockings will have disintegrated by that time.

However, the prepared tree wraps are longer lasting, and should be removed in the early spring of the following season, preferably during cloudy weather so that the bark will have time to adjust before the sun gets too bright.

To wrap a tree trunk, begin at the bottom and bandage the trunk like you would your leg with an Ace bandage. Continue this way up to the first branch; secure it there and at the bottom with a piece of nylon stocking.

THE CARE AND FEEDING OF YOUR FLOWERING TREES

Trees Get Hungry Too!

Trees cannot live on rain alone; to thrive and survive, they must be regularly maintained, and that means fed. Over the years, I have found that trees fed twice a year perform at peak all season long.

To feed flowering trees within an existing flowerscape, first I use a root feeder in the early spring with fruit tree cartridges even though they may not be fruit trees. Then I foliar feed with this timely tonic.

I personally do not feed my trees after August 15 in areas where the temperature drops below freezing in the winter because the fertilizer will stimulate new growth that can freeze in the coming cold weather.

TIMELY TONIC

Foliar feed your trees every 3 weeks during the growing season with this tonic:

1 oz. of shampoo,
1 oz. of ammonia,
1 oz. of whiskey,
1/2 can of beer,
1 oz. of hydrogen peroxide,
1 oz. of gelatin, and
4 tbsps. of instant tea,
all dissolved in
2 gallons of warm water.

Each tree should get up to a quart and-a-half once in the spring and again on June 15, no matter where you live in the good old U.S.A.

One of the most important things a tree needs during the summer is water. Eighty to ninety percent of tree problems are due to water supply problems. How do you tell if the tree needs water? Here are some of the visible signs:

- Wilting leaves—Temporary wilting is the drooping of leaves during the day, and recovery during the night. Permanently wilting trees do not recover at night. Prolonged, permanent wilting will kill trees.

- Leaf Shedding—Leaves may be shed while they are still green in severe drought conditions.

- Leaves may also turn yellow or brown, appear scorched (brown around the edges), or even show signs of early fall coloration.

- The tree may produce a large number of seeds prematurely.

All of these signs tell you that your tree is under stress, and could be irreparably damaged by the lack of water, or insects and diseases taking advantage of the tree in its weakened state.

Trees Like A Drink Now And Then

Trees require a substantial amount of water to carry on their normal functions; however, the amount of water required varies greatly with different species of trees and with different soil conditions.

Many of the newer subdivisions have predominantly clay soil. If that's the case where you live, then overwatering is one of the major reasons trees die.

Trees planted in clay should be watered only once a week, and then only if there has been no substantial amount of rainfall during the week. When little or no rain has fallen, and the soil around the tree's root system is dry to a depth of 6 to 8 inches, a hose should be allowed to run at the base of the tree for fifteen to twenty minutes at low pressure.

In areas that have sandy or gravel-rich soil, overwatering is not the problem it is in those areas having clay soil. However, even with the better drainage provided by a sandy soil, trees planted in these conditions should be watered not more than once a week with a hose for fifteen or twenty minutes at low water pressure, and should not be watered in weeks in which there has been a heavy rainfall.

Don't Forget To Wash Behind The Ears

Plants, like people, cannot properly function if they do not practice good personal hygiene. This means periodic baths. Oh yes, my soil brothers and sisters, your entire garden needs to be bathed regularly with soap and water, and a light disinfectant.

In the fall of the year, after all the leaves have fallen from the trees, but before the temperature falls below freezing, you should spray all of your flowering trees with one cup of Shampoo mixed in 20 gallons of water, followed by a Dormant Spray. This will kill any bugs that are hibernating there.

In the spring, you should repeat the same program as soon as the temperature stays above freezing for twenty-four hours. Then as soon as the buds have set, but before the tree begins to flower, make my **All Season Clean-Up Tonic:**

**1 cup of Shampoo,
1 cup of chewing tobacco
juice, and 1 cup of antiseptic
mouthwash in a 20-gallon hose-end
sprayer jar, filling the balance of
the sprayer jar with water.**

With this mixture in hand, wash down your flowering trees as well as the rest of the dormant flower garden.

THUG BUSTERS

AMMONIA

To keep wasps away from the ripening fruit on your fruit trees, mix equal parts of ammonia and water, and fill several cans with the mixture. Hang the cans among the fruit trees for a sure-fire repellent.

BUG SPRAY

Mix 1 cup of garlic juice, 1 cup of antiseptic mouthwash, and 1 cup of Shampoo in a 20 gallon hose-end sprayer. This tonic controls aphids and most other pests that come to dine on your plants. Also, Tobacco Dust sprinkled on plants repels many insect pests.

PETUNIA POWER

A bed of perky petunias around your apple tree will repel many of the insects that are drawn toward the fruit.

MOTH BALLS

Place moth ball crystals around the bases of peach trees and cover with dirt to fight peach tree borers; then paint the trunks of all fruit trees, especially peaches, plums, and apricots, on the south and west sides with a water-based white paint to help prevent sunscald.

Then during the season, every three to four weeks, wash everything down in the evening with one cup of Shampoo mixed in 20 gallons of water.

Take Control Of Insects And Disease Before They Control You

VARMINT CONTROL

To keep cats and squirrels from climbing trees, place a 12" wide piece of sheet metal around the trunk, 6' to 7' off of the ground.

When using chicken wire to prevent rabbit damage to tree trunks, place 4 sticks (the diameter of your little finger) between the tree and the chicken wire. This prevents the rabbits from getting to and damaging the bark.

If you follow my general hygiene program, you will seldom have a tree problem. If you do, I want you to spray a solution of Tomato and Vegetable Dust, mixed at 6 teaspoons per gallon, with an ounce of Shampoo per gallon, every 14 days throughout the growing season.

Organic Approach

There are many persistent bugs in any garden, and if you are faced with one or more, simply take this safe, sane, and aggressive approach:

1. Begin with a light application of Diatomaceous earth (DE) and/or para-dichlorobenzene crystals (better known for their use in moth balls). Mix one cup of crystals with 3 cups DE and sprinkle it on the soil in a 3-foot circle beneath the flowering trees in both the spring and fall.

2. Spray your troubled tree early in the season with a solution of 1 cup of Shampoo and 6 tablespoons of Tomato and Vegetable Dust, mixed into a paste, and then applied with a 6-gallon hose-end sprayer, in the evening, every three weeks throughout the growing season.

3. Sprinkle Dursban® or diazinon granules as directed onto the soil, from the trunk out past the weep line (the line representing the furthest outreach of the tree's longest branch) in both spring and fall.

4. Add an all-purpose liquid Fruit Tree Spray at the recommended rate to my Clean-Up Tonic for fast, easy insect control.

These few steps can control or head off most insect and disease problems before they get out of hand.

Chemical Controls

You should always remember that the spraying of any chemical is a very dangerous proposition that could cause serious injury or death. The dangers, however, can be reduced if you follow a few simple rules.

Safety First!

1. Read the instructions on the label every time you use a pesticide, no matter how many times you have used the material in the past.

2. Always follow the mixing and application instructions on the package to the letter.

3. Never leave any materials in your sprayer for any length of time.

4. Never apply any materials under windy conditions.

5. Never spray around pets or children.

SUPER GROWING SECRET

The spraying of trees and shrubs is a monthly chore during the growing season, and as a tree grows, the chore and the expense grows along with it. So, when a tree grows to a size where it cannot be sprayed from the ground, it should only be treated when a serious disease or insect problem has been identified.

Small trees and shrubs should be sprayed every two weeks throughout the growing season with my All Season Clean-Up Tonic. By spraying your plants twice a month, insect and disease problems can be effectively controlled. Remember to spray after 7:00 p.m., when it's cool and comfortable for you, and the bugs will be at home.

6. Always shower after using any chemical control.

7. Never wash the clothes that were used while spraying chemicals with the regular family laundry. You should set aside a special set of clothes for spraying.

8. Finally, never mix pesticides unless your instructions call for it.

Herbicide Damage

USE

COMMON

SENSE WHEN

APPLYING

CHEMICAL

CONTROLS

Herbicide damage to trees and other plant materials is on the rise everywhere. The reason for this is the increased use of herbicides by homeowners to control the weeds in their lawns. This damage to trees and shrubs can often be identified by the discoloration and premature dropping of foliage and, in many cases, a twisting or curling of the new growth. Wetting the ground with a heavy concentration of weed-killing chemicals may result in their leaching down through the soil to where they can be absorbed by the root systems of the surrounding trees. So, herbicides should be used cautiously, applying them only to the foliage of the weeds that you want to destroy.

Herbicide injury may also occur from exposure to spray drifts, or excessive herbicide mist. To avoid this type of injury, it is important to use low-volatile materials, and apply them when there is little or no breeze. A coarse spray applied under low pressure will also limit the amount of spray drift.

Cherry

Still another way to avoid or minimize damage is to use only the more specific or selective herbicides. Broad spectrum chemicals will kill all of your weeds, but they will also kill your trees, shrubs, and flowers if the material is not applied carefully.

Root Prune— Get To The Root Of The Matter

Root pruning is something that people hear me talk about, yet they don't understand it. Root pruning is a pedicure for your trees to stimulate new root growth. This job should be done in early spring and should be made part of your regular feeding program. Here's what you should do:

1. Cut The Soil—while the tree is dormant*, plunge a flat-backed spade or shovel with a sharp edge into the ground out at the weep line (a line around the tree out at the furthest extension of its branches) all the way around the tree.

2. The Dry Mixture—Sprinkle one-half pound of Epsom salts per mature tree into the cuts. Epsom salts will deepen the tree's color, thicken its foliage, petals, and bark, and increase its root growth.

3. Drill The Holes—Then drill holes, one inch in diameter, 10 to 12 inches deep, 18 inches apart, in a circle 9 inches beyond the weep-line cut.

4. The Final Feeding—Break up tree spikes into thirds, drop one piece into each hole, and pour in a solution of **2 oz. of Shampoo and 2 oz. of instant tea in a gallon of warm water** into each hole. Cover the hole with soil.

Pruning—
It's A Real Cut Up!

Generally speaking, pruning is an annual chore. Putting off or avoiding periodic pruning may not have serious results for a healthy tree, but weaker trees may have dead branches or structural faults (such as low-hanging, contorted, or sharp branches) which may be a hazard for those who pass underneath them. Pruning can also, in many cases, promote heavier flowering and fruiting.

*The dormant season is late autumn, after the leaves have fallen, to early spring before the sap begins to rise.

GREEN THUMB TIP

Diseases can be spread from one tree to another by dirty pruning tools. So immediately after pruning a tree that may be diseased, wipe off the blades of your tools with denatured ethyl alcohol. It's also a good idea to disinfect all borrowed or rented tools with alcohol before using them on your own trees. You never know where they've been, or what they've been in contact with.

OIL YOUR

TOOLS BEFORE

PUTTING

THEM AWAY

Locust

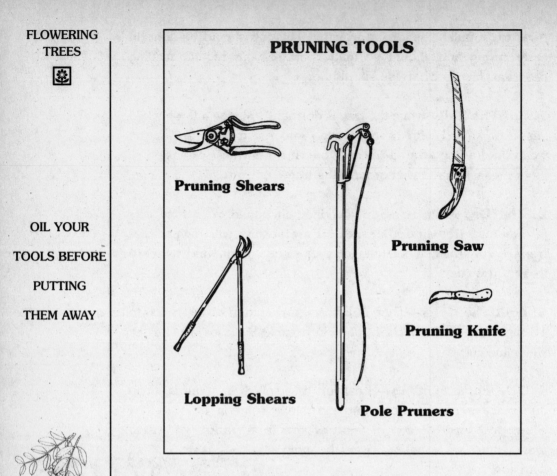

PRUNING TOOLS

Pruning Shears

Pruning Saw

Pruning Knife

Lopping Shears

Pole Pruners

You'll need pruning shears, a pruning knife, lopping shears, pole pruners, and a pruning saw to prune your trees properly. All of these tools should be sharpened and oiled regularly with WD-40® It is also a good idea to sterilize the tools with rubbing alcohol in order to prevent the transfer of infectious diseases from one tree to another.

All cuts should be made flush to a larger branch or the trunk. Avoid leaving stubs because they do not heal over, and are likely to provide a channel for wood-rotting fungi to enter the heartwood of the tree.

All wounds over one inch in diameter should be covered with pruning paint. A coat of any asphalt varnish base paint or a mixture of 3 drops of liquid Sevin to 8 ounces of interior latex paint will also do a good job.

PRUNING PRINCIPLES

TREE	WHEN TO PRUNE	HOW TO PRUNE
Carob	After flowering	Repair when necessary
Catalpa	While dormant	Repair when necessary
Chestnut	When necessary	Repair when necessary
Citrus trees	After harvest	Shape and thin occasionally
Eucalyptus	When necessary	Repair when necessary
Flowering cherries, peaches, etc.	After flowering	Shape and thin occasionally
Flowering dogwood	After flowering	Repair when necessary
Fringe tree	After flowering	Repair when necessary
Goldenrain tree	After flowering	Seldom required; repair when necessary
Hawthorn	After flowering	Repair when necessary
Jacaranda	When needed	Repair when necessary
Japanese pagoda tree	Should not be pruned	
Laburnum	After flowering	Repair when necessary
Linden	Should not be pruned	
Magnolia	After flowering	Prune above outside limbs
Mountain ash	After flowering	Repair when necessary
Myrtle	After flowering	Prune often to control rapid growth
Orchid tree	Late spring	Shape and repair when necessary
Redbud	After flowering	Shape when young
Royal poinciana	After heaviest flowering	Repair when necessary
Serviceberry	After flowering	Repair when necessary
Silk tree	After flowering	Repair when necessary
Silver bell tree	After flowering	Repair when necessary
Smoke tree	Early spring	Cut out second-year wood; thin first-year wood
Snowbell	After flowering	Repair when necessary
Sorrel tree	After flowering	Repair when necessary
Stewartia	While dormant	Repair when necessary
Toyon	After flowering	Repair when necessary
Tree lilac	After flowering	Seldom needed
Tulip tree	Should not be pruned	
Whitebud	After flowering	Repair when necessary
Yellowwood	After flowering	Repair when necessary

Preparing for Winter— Button Up Your Overcoat

Trees vary in their hardiness, which may not be so much affected by latitude as it is by exposure to winter winds, sudden drops in temperature, and drought. So, as I said at the outset, select only those kinds of trees that are considered to be hardy to your particular area.

A tree's hardiness can be weakened through overprotection or by applying fertilizer at the wrong time of the year. A tree planted near the home may be sheltered from the cooling fall winds that help induce dormancy. Then if the sap is still running when winter settles in, the tree can freeze, causing irreparable damage. Heavy fertilization in late summer can produce new growth which may not have time to mature before winter frosts. In areas where heavy winter snowfall may be expected, it is important that the trees be pruned so that their branches can withstand the weight of snow and ice. In windswept locations, it may be necessary to protect young trees with guy wires until the roots are firmly established.

In most cases, the application of an anti-transpirant spray like Weather-Proof™ is needed to protect foliage and wood from drying winter winds. Whatever you do, follow the checklist to make sure that your trees are buttoned up before the cold weather sets in.

WINTER CHECKLIST

✓Dormant spray—With an all-seasons horticultural or dormant oil in late fall.

✓Water—soak the soil well before the ground freezes.

✓Extra mulch—to keep moisture in the ground.

✓WeatherProof—locks moisture in, seals the elements out.

✓Wrap trunks—to prevent splitting, cracking, and sunscald.

✓Stake young trees—so they don't get whipped about in the winter wind.

✓Burlap screens—protect against sun, wind, salt, and pollution damage.

The Anchors

Flowering trees are the anchors in any landscape plan. It doesn't matter if it's a single flowering tree in the center of the yard with a white petunia collar cluster around it, or a flowering tree in the midst of your flower garden. Everything else around it should be balanced in terms of color, size, and shape.

So, go on, add a flowering tree or two to your little corner of the world. The beauty, joy, and comfort it will bring you for many years to come will be well worth the effort. I guarantee it!

❧ ❧

TREES

DETERMINE

LANDSCAPE

SUCCESS

Pear

FLOWERING SHRUBS
Blooming Walls

SHRUBS

ARE

THE

BIGGEST

BANG

FOR YOUR

BUCK!

There are three groups of plants in any flower or landscape that give you the biggest bang for your buck—**evergreens, perennials, and flowering shrubs**. Of the three, flowering shrubs are really the best flower investment for your money. In addition to bringing color and drama to your landscape, they can function as noise barriers and windscreens, protecting other plants in the landscape; they can take the place of trees in small yards or patios; and they can direct or discourage traffic. They fill up a great deal of space at very little investment, and will live for years and years with very little care and attention.

Flowering shrubs are not only valuable for their spring flowers; in many cases, planting a wide variety of shrubs can give you a flowering display throughout the year, depending upon where you live. Many of the flowering shrubs—like blueberries, elderberries, and currants—offer the added bonus of bearing fruit. There are over 250 varieties of such fruit- and berry-bearing shrubs. They are excellent for attracting birds, but keep in mind that they will also draw a great number of unwanted guests like mice, rabbits, and porcupines, to name a few. I also want to caution you that not all fruits and berries are safe to eat, so please keep an eye on small children in your garden if you're not sure of the toxicity of the berries on your shrubs.

While we're most interested in the blossoms, berries, and foliage the flowering shrubs provide, let's not forget the visual contribution these same plants can provide during the winter months. The texture, shape, and color of a shrub's trunk, branches, and bark can lend interest and beauty to an otherwise drab, flowerless, and leafless winter landscape.

SELECT YOUR SHRUBS WISELY

Size It Up

When you select a flowering shrub, make sure you know what you're getting into—don't be swayed by a pretty face. You must inquire as to the average mature height and width of a plant in order to know how close to cluster or row plant it. You will also need these facts in order to know how close you may plant it to walls, walks, and driveways. It amazes me to hear how many people have to remove trees, shrubs, and evergreens every year because they overgrew the driveway or front door.

I find that most second and third homeowners lean toward the purchase of larger, more mature flowering shrubs. They often secure—either through the necessity or generosity of friends or neighbors—"move outs," full-grown shrubs that are in the way of new construction or don't fit into a new landscaping plan. These are, as a rule, excellent additions to your garden if you have equipment to move them, and the space to accommodate them.

If this opportunity doesn't present itself and you can't afford mature shrubs, I recommend that you wait and save until the fall sales begin to purchase more mature plants. The chances of them surviving into next year are much better, and in the end, though they are more expensive, they are a better investment.

Shrub Form

Basically, you will find the flowering shrub family divided into three main forms:

Standard—This simply means they grow very tall and large, and generally reach maturity from a cutting in anywhere from three to five years.

Dwarf—This group is more likely to grow short by virtue of heredity, as opposed to grafting or the use of chemicals that can reduce or inhibit the growth of woody caned, flowering shrubs. Dwarf shrubs, as a rule, grow under 3 feet tall; there are over 100 varieties to choose from.

Vine—Honeysuckle and wisteria are two examples of flowering vine or "climber" shrubs. There can be some disadvantages in their use—certain types have been known to tear down a fence or crush an arbor or trellis in one season. However, if they are properly trained and pruned, they can be a pleasant addition to any flowerscape.

BLOOMING BASICS

You also need to know the following about each plant:

(1) whether the plant blooms;

(2) when, and for how long it blooms;

(3) the color of the blossoms and foliage; and

(4) whether the flowers are fragrant.

FLOWERING
SHRUBS

SHRUBS'

BAD HABITS:

FAST,

UNEVEN

GROWTH

AND

SUCKERING

Survival Tactics

Finally, make sure the plant you are buying or ordering is hardy in your area—there's nothing more frustrating than buying a plant that doesn't survive its first winter. Other conditions you must consider are how much shade you have, and whether your plants will have protection from any continuous prevailing wind. So, please, before you invite a flowering shrub to live in your garden, make sure the friendship will last.

You've Got to Take
The Good With The Bad

I wouldn't be doing my job if I only told you the good things about flowering shrubs because some of them have a couple of bad habits—like not staying where you plant them.

Most flowering shrubs really want to please you, but like growing teenagers, they have a tendency to literally sprout up overnight and become a gangly-looking mess if you don't keep them neat and trimmed.

Another bad habit is that they will send out shoots beneath other trees, shrubs, and flowers in an insidious attempt to propagate themselves; this behavior is known as suckering. You must be alert to it, and cut the suckers off at ground level as soon as they develop.

When selecting any shrub, especially flowering shrubs, make sure you understand the time and effort needed to keep it in good shape. Read the care and planting instructions that accompany most flowering shrubs. If you do, then both you and your new plant will be happy.

Let Your Imagination Run Wild

Most landscape architects and designers will combine several different varieties and forms of the same flowering shrub, creating a palette of texture and color. You may want to try the same thing in your own garden, planting several varieties of, say, lilacs or azaleas or clematis, either subtly varying the color (planting, perhaps, only shades of pink) or boldly combining numerous hues. You can also compose a planting of the single- and double-flowered varieties of a particular shrub.

There are nearly a hundred, maybe even more, garden catalogs available just for the asking that will show and tell about virtually every variety available in this country. Send away for a few, and enjoy some armchair perusing.

The following charts list the most popular and widely available flowering shrubs. I've divided the information up several ways so you can quickly and easily find out exactly what you need to know when buying a particular shrub. And make sure you check your zone hardiness against their needs so that your newly planted shrubs live for many glorious years to come.

KEY: Zone hardiness indicates the coldest climate area plants can survive

COLOR:	Y = *Yellow*	R = *Red*	W = *White*	P = *Pink*
	L = *Lavender*	B = *Blue*	G = *Green*	

FLOWERING SHRUBS

HOME GARDEN NAME	ZONE	COLOR OF FLOWERS	FRUIT BEARING
Andromeda	5	W	
Azalea	5	Many	
Barberry	3	Y	✓
Beach plum	4	W	✓
Beautybush	5	P	✓
Blueberry	4	W	✓
Blue spiraea	5	B	✓
Bottlebrush buckeye	5	W	✓

FLOWERING SHRUBS

HOME GARDEN NAME	ZONE	COLOR OF FLOWERS	FRUIT BEARING
Broom	6	Y,R,B	
Butterfly bush	6	L	
California lilac	4-8	B	
Camellia	7	P,R,W	
Cherry laurel	6	W	
Chinese redbud	6	L	
Cotoneaster	4	P	✓
Crape myrtle	7	P,R,L,W	
Daphne	5	R,P,L,W	✓
Deutzia	5	W,P	
Firethorn	6	W	✓
Flowering almond	5	P,W	
Flowering plum	6	P	
Flowering quince	5	R	
Forsythia	5	Y	
Gardenia	8	W	
Genista	2	Y	
Glossy abelia	5	P	
Hardy orange	6	W	✓
Heath	6	R,W,L	
Heather	5	R,L,W	
Holly olive	7	G	✓
Honeysuckle	3	P	✓
Hydrangea	3	W,P,B	
Japanese snowbell	6	W	
Jetbead	6	W	
Kerria	6	Y	
Korean abelialeaf	5	W	
Kousa dogwood	5	W	
Leatherwood	6	W	
Leucothoe	5	W	
Lilac	3	P,L,W,R	
Mock orange	4	W	
Mohonia	5	Y	✓
Mountain laurel	4	P,W	

FLOWERING SHRUBS

HOME GARDEN NAME	ZONE	COLOR OF FLOWERS	FRUIT BEARING
Ocean spray	5	W	
Parrotia	6	R	
Pearlbush	5	W	
Photinia	7	W	✓
Privet	4	W	✓
Pussy willow	5	Gray	
Rhododendron	5	R,L,P,Y,W	
Rock rose	8	P	
Rose	5	Y,W,P,R	
Rose acacia	6	P	
St.-John's-wort	6	Y	
Sand myrtle	6	W	
Sapphireberry	6	W	✓
Shadblow	4	W	✓
Skimmia	7	Y,W	✓
Smoke tree	5	G	
Snow wreath	6	W,G	
Spicebush	4	Y	✓
Spike heath	6	P,W	
Spiraea	4	W,P,R	
Star magnolia	5	W	✓
Stewartia	7	W	
Strawberry shrub	5	Y	✓
Summersweet	4	W	
Sun rose	6	Y,R,W	
Sweet spire	6	W	
Tamarisk	5	P,R	
Trailing arbutus	3	W,P	
Tree peony	5	W,P,Y	
Viburnum	5	W,P	✓
Vitex	5	L	
Weigela	4	P,R,W	
Winter hazel	6	Y	
Winter jasmine	6	Y	
Witch hazel	4	Y	

HARDY FLOWERING SHRUBS BY ZONE

ZONE 3
Bush cherry
Greenweed
Manchu cherry
Tamarisk

ZONE 4
Hardy heather
Lilac

ZONE 5
Azalea
Beautybush
Double-file viburnum
Double kerria
Flowering almond
Flowering quince
Fringe tree
Mock orange
Pussy willow
Rose of Sharon
Spring witch hazel
Wright viburnum

ZONE 6
Butterfly bush
Chaste tree
Chinese Judas tree
Evergreen candytuft
Franklin tree
Hydrangea
Lanceleaf phillyrea
Nippon spiraea
Sargent crab apple
Star magnolia
Weigela hybrids

ZONE 7
Autumn sage
Crape myrtle
Fuchsia
Hebe
Laurel rock rose
Spanish broom

ZONE 8
Broom
Ceanothus
Evergreen mock orange
New Zealand daisybush
Oleander
Pomegranate
Willmott blue leadwort

ZONES 9-10
Bottlebrush
Flame-of-the-woods
Flowering plumbago
Flowering senna

FLOWERING SHRUBS
FOR PROBLEM AREAS

Damp Soil

Zone 3
Bayberry
Viburnum
Vinebark

Zone 4
High-bush blueberry
Rosebay rhododendron
Summersweet

Zone 5
Allspice
Drooping leucothoe
Heather
Mock orange
Mountain laurel
Pussy willow
Red-veined enkianthus
Rhododendron
Shadblow

Zone 6
American andromeda
American holly
Darwin barberry
English holly
Hydrangea
Japanese andromeda
Red chokeberry

Rhododendron
Star magnolia

Zone 7
Camellia

Zone 8
Japanese viburnum

Zones 9-10
Sweet viburnum

Dry/Poor Soil Conditions

Zone 3
Bayberry
Bush cinquefoil
Greenweed
Ninebark
Shrub rose
Siberian pea
Tamarisk

Zone 4
Dryland blueberry
Lilac
Shrub elaegneus

Zone 5
Forsythia
Jetbead
Quince

Zone 6
Broom
Butterfly bush
Lavender
Rosemary
Rose of Sharon
Winter honeysuckle

Zone 7
Chaste tree
Crape myrtle

Zone 8
Blue leadwort
Japanese pittosporum
Myrtle
Oleander
Pomegranate

Zones 9-10
Bottlebrush
Jerusalem thorn
Lantana
Shrub acacia

Time to Choose

You've looked at all the pictures in the catalogs and books, you have checked all the lists of suggested flowering shrubs in this and other books, and now it's time to choose. But first you must ask yourself a hard question and answer it truthfully—<u>do you have the time and patience to really prepare your soil before planting</u>? What this means is that you are aware of the basic needs of the shrubs you have selected, and are willing to dig adequate holes, prepare compost, balance the soil, and improve the drainage when necessary to ensure that your new flowering additions have the very best start. If your answer is yes, then you can pick any plant on the list for your hardiness zone. But if you must work with poor soil and/ or drainage as it is now, your choices will be limited to those in the Problem Area Chart.

THE BEST

PLANTING

TIMES—

LATE FALL

AND

EARLY SPRING

PLANTING—THERE IS A SEASON FOR <u>ALL</u> THINGS

Planting time is as important as planting method. With the quality of today's nursery stock and the improved methods of growing and transporting, a whole new world of home landscaping has been opened up for the do-it-yourself gardener. There are corporate giants in the nursery industry just as there are in the auto, apparel, and electronics industries: Select, Greenleaf, Monrovia, Midwest, and Boise Cascade grow and distribute millions upon millions of healthy, hardy plants ready for your garden. But if you don't plan or properly plant, these shrubs will pass away in your yarden in less than a month. So check the section covering planting containers for flowering trees, and use this as a guide for all flowering shrubs. If you do, you and your plants can be confident that their life will be a long and healthy one.

Planting Tips

An old friend of mine once said that most new home owners get plenty of practice planting because they select the wrong plant, plant it in the wrong spot the wrong way, and then when it dies, they have to replace it. That's an awfully frustrating and expensive way to learn the proper planting practices. Let me give you a leg up with my general guidelines:

Six Simple Steps To Super Shrubs!

Step 1. Dig all holes wider than needed.

Step 2. Dig them twice as deep as needed (I call this digging a $10.00 hole for a $5.00 plant).

Step 3. Mix $1/2$ cup of Epsom salts per 2 bushels of compost in a separate container before you refill the hole.

Step 4. After planting the shrub, fill the hole with a mix of 50% compost and 50% soil, tamping it down as you go.

Step 5. Water well to remove all air pockets.

Step 6. Mulch the plant with shredded wood bark.

They're Not Chow Hounds!

It's hard to believe when you consider their rapid and luxuriant growth, but flowering shrubs are not as big of eaters as their friends, the flowering trees. As a rule, you can feed your flowering shrubs every other year with a root feeder, using 3 spikes or 2 or 3 handfuls of any slow-release lawn food sprinkled onto the soil out at the tips of the farthest branches.

I have found, though, that with the addition of two simple steps, you'll have the healthiest, most robust, flower-producing shrubs around.

Step 1. Feed them my Super Shrub Tonic every three weeks thoughout the growing season; and

Step 2. Give them a good root pruning every other year.

SUPER SHRUB TONIC

**1 can of beer,
1 cup of fish fertilizer,
1 cup of ammonia,
$1/2$ cup of Shampoo, and
2 oz. of hydrogen peroxide
in a 20 gallon
hose-end sprayer.**
Spray the plants to the point of run-off.

281

Mix up a batch of my Super Shrub Tonic and feed your shrubs, as well as everything else in your yard, with it every three weeks during the growing season. Be sure to place a white golf ball into all sprayer jars that do not contain weed killer; this will keep the solution thoroughly mixed.

Root Pruning— Getting Deep

You only want to do this to mature, healthy shrubs that have been in place at least three years. This is the equivalent of a pedicure to humans.

ROOT PRUNING TONIC

1 can of beer,
1 oz. of Shampoo,
1 oz. of ammonia,
1 oz. of hydrogen peroxide,
1 oz. of whiskey, and
4 tbsp. of instant tea in
2 gallons of very
warm water.

To root prune, you simply take a flat-back spade with a razor-sharp edge, and plunge it into the ground out at the tip of the farthest branch as deep as it will go, in a circle all the way around the shrub. Once that's done, I want you to pour $1/4$ pound of Epsom salts evenly into the cuts, all the way around that shrub. Then pour a quart of my Root Pruning Tonic into the cut over the Epsom salts.

Pruning—It's Important To Remain Shapely

There is a right way, a right time, and a right tool for pruning flowering shrubs. Why prune your shrubs? To keep them looking young and fit, not old, sloppy, and out of control.

Annual growth on older stems becomes less every year, which means that new growth will grow out of the center of the crown (the top of the stem or branch), where it generally won't get enough light. In its reach for the sun, the new growth will get long and skinny with little or no foliage.

In most cases, you need to prune one or two of the older stems to the ground each year; this is best done during the early spring or late fall, while the plant is dormant. After the shrub has flowered, the young wood can be shaped. There are, however, a number of shrubs whose growth should not be pruned back until after flowering. They're listed on the accompanying chart.

Remove dead wood or broken branches whenever they appear; also, make sure you seal all wounds with my Wound Sealing Tonic which is made by mixing:

**3 drops of Sevin® and
3 drops of antiseptic mouthwash
in 8 oz. of interior latex paint**

Use an old rag or sponge-type paint brush to apply it. Dab a little bit of this mixture on each cut to ensure proper healing.

THE PROPER CUT

Pruning new growth is easy. Position the cut to a bud as new growth comes from the buds. Be careful not to make the cut too close or too far away from a bud. With by-pass pruners, position the hook to the discarded side of the branch so as not to damage the bark of the remaining branch.

Too long—
Causes die
back.

Too close—
Interferes with
bud growth.

Too slanted—
Exposes excess
wood tissue to
damage.

Ideal—
Promotes
healthy
growth.

PRUNE AFTER BLOOM

Akebia

Amelanchier (Shadblow)

Azalea (Hardy Ghent, Mollis)

Benzoin (Spicebush)

Calycanthus floridus (Sweet shrub, Strawberry shrub)

Caragana (Siberian pea)

Celastrus (Bittersweet)

Cercis (Judas tree, Redbud)

Chaenomeles (Flowering quince)

Chionanthus (White fringe)

Cornus (Dogwood, without berries)

Crataegus oxyacantha (English hawthorn)

Daphne (Garland flower)

Deutzia

Exochorda (Pearlbush)

Hydrangea hortensia

Kalmia (Laurel)

Kolkwitzia amabilis (Beautybush)

Lonicera fragrantissima (Bush honeysuckle)

Magnolia

Philadelphus (Mock orange)

Pieris (Andromeda)

Potentilla (Cinquefoil)

Prunus (Flowering almond, Cherry, Plum)

Rhododendron

Ribes (Flowering currant)

Rosa

Spiraea (Spring-flowering)

Spiraea Prunifolia (Bridal-wreath)

Spiraea thunbergii

Spiraea x vanhouttei

Syringa (Lilac)

Tamarisk (Spring-flowering)

Viburnum carlesii

Viburnum lantana

Viburnum opulus (Cranberry bush)

Weigela (formerly *Diervilla*)

Insect And Disease Controls

There are no shrubs I know of that do not have a problem or two with insects or disease from time to time, so why not take an aggressive approach to these problems in the beginning? Here's what you should do in three easy steps:

Step 1. To start my program, I dormant spray all of my woody caned shrubs after they have lost their leaves in the fall and again before they bud out in the spring with Dormant Spray. You can purchase it as two separate chemicals, or as one under the name of Horticultural Oil, Eco-Oil or All Seasons Hort/Dormant Oil. This control actually smothers any bugs that are hiding in the nooks and crannies.

Step 2. Then, I spray all of my shrubs starting in early spring with this Timely Tonic. I use a 6-gallon insecticide sprayer with a red golf ball in the sprayer jar to keep the solution mixed. And I spray it after 6:00 p.m., to make sure that I catch the insects off guard.

TIMELY BUG TONIC

1 cup of chewing tobacco juice,
1 cup of antiseptic mouthwash,
1 cup of Shampoo, and
6 tsps. of Tomato/Vegetable dust
per gallon of water.

If you use this tonic, you will seldom have a sick shrub.

Step 3. To destroy insect problems below ground, apply Dursban®, Merit®, or diazinon to the soil beneath the plant from its trunk out beyond its weep line as soon as the soil is free of snow. Caterpillars and bagworms can be safely controlled with *Bacillus thuringiensis* (Bt). And for borers, apply 2 cups of borer crystals or **mothballs** (paradichlorobenzene) to the soil beneath the infested shrubs.

FLOWERING
SHRUBS

PLANTS FOR

FREE—

PROPAGATE BY

CUTTINGS

EXPANDING YOUR
SHRUB FAMILY

What I'm referring to is plant **propagation.** You can grow your own shrubs from what are known as softwood cuttings and hardwood cuttings. It always fascinates my neighbors to watch me take these cuttings from my shrubs, work a little garden magic on them, and then pass plants out for free. I can do this because they cost me nothing; so can you. Here's what you should do:

Softwood Cuttings

Softwood cuttings are slips taken from the adult plant's soft growth. Most all of your flowering shrubs will yield this type of cutting. Here's a step-by-step guide:

Step 1. Take your cuttings in May and early June from new growth <u>after</u> the shrub has flowered. They should be 3 to 6 inches long, and the bottom 3 layers of leaves should be removed.

Step 2. Dip the cutting first into water, then into about a half inch of a root stimulant product called Dip 'n' Grow.

Step 3. Shake off the excess, and place the cutting into a pre-poked, pencil-sized hole in your rooting material—sharp sand works best—covering at least one or two of the nodes, or leaf breaks. The best air temperature for rooting is 60-70°F, while the soil should be 5 degrees warmer.

Step 4. Keep the soil shaded and always damp, but not soaked, the first few days. Sprinkle the foliage often to encourage humidity.

Step 5. Move the cuttings into the light as they progress in rooting.

Step 6. When roots are well established, pot them up and move them into the garden. I plant pots and all into the soil to protect them.

The following is a list of those shrubs that you can take softwood cuttings from:

SHRUBS FOR SOFTWOOD CUTTINGS

HOME GARDEN NAME	PROFESSIONAL NAME
Azalea	
Barberry	*Berberis*
Beautybush	*Kolkwitzia amabilis*
Bittersweet	*Celastrus*
Boxwood	*Buxus*
Broom	*Cytisus*
Butterfly bush	*Buddleia*
Camellia	
Crape myrtle	*Lagerstroemia indica*
Dogwood	*Cornus*
Firethorn	*Pyracantha*
Fringe tree	*Chionanthus*
Golden bells	*Forsythia*
Heather	*Calluna*
Hemlock	*Tsuga*
Holly	*Ilex*
Honeysuckle	*Lonicera*
Hydrangea	
Jasmine	*Jasminum*
Juniper	*Juniperus*
Leucothoe	
Lilac	*Syringa*
Mock orange	*Philadelphus*
Oleander	*Nerium*
Oregon laurel	*Arbutus menziesii*
Pachysandra	
Privet	*Ligustrum*
Rhododendron	
Rose	*Rosa*
Rose of Sharon	*Hibiscus syriacus*
Senecio	
Sequoia	
Silver vine	*Actinidia polygama*
Spiraea	
Spruce	*Picea*
Strawberry tree	*Arbutus unedo*
Viburnum	
Weigela	
Winter creeper	*Euonymus radicans*
Yew	*Taxus*

287

Hardwood Cuttings

This type of cutting is even easier to propagate than soft-wood cuttings. Take hardwood cuttings in late fall or winter. Cut slips 6 to 8 inches long, tie them in bundles, and store them in the basement in a box covered with peat moss until spring.

After the last chance of frost has passed, remove the cuttings from the peat moss, dip one end in a rooting hormone, and then plant the slip in your garden, leaving about half of the stem above the ground.

Here's a list of the hardwood cuttings you can take:

SHRUBS FOR HARDWOOD CUTTINGS	
HOME GARDEN NAME	**PROFESSIONAL NAME**
Barberry	*Berberis*
Burning bush	*Euonymus*
Catalpa	
Crape myrtle	*Lagerstroemia indica*
Deutzia	
Dogwood	*Cornus*
Elder	*Sambucus*
Firethorn	*Pyracantha*
Flowering quince	*Chaenomeles*
Golden bells	*Forsythia*
Hazel	*Corylus*
Honeysuckle	*Lonicera*
Lagerstroemia	
Ninebark	*Physocarpus*
Oleander	*Nerium*
Poplar	*Populus*
Privet	*Ligustrum*
Russian olive	*Elaeagnus angustifolia*
Viburnum	
Weigela	
Willow	*Salix*
Wisteria	

LET ME INTRODUCE YOU...

I just love shrubs, and want you to do the same. So, to introduce you to my all-around favorite flowering shrubs, I've put together the following list. Keep in mind that these shrubs are not necessarily any better than the dozens of others you have to pick from; it's just that over the years, they have performed consistently well.

Almond

Flowering almonds *(Prunus triloba plena)* grow into low bushes, though under favorable conditions, they may grow 10 feet tall or more. They bear a profusion of pink, rosette-shaped flowers that are borne in small clusters densely packed along the branches in early spring before the development of the leaves. The flowering almond makes a good subject for espaliering. Trained against a wall in this manner, flowering almonds should be pruned each year after flowering.

Young plants may be easily transplanted in the spring, even if bare-rooted. They prefer light, well-drained soil in full sun. They are grafted on wild stock, so take care to remove all suckers which arise from below the point where they were budded. Most tragedies with flowering almonds occur because this task is neglected, and the wild stock takes over.

A LIST
OF
CONSISTENT
PERFORMERS

Azalea

Azalea
(Rhododendron)

Azaleas are capable of yielding an extraordinary harvest of beauty, but they do not offer it freely—it must be earned. But to those who fall in love with this lovely flower, no effort is too much!

So that there will be no confusion, let me say that botanists now classify all azaleas as rhododendrons. This includes not only the evergreen kinds, which have large, leathery leaves, but also the deciduous or leaf-losing varieties.

Azaleas, which flower in spring or early summer, may grow only 18 inches tall, or attain a height of 15 feet or more, depending on the variety.

The soil for azaleas should resemble, as nearly as possible, that in which they grow naturally—a cushion of acid leaf mold. It should contain a large percentage (60-90) of organic matter. This may be leaf mold (especially that of oak leaves), peat moss, decomposed pine, hemlock, or spruce needles, or a mixture of any of these. Good quality soil and a little sand should make up the rest.

Azaleas are "surface-rooters," but you should give them at least 18 inches of this compost and a good surface mulch of partially decayed leaves so their roots will remain cool and moist during the hot summer months. They should also have mulch in winter for protection against severe cold. Most azaleas grow naturally in light, open woodlands, or on the fringes of the woods. If shade is too heavy or continuous, they will not flower freely. On the other hand, they do not like the scorching heat of summer. Place them where they will receive some shade or in an area to the north or northeast of the house where they will receive some sunlight for part of the day, but shade the rest of the time.

Since azaleas have many feeding roots close to the surface, mulching is preferable to cultivation for keeping down weeds.

Hardy azaleas may be raised from seeds sown in pots or shallow flats in February, March, or April. Fill the flats or pots with good soil covered with a half inch layer of sphagnum moss which has been rubbed through a $1/4$ inch mesh or sieve, and place them in a slightly heated greenhouse or coldframe.

FEEDING TIME FOR AZALEAS

An annual application of fertilizer is recommended at approximately half of the rate of other woody plants. Use fertilizers such as cottonseed meal, special azalea or rhododendron fertilizer, or any other acidic fertilizer. Coffee grounds are especially good for these plants, so sprinkle them liberally on the soil.

If the plant's foliage should turn yellow between the veins, iron is most likely deficient, and should be applied as a foliar spray and soil drench. Liquid Iron is about the best product for this application, and will restore that deep green color overnight.

For cuttings, choose half-ripe (new, strong growth) or semi-woody (several weeks older) shoots of the current year's growth in July, taking 2 to 3 inch long slips, each with a very thin heel or piece of the old branch. Place them in a greenhouse or coldframe in a mixture of sand and peat moss. Keep the frame closed for three to four weeks to encourage the cuttings to form roots, watering them immediately after insertion and keeping them evenly moist, spraying daily, if necessary.

Barberry

(Berberis)

There are many good reasons for growing barberries. Some varieties are famous for their beautiful and fragrant flowers, while others are covered with bright-colored fruits later in the year.

The evergreen barberries, which retain their leaves through the winter, are exceedingly handsome. One of the hardiest of these is *B. julianae*, which comes from China.

Among the red-fruited barberries, *B. wilsonae* is a dense shrub about 3 feet tall with very spiny branches that bears coral red fruit in autumn. The berries are bundled rather than clustered, and are preceded by yellow flowers. The ripe fruits will yield a good jelly. A choice brandy is also made from the berries, and special, large-fruited types have been developed for this use. The soft, inner bark of the barberries is said to have a healing effect if rubbed on chapped hands or lips.

BARBERRIES AT-A-GLANCE

✓ Beautiful, fragrant flowers
✓ Easy-to-grow
✓ Pruning rarely required
✓ Excellent hedges

Barberries will thrive in a wide range of soils, from sandy loam to clay. They are easily transplanted and are tolerant of light shade. They will, however, display more brilliant autumn color if grown in full sun. The evergreen types are best planted in spring; the deciduous, or leaf-losing, types may be either fall- or

Barberry

291

spring-planted. This shrub will grow into a well-shaped bush naturally, so pruning is rarely required. If cutting back becomes necessary, do it as soon as the flowering period is over. Barberries make excellent hedge plants, generally requiring only one annual clipping.

Increase your supply of barberries by sowing seeds as soon as they have ripened or in early spring. Sow them in flats or pots filled with **two parts good garden loam, one part leaf mold and one part sand,** and place them in coldframes. Pick out the young plants, and pot them singly in small pots when they are large enough to handle. Later, they may be transferred to the nursery border.

All barberries may be increased by cuttings. Take slips 3 to 4 inches long in July or August, and place them in a bed of sand or a mixture of sand and peat moss, preferably in a coldframe. Cuttings take about six months to become sufficiently rooted for transplanting. You may also detach suckers from large plants to form new bushes.

Beautybush
(Kolkwitzia Amabilis)

Beautybush is a deciduous shrub from China that belongs to the honeysuckle family. The flowers of the beautybush are borne in great profusion in early June, and though smaller and far more abundant, greatly resemble those of weigela. The bell-shaped flowers are a lovely pink with a golden throat. They contrast beautifully with the soft, gray-green foliage that stays on the bush into autumn. The beautybush also has a distinctive bark which peels away from the stems in large flakes.

POLLUTION-PROOF PLANTS

Those of you who live near industrial areas where air pollution is a problem should select shrubs with special care. Experience has shown that some shrubs are exceptionally tolerant of toxic fumes and dust. Those that should perform satisfactory in heavy air-pollution areas include:

Five-leaf aralia
Japanse barberry
Siberian pea tree
Tatarian dogwood
Winged euonymus
Showy border forsythia
Inkberry
Drooping leucothoe
Honeysuckle
Bayberry
Shrubby cinquefoil
Alpine currant
Arrow-wood

Beautybush is a vigorous shrub, growing 8 to 9 feet tall, but it can be pruned back to a lower height if desired. Since it can grow quite tall as it matures, it is advisable to place it in the background of the border.

This shrub is perfectly hardy and will thrive in any fair, well-drained garden soil in full sun or very light shade. It may be propagated by either cuttings or seeds, but cuttings are preferable because seedlings will show great variations both in color and flower size.

Broom
(Cytisus)

The brooms are delightful plants, bearing pea-like flowers of many colors. One of the most effective, the spike-broom, is distinguished by erect, spike-like racemes of honey-scented yellow flowers, at their showy best in July.

Broom

Brooms, which reach a height of 4 to 5 feet tall, have rather dull, 3-fingered, gray-green leaves. They can be used as a light, flowery garden hedge if placed in a sunny location. Prune them back to the desired height after the flowering season. Brooms do best in well-drained, rather light soils, but clay can be made more suitable by adding sand and compost.

The wild types may be propagated by seeds sown in pots or flats as soon as they have ripened. Soaking the seeds twenty-four hours before planting aids in germination. Varieties which do not come true from seeds should be increased by means of cuttings. Place them in a bed of sandy soil in a cold-frame in August, or in a shaded spot outdoors. Make the cuttings from firm summer shoots. They should be 3 to 4 inches long and have a small piece of the older wood attached.

SOAKING SUCCESS

You should always water your shrubs with soaker hoses which allow water to bubble out on top of the ground, rather than run off. Also, the soil is not disturbed by a huge, high pressure volume of water.

How can you tell if you've soaked the soil long enough? Scoop up a handful of soil about 3 inches down. If you can shape it into a tight ball, chances are your soil is wet all the way down to the roots. If not, then you need more water.

293

Brooms do not transplant very successfully, so they should be grown in pots until they are large enough for planting in their permanent location. For the first two or three years, the new shoots on the young plants should be cut back several times during the growing season to ensure the formation of well-branched plants.

Buckeye

Bottlebrush buckeye *(Aesculus parviflora)*, which grows 7 to 10 feet tall, is at home in small gardens, and is excellent for use as a lawn specimen. The erect, foot-long, candlelike spires of white blossoms produce a striking effect in July and August, especially since they come at a time when few other things are in bloom.

The buckeye matures into a large, billowy shrub, increasing in width by means of suckering roots. Left to itself, in time it will take over a large area.

Its leaves are 5- to 7-fingered, and are somewhat coarse and plain. They turn an attractive yellow-gold in autumn, again adding color to your garden.

Buckeye is native to the southeastern United States, but is reliably hardy further north. This shrub will grow readily in average soils. It is most happy in open situations but will do quite well in light shade.

Butterfly Bush
(Buddleia)

These lovely, colorful, summer- and autumn-flowering shrubs are easy to grow, and have great value in the home garden. Many are hardy; others are suitable for outdoor planting only in mild climates. Most are deciduous, or leaf-losing. There is considerable variation in their height, which ranges from 3 to 15 feet tall at maturity. The blossoms come in many exquisite colors, including deep rose-purple, white, purple, flaming violet, pale lilac, and many shades in between, some of which are made even more striking by orange eyes. A very graceful Chinese type, the weeping willow or fountain buddleia *(B. alternifolia)*, grows 10 feet tall, and bears delicate clusters of mauve flowers in June.

Most buddleias will grow in ordinary garden soil to which some organic matter has been added, preferably decayed manure. They may be planted in either spring or fall.

It is important to prune this shrub correctly. The types which flower in late summer and autumn should be pruned each spring by cutting back the shoots or the previous year's growth to within 2 or 3 inches of the older wood. Spring bloomers should be pruned back after they bloom.

In severe climates, the bush may be killed back to the ground during the winter, but as long as the roots survive, new growth will be produced, and it will bloom every summer. Mulching the plants during the winter months is of great benefit, particularly in climates where the ground is subject to hard freezing.

Buddleias are readily propagated by cuttings. These cuttings, which may be either half-ripe wood or semi-woody side shoots, should be 5 to 6 inches long. Place them in a coldframe or outdoors in a sheltered, shady location, and keep them moist.

Buddleias are always happiest and most effective in a sunny location. As an extra added benefit, they also add to the beauty of your garden by attracting large numbers of butterflies during the day, and numerous moths at night.

PLANT

BUDDLEIAS

TO ATTRACT

BUTTERFLIES

FRAGRANT, INEXPENSIVE BEAUTIES

If you are looking to cut down on the grass area to be cut, flower beds that always need your attention, or evergreens that always need trimming, then try a couple of these fragrant, inexpensive beauties. Make sure that you make note of both the common as well as the botanical name so when you go hunting, you'll know what you're looking for.

Beautybush (*Kolkwitzia amabilis*)—This shrub grows 8-10' tall, with pink flowers in June. Beautybush is part of the honeysuckle family, and is great for early indoor blooms. Hardy in Zone 3 and south.

Butterfly Bush (*Buddleia davidi*)—This plant grows from 6-10' tall, with lavender flowers in late June until frost. Hardy in Zone 5 and south.

Clammy Azalea (*Rhododendron viscasum*)—Also known as swamp honeysuckle, this grows 6-10' tall, with white to pink flowers in June. Hardy in Zone 3 and south.

Cranberry Bush (*Viburnum trilobum*)—This shrub also goes by the name of high cranberry. It grows 8-10' tall, with blooms in late May-June. It has the famous Thanksgiving berries.

Japanese Quince (*Chaenomeles lagenarice*)—Grows from 4-6' tall, with scarlet red flowers in April and May. Hardy in Zone 4 and north.

Sweet Peppertwist (*Clethra alnifolia*)—Also known as spiked alder, it grows from 3-10' tall, with white and pink flowers from August to October. Hardy in Zone 2 and south.

Winged Euonymus (*Euonymus alatus*)—Grows 5-10' tall with yellow flowers. Hardy in Zone 3 and south.

Cherry Laurel
(*Prunus Laurocerasus*)

Cherry laurel is greatly valued as a hedge shrub, as a screen plant, and for its shade. Left unpruned, it will form a large evergreen bush about 15 to 25 feet tall; however, it is most effective as a dense hedge. There are several named varieties which vary in habit of growth and size of leaves. Some have narrow leaves of a rich green, while others have large, glossy leaves.

Cherry laurels are easy to grow in any reasonably fertile, well-drained soil. They will thrive in sun or shade, and stand pruning well. Plant them in early spring just before new growth begins, or in early fall after the season's growth is completed. The planting should be done while the soil is still warm enough to encourage the development of new roots, so it may establish itself before cold weather. Newly planted laurels should be watered freely, especially when planted in late summer or fall.

Cotoneaster

Cotoneasters are quite a large genus, and since some members are far more attractive than others, you should choose your variety with care. Some species are hardy, but most cotoneasters are more vigorous and beautiful when grown in the milder parts of the country.

There are both deciduous and evergreen cotoneasters. They are valued chiefly for their red berries in fall, though some have attractive white flowers in spring that resemble spiraea blossoms. Generally speaking, the deciduous types are hardy in the North, while the evergreen types are more suitable for southern gardens.

Cotoneasters vary in height from a few inches to many feet. For this reason, their uses in the garden are many and varied, some being ideal for the shrubbery border, others for the

SNAKE ALERT!

Are snakes a problem in and among your shrubs?

Get rid of them by sprinkling a mixture **of 50% beach sand and 50% Diatomaceous Earth** in a 2" band around the affected area. They won't dare cross that line!

COTONEASTERS ARE GREAT FOR SLOPES AND HILLSIDES

RECOGNIZE A BARGAIN—OR A BUST!

I get so mad when I go to a retailer who advertises top-quality nursery stock at rock-bottom prices, only to find that he had rock-bottom quality at top prices. If you purchase a poor-quality, sick plant for pennies, <u>you've paid too much!</u> Here are some tricks to beware of:

✓ Oversized plants in undersized containers or balls. These are often sold to inexperienced buyers who think that more growth means more tree. The grower has to get these big plants out of his fields to make room for more merchandise, and he keeps the size of the soil ball down to keep the weight low, so he pays less for freight. The problem is that there isn't enough root stock left to support a plant this large, and so, it dies soon after planting.

✓ Bare-root plants that have been transplanted into containers and placed on sale before they have developed enough root stock to sustain the plant.

✓ Infected nursery stock that has been shipped to the retailer instead of being treated or destroyed. You and your yard pay the price.

✓ Placing undersized plants in oversized containers, that are then sold by pot size, and not plant size. Be sure of what you're paying for.

rock garden, and still others as specimen shrubs. Some work well as hedges and others in an open, naturalized, woodland setting.

Cotoneasters are very easy to grow, thriving in almost any kind of soil, even in poor soil where other shrubs find it difficult to become established. You will, however, be rewarded with better plants if some decayed manure of organic matter is added to the soil. Cotoneasters may be planted in fall or spring. Small potted plants are the most successful.

Pruning is not a great problem, as cotoneasters require very little. With the deciduous varieties, thin out any crowded branches, and shorten those that have grown too long. Do this in late fall or during the winter. The evergreen kinds should be pruned about the middle of April.

Cotoneasters may be propagated by seeds or cuttings. The seeds should be sown in late autumn in a coldframe or greenhouse in pots of sandy soil. Cuttings 4 to 6 inches long should be taken from shoots of the current year's growth. They may be grown in the greenhouse or in a sheltered location outdoors if winters are mild.

Crape Myrtle

(Lagerstroemia Indica)

If "beauty is its own excuse for being," then surely this shrub needs no other. It has long been a southern favorite, and is probably more widely planted than any other woody perennial. In regions of little rainfall, this stately queen will stand up and bloom when other plants falter and fail.

Standard-sized crape myrtle will grow as tall as 25 to 30 feet. Though there are varieties that produce white or light violet flowers, the preferred color seems to be a luscious shade of watermelon pink. The closely-packed clusters of flowers, each individual one about an inch wide, really do resemble fluffed-up crepe paper. Moreover, the season of bloom usually extends from July to September, when few other flowers are seen.

Crape myrtles are by no means confined to the South. In fact, in sheltered places, specimens will survive all but the most severe winters, even as far north as New York City. Should the tops be winter-killed, prune back the dead wood in spring; this will encourage the development of new shoots that will bloom the same season. In milder regions, crape myrtle plants should be shaped each year for balanced growth, pruning away weak and superficial shoots. Do this <u>before</u> spring growth starts, never after.

GREEN THUMB TIP

Shrubs, like everything else, tend to grow up to be what they're meant to be. You can shorten a cocker spaniel's tail, give him little pointed ears and shear off a lot of hair, but that won't make him a bulldog. Likewise, no amount of pruning is going to make a crape myrtle a privet hedge. Shape the crape myrtle to point out its own lovely lines; don't try to cut it down to the ground every time it reaches for the sky.

Crape myrtle

Those of you who live in severe climates may still enjoy crape myrtles by setting the dwarf varieties in tubs and boxes, and moving them to a frost-free environment in the winter. Be sure to keep them nearly dry.

No shrub is easier to propagate than a crape myrtle. I have started dozens of new plants by simply inserting cuttings in the ground in the fall of the year. These cuttings, 12 to 15 inches long, should be inserted to a depth of about 6 to 8 inches in a shady location, and be kept fairly moist. They will root readily and may be moved to a permanent location the following spring.

CUT BACK

DEUTZIA

IMMEDIATELY

AFTER

FLOWERING

Deutzia

Deutzias are splendid for spring and early summer flowering, producing white, pink, rose, or purple flowers. Otherwise they are undistinguished. The majority are of imperfect hardiness in most sections of the country, though easily grown in the South. If you want to grow them, be sure to give them a sheltered location, and a lot of mulch during the winter months.

Deutzias grow about 3 to 5 feet tall on average, but some species reach a height of 10 feet at maturity. They prefer a sunny location, but will tolerate light shade.

If you want your plants to flower freely every year, encourage them to form well-ripened wood. You can do this by cutting back the old shoots to the point where vigorous young ones are developing as soon as the flowering season is over. The shrub will also benefit from an occasional application of well-rotted manure or organic matter.

Deutzia

It is easy to increase all of the deutzias by means of cuttings, which should be of soft shoots about 3 to 4 inches long. Take cuttings in May or early June, or take them of firmer wood in July. Place them in a greenhouse or coldframe in a bed of sandy peat. When well-rooted, set the young plants in the nursery border, pinching off the ends of the shoots so the plant will be bushy. They are usually large enough for permanent planting when about two years old.

Dogwood

Kousa, or Japanese dogwood *(Cornus kousa)*, is the Oriental version of our own beloved native species. A comparison of the two shows that each has its own benefits. In its native land, the kousa dogwood will make a spreading tree some 20 feet high, but generally, it doesn't get nearly so tall in the United States.

Our native dogwood blooms in spring, while kousa is at its showy best in late spring or early summer. The flowers are borne over a long period of time, and are creamy white in color, often fading to a clear, soft pink. It is worthwhile to grow both species together to prolong the blooming season of this lovely flowering shrub.

The petals of the kousa dogwood blossom are narrow and pointed, whereas those of our native species are rounded and notched. The leaves are smaller, and not quite as coarse as those of the American species. They are, however, less brilliant in autumn, turning brownish purple, rather than yellow and red.

The fruits of kousa dogwood also differ. Instead of consisting of individual red berries, they are fleshy, pinkish red "heads," somewhat resembling strawberries in appearance. They usually ripen in August.

If you are using the kousa dogwood in your landscape, remember that there are subtle differences in appearance according to the angle from which it is seen. Its beauty is shown off to better advantage if it is looked down upon rather than up at.

THUG BUSTERS

Dogwoods are especially susceptible to one serious insect pest—the Dogwood borer larvae. If not properly maintained, the tree can lead to general decline. Dogwood borers are mainly a problem to trees which have been physically injured because the larvae need an injured area in order to penetrate the bark. These insects and their damage can be reduced by:

✓avoiding physical injury,

✓bracing newly planted trees to prevent wind damage, and

✓wrapping the trunks of newly transplanted trees with burlap or tree wrap paper for the first full year of growth.

301

Dogwoods may be planted in either spring or fall and may be increased by hardwood cuttings taken in October or November. Another easy way to propagate them is by layering; the trees do this naturally when their branches touch the ground.

Little pruning is needed beyond shaping the trees occasionally or cutting out suckers to prevent the spread of the bushes beyond their allotted area. Pruning should be done after the plant has flowered.

Forsythia

Forsythias are beautiful, hardy, deciduous shrubs. Cherished everywhere as joyful evidence of spring's return, forsythias bear a profusion of golden yellow flowers in March which usually last well into April.

The upright species are very handsome in or out of flower, and have a broad, sweeping growth habit. The leaves, which soon follow the flowers, remain green until late fall. The height varies according to variety, with the dwarfs being only 2 feet tall, while others grow as tall as 10 feet.

Forsythias grow easily in any good garden soil, but are more vigorous and flower more freely if you dig in some peat, compost, or well-decayed manure, and mulch them well in late spring or early summer.

Forsythia

All the members of this good-natured family are easily transplanted, and grow equally well in full sun or light shade. Planting may be done in spring, but late fall is best. Forsythias are dependable bloomers, rarely injured by severe winters unless they are planted in exposed places or in low-lying frost pockets. If freezing does occur, you may get little more than token blooming that particular spring, but this is rare.

Pruning should be done annually as soon as the flowering season is over. The flower buds for the next year develop on the short side shoots of the old branches. If forsythias are cut back during the dormant season, the greater part of their floral display will be sacrificed.

Forsythia may be propagated by either cuttings or layering. Softwood cuttings, which will root readily, may be made in June or July. These cuttings, 3 to 4 inches long, should be inserted in a propagating case in a greenhouse or coldframe. Semi-woody cuttings may be made later in the season and inserted outdoors or in a coldframe. You can even make cuttings of mature wood and insert them in sandy soil as late in the year as October or November, and they will root easily.

BRINGING SPRING INDOORS

There's no sight more welcome than the first flowers of spring, but you don't have to wait until late March or April to enjoy fresh blooms indoors.

The best time to cut branches for forcing is usually in February or March when the temperature climbs above freezing for a day or two. Good choices for forcing are forsythia, witch hazel, and flowering cherry.

Select branches that have the most buds, and make a clean, cut flush against the trunk of the tree so that no stub is left. This procedure ensures quick healing with little danger of insect or disease damage. Seal all cuts with a mixture of antiseptic mouthwash and latex paint.

After gathering the branches, crush or split the lower stems a few inches from the bottom to increase the area exposed to water for better absorption. Place the branches in a bucket of room-temperature water, and store in a cool place (60-65° F). A warm room will help produce flowers more quickly, but they will not be as large or as abundant. Change the water once a week. Your beautiful blooms should appear in 2 to 3 weeks.

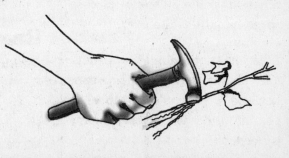

Heath

(Erica)

These are acid-loving plants for sunny locations. They may be either deciduous or evergreen; all have very beautiful, creamy white flowers.

The hardy species are dwarf shrubs, especially valuable for gardens where there is no lime in the soil, like on peaty land. The tender heaths grow quite slowly, especially when young, and require careful cultivation. Because they're so finicky, they have declined in popularity in competition with the more quickly grown plants.

Both the hardy and tender types can be increased by cuttings of short side shoots that are just starting to get firm. These side shoots should be only about an inch long. Remove the leaves from the lower $2/3$ of the stem, taking care that the delicate bark is not torn. Insert the cuttings in sandy peat which has been made firm and covered with a layer of sand. (They will take root most easily in a propagating frame.) The cuttings will take several weeks to root, and should be watered carefully.

Heather

(Calluna)

While the common name "heath" is applied to the *Erica* genus, "heather" is reserved for the genus *Calluna*.

LIMITING SHRUB MAINTENANCE

Avoid such shrubs as hydrangea, eugenia, privet, and many deciduous flowering shrubs that need regular pruning.

For color and visual interest, plant flowering shrubs like azalea, lavender, rosemary, and gardenia. Less trouble than annuals, these may be good choices for an easy garden, depending upon where you live.

Avoid trees and shrubs that create litter. All deciduous trees drop leaves, and flowering trees like acacia, olive, and jacaranda (all warm-climate plants) also drop blossoms and seed pods. I still bear a grudge against an acacia tree planted near a patio that required daily clean-up almost seven months of the year.

As a final note, don't plant trees and shrubs too close together because you won't be able to get in to do whatever pruning is needed.

Heathers are hardy, rather small evergreen shrubs which grow wild in many parts of Europe, and in a few places in North America. The name Calluna is derived from "kallunein," meaning "to sweep," for the branches were frequently used as brooms.

With their short, spikey leaves and lavender blossoms, heathers look their best when grown in irregular masses, making excellent ground covers where the soil is acidic and well drained. Do not try to grow them in wet, poorly-drained land.

They should be planted in early fall or spring and set about a foot apart. Each spring, before new growth becomes apparent, the shoots of the previous season should be cut off close to the base of the plants.

Take 4- to 6-inch cuttings in July or August, and place them in a greenhouse or coldframe in a mixture of sand and peat moss.

Honeysuckle
(Lonicerea)

Japanese honeysuckle *(L. japonica)* is the common, half-evergreen twining shrub that has become naturalized over a large portion of the United States. Few plants give so much satisfaction for the small amount of care required. Its characteristic fragrance makes honeysuckle perfect for entrance plantings. The flowers open white, but change to creamy yellow as they age.

It may also be used as vine, as a hedge or ground cover, or even as a low bush. It can be propagated by layering or seeds.

Everblooming honeysuckle starts blooming in spring and continues throughout the growing season. The buds and outer parts of the bloom are an

SHRUB-A-DUB-DUB

Every now and then, I give my shrubs a bath as well as a drink! It gets rid of dust, dirt, and pollution, and helps keep insects away. So, add a little liquid soap or baby shampoo to your regular water. Your shrubs will love it, but the bugs will be doing the "green apple shuffle" to the bug bathroom.

attractive purplish red color, and the inner part is yellow. This honeysuckle is slow-growing and not as vigorous as the Japanese type. It may also be used as a ground cover or low hedge but will take longer to cover. It may be propagated by cuttings of young spring growth.

A third type, the trumpet honeysuckle, is native from Connecticut to Florida and Texas. It is a twining vine, and the bloom is an attractive orange-scarlet on the outside and yellow on the inside. It blooms in spring and early summer, with a scattering of blossoms in the fall. It grows best in moist soil.

Hydrangea

This genus of handsome shrubs includes both hardy and tender members, and even several woody climbers. A few of the tender types are evergreen, but most are deciduous. When anyone thinks of hydrangeas, they almost invariably picture the blue ones, though the pink color is just as lovely. Remember that pink-flowered hydrangeas will bear blue blossoms where the soil is either naturally acidic or treated with one of the chemical bluing powders sold by garden supply centers for this purpose.

Hydrangea

Hydrangeas produce their largest flower clusters at the tips of the shoots formed during the previous season. If these terminal buds are destroyed by either excessive winter cold or untimely pruning, you will have little bloom. Prune in summer as soon as the flowering season is over. Remove all of the old shoots which have flowered down to a point on the stem where the new growth is developing. Also, cut out weak and crowded shoots. Leave the strong new shoots at the base of the plant and on the lower parts of the old stems, for they will produce the next season's bloom. Never prune in late fall, winter, or spring if you want flowers the next year.

COLOR CHANGE

To change hydrangeas color, mix iron filings into the soil, or water it with alum (1 tsp.) or aluminum sulphate (3 oz.) dissolved in a gallon of water. But be careful! White-flowered types will not turn blue, but rather, they will become an unattractive slate color.

I have found that tipping a bushel basket over my hydrangea plant, and then covering it with leaves affords excellent winter protection. I always uncover it as soon as the weather warms up, and often find that it has made good growth inside the basket.

Cuttings are the easiest way of increasing your stock. Take 4- to 6-inch cuttings from the ends of the non-flowering shoots any time from April to August, being careful to retain 2 or 3 pairs of leaves on each cutting. Remove the bottom pair of leaves, and cut the stem across just below a joint. Insert it in a bed of sand in the greenhouse or in a coldframe. Keep it closed until the cuttings are well rooted, except to moisten at intervals as needed.

When the cuttings are rooted, gradually let more air in, and when the young plants are hardened off a bit, pot them up separately in small pots. They should be planted in a compost of peat, leaf mold, and sandy, lime-free (if you want blue hydrangeas) loam. If you want pink or white hydrangeas, use fibrous loam, which contains lime.

Lilac
(Syringa)

Lilacs have come a long way and, while the older, single varieties still have much to recommend them, I am inclined to cast my vote for the newer, smaller hybrids which seem far better suited to the home landscape. These are just as

SUNNY SIDE UP

Full Sun Means 360°

When you read a planting instruction tag that calls for "full sun," I know what most of you have in mind. You wonder what difference a little shade makes. The answer: the difference between beautiful and ugly! Here is a very simple explanation that an old forester I once worked for gave me:

Full-sun-loving plants in the shade will grow tall, thin and ugly.

Shade-loving plants in the sun will be short and dumpy.

So, your shrubs a favor: respect their preferences, and they will repay you tenfold with performance!

fragrant as the older varieties, are available in a number of luscious colors—red, white, purple, blue, and magenta—bear double blossoms, and bloom over a longer period of time, usually half the summer. Though they will grow 8 to 10 feet tall at maturity, judicious pruning can keep them within bounds. If you select "own root" shrubs (many growers graft lilacs for quicker production), your lilacs will be long-lived plants with no wild sucker growth from the understock.

Lilacs are useful as either specimen plants or, planted 5 feet apart, will make a dramatically beautiful flowering hedge. Grow them in single color masses for the most striking effect.

My one minor objection to lilacs is their unsightly seed capsules, particularly noticeable in the double-flowered types. If you find these bothersome, clip them off with a long-handled tree-trimming tool.

Lilac

The Persian lilac is, in my opinion, the best of the older lilacs, and it is singularly beautiful when in flower. Its slender branches form a shapely bush and it grows to a mature height of about 4 to 5 feet. Its flowers, borne in small, sweetly scented clusters, are lavender or white.

Propagate lilacs by softwood cuttings.

CUTTING LILACS

Tall, spindly lilacs are the result of improper cutting. Proper cutting requires removing branches from all portions of the plant equally. Tip end cutting on most shrubs is okay, and long stems should only be taken when the shrub is heavily overgrown. In that case, the stem should be cut back as far as possible to ensure graceful shaping.

Mock Orange
(Philadelphus)

I am less fond of mock oranges than other flowering shrubs. They are undeniably fragrant, and their white flowers in May and June are attractive. However, after the blooming period is over, the foliage is not particularly beautiful, and they look somewhat ungainly during the winter months when their leaves have fallen.

To many, their exquisite fragrance is reason enough to plant them. If you want them because of this, choose from the smaller varieties, which range in height from 4 to 7 feet. There are also dwarfs that grow less than 4 feet tall and some lovely double-flowered varieties which are more appropriate to a larger lot. The 'Aureus' variety has golden leaves, with its color at its best in spring.

Mock oranges are great for naturalizing. The smaller ones may be used in the foreground of the border, the taller types in the back. Branches of mock oranges provide ample material for cutting, and they do a wonderful job of perfuming the rooms in which they are placed.

They are also easy to grow because all mock oranges may be transplanted bare-rooted in the spring. These shrubs thrive in full sun, but will adapt to light shade. Any garden soil will do for them, but they must be given adequate moisture.

Since blossoming occurs on the branches of the previous year's growth, pruning should take place immediately after flowering so that a good supply of vigorous flowering wood may be produced during the summer growing period.

Propagate mock oranges by taking hardwood cuttings.

SPECIAL SHRUBS FOR SPECIAL PLACES

Often taken for granted, shrubs are frequently thought of only as hedges, foundation plants, fences, borders or lawn specimens, while their beauty, drama, and special traits are overlooked. The fact is, ornamental shrubs have many unique features and deserve to be carefully selected so their highlights can be featured. Consider some of these factors when adding or replacing shrubs in the garden.

- If your favorite reading chair rests near a window, plant a shrub with fragrant flowers right underneath it, and enjoy the aroma of viburnum, lilac, or mock orange.

- If you're a bird lover, chokeberry, honeysuckle, or bayberry will attract fine-feathered friends to your garden.

- In limited spaces, try heath, heather, or crape myrtle for gardening versatility.

Mountain Laurel

(Kalmia Latifolia)

The best-known and most attractive of the kalmias is the mountain laurel. This native of eastern North America may grow as tall as 20 feet under ideal conditions, but usually forms a shrub 6 to 10 feet high.

When not in flower, mountain laurel bears some resemblance to the rhododendron with its leathery, 3- to 5-inch-long leaves. The blush pink flowers are cup-shaped, often an inch across, and are borne in clusters in late spring. Some of the dwarf varieties have flowers of deeper pink; others have dense clusters of a vivid rose red.

MOUNTAIN LAUREL AT-A-GLANCE

✓ Hardy, deciduous

✓ Acidic soil

✓ Plant in April or October

✓ Little pruning required

✓ Propagate by cuttings, layering, or grafting

All the kalmias are hardy, deciduous shrubs, and do best in acidic or lime-free, loamy soil. If you want to grow them successfully, dig in plenty of peat moss or compost in the soil prior to planting, and add coffee grounds and oak leaf mulch.

Plant mountain laurel in fall or spring; October and April are considered the best months. The roots are apt to be thin and fibrous, so pack the soil firmly about them.

Pruning is seldom necessary and is usually done only for the purpose of training back long shoots to maintain the bush in a more shapely form. Older bushes that have become misshapen may be cut back to the ground, and they will renew themselves by sending up new shoots from the base of the plant. Any necessary pruning should be done after the plant has flowered.

The best means of increasing mountain laurel is through seeds sown in early spring. Place them in shallow flats or pots of sandy, peaty soil in a cool greenhouse, and keep them moist.

Mountain
Laurel

Propagation may be accomplished by cuttings, layering, or grafting. Layering is an easy way to increase your stock. Lay down a low-growing branch and make a slit in the stem just beneath a joint about 12 inches from the tip. Bury the cut section 2 or 3 inches below the soil and keep it moist. When roots have formed, cut from parent plant and remove to a new location.

Pearlbush
(Exochorda)

The pearlbush is valued for its short panicles of large white flowers borne in early June. The pretty green leaves are just developing at this time, so the flowers are prominently displayed.

This shrub will require a little patience on your part, as it may tend to look somewhat untidy and rather leggy in its early stages of growth. It will, however, overcome this adolescent awkwardness as it matures, forming a tall, upright shrub of broad-oval form, 12 feet tall or more. Because of its erect growth, it is attractive even during the winter months after its leaves have fallen.

These shrubs are accommodating and will thrive in most good garden soils, preferably enriched with an occasional top dressing of decomposed manure or good compost. Plant them in open spots where they will receive full sun. Pruning should be done following the flowering period. Cut out any weak or crowded branches and shape the bush to a sturdy, more desirable form.

Take cuttings 3 to 5" long which will root readily if placed in a propagating frame in July or August. Seeds may be sown under glass as soon as they have ripened. It is sometimes possible to detach suckers from older plants in late fall.

HERE'S THE DIRT

Rhododendrons, azaleas, blueberries, mountain laurel, sourwood, hollies, and wintergreen are closely related. All demand porous, very acidic soil, of not less than two-thirds organic matter. Plentiful moisture is a must all year long, partly retained under a deep mulch of rotting oak leaves or pine needles. Standing water will kill these plants in a matter of days; there must be rapid drainage of excess water above and below the surface at all times.

Pearlbush

Privet
(Ligustrum)

Most of us think privet is synonymous with hedge, and it's rather a shame that this excellent shrub has been typecast, for some varieties are beautiful enough to be grown as specimen plants. If given plenty of space to develop, privet will form a handsome bush. It suffers from crowding and hard pruning. Pruning, when it becomes necessary, should be done after its flowers have faded.

Used as a hedge, privet must be kept within bounds by regular trimming. As a hedge plant, it is unquestionably king. However, consider using it for untrimmed screens or in a group planting, where its handsome leaves will show up to good advantage. Though trimming is necessary, privet also makes neat, easily kept foundation plantings. I am glad to see that the fad for shaping privet into globes, cubes, or animals has passed.

Privets bear small spikes of white or creamy white flowers in summer which are very dainty in appearance. Their only disadvantage is a disagreeable odor, though this is true of every species of privet. The flowers are followed by large, quite decorative clusters of blue-black berries which birds adore.

All privets are easily transplanted and accommodate themselves to average garden soils. They may be planted in spring or fall.

You may increase your stock by sowing seeds, but since cuttings are so

THUG BUSTERS

From the kitchen cabinet:

Liquid Dish Soap—Use it as an insect preventer. Mix 1 tsp. to the quart, 1 tbsp. to the gallon, or 1 cup per 20 gallons of water, and spray on everything in your garden—trees, shrubs, flowers, vegetables, fruit trees, lawn, and roses to keep them in the pink!

Cayenne (red) pepper—Sprinkle this spice in and around your shrub beds to keep cats and dogs from using them as a dumping ground. Also, dust the plants with cayenne pepper in the morning while the plants are still wet with dew to keep insects or worms off of flower bushes.

Salt—Keep the shaker handy; a little bit sprinkled directly on destructive slugs will melt them into a gooey mess. Hey, nobody said thug busting was pretty!

easily rooted this is a more practical method of propagation. Take cuttings 3 to 4 inches long in summer and plant them in a coldframe in Pro-mix. Keep them shaded and moist until roots have formed.

Pussy Willow

(Salix Caprea)

Few early spring plants are more charming than pussy willows, especially the newer kinds like the French Pink. Huge, fuzzy catkins of silvery gray gradually turn to a silvery pink, then to a deeper rose pink peppered with hundreds of golden stamens, finally becoming solid gold. Pussy willow is highly prized for indoor bouquets—and with good reason. For early indoor bloom, cut branches and place them in a container of water in a sunny, warm window around the middle of January. Children have a lot of fun watching the catkins develop.

The pussy willow has many uses. It may be used as a specimen plant or in the foreground of shrubbery. A pair, used on either side of a doorway, will add a bit of garden magic in spring. Or use them as a low-growing hedge, clipping them into shape when necessary.

One of the best types of this engaging little shrub grows about 5 feet tall, and eventually broadens out to become the "Mr. Five by Five" of the plant world. This rounded, symmetrical bush has numerous slender twigs with narrow, pointed, gray-green leaves.

The pussy willow, like most willows, prefers wet soil, but will grow reasonably well even in light, sandy soil, provided it is not allowed to completely dry out.

Pussy willows are easily propagated by cuttings of ripened wood, the usual length being 9 to 12 inches. Stick them in water until the roots develop, then plant them in nursery rows or where the new plant is to grow in the future. Keep the soil moist even after roots have formed.

PUSSY WILLOWS ARE PRIZED FOR INDOOR BOUQUETS

313

Quince
(Chaenomeles)

The Japanese quince has a lot going for it. One of the loveliest of the early-spring-flowering shrubs, it forms a bush about 10 to 12 feet high. There are a number of beautiful varieties, and you have a choice of white, pink, or crimson flowers. There is even a lovely semi-double type, rosea-plena. To make things even more interesting, its pretty flowers are followed by aromatic fruits which may be used for making a delicious jelly.

I have grown flowering quince as a hedge shrub and recommend it highly. Little pruning is necessary to keep it compact, and in many situations the spiny branches are an advantage, especially when you're trying to keep kids, cats, dogs, or rabbits out of your yard. When so grown, it will flower well in spring. You can also encourage flowering by pruning the side shoots in early summer to about five leaves, and then cutting back to two buds in winter. Quinces may be espaliered.

Flowering quince, sometimes called "japonica," belongs to the rose family. It will thrive in ordinary loamy soil and is very showy if grown in a sunny position in the open garden. Flowering quince is hardy, but loses its leaves in winter, revealing shapely and attractive branches.

You may easily increase your stock by layering the branches in autumn

IRON-POOR SAP

Trees, shrubs, evergreens, and grass all need a substantial amount of iron in their diet in warm weather, which in the South and West, means all year long. If they don't get this iron, they will suffer from chlorosis, which is a yellowing of the foliage. In the cooler areas of the country, you generally don't have to worry about this until just after the forsythias bloom.

Early February is the time to spray the foliage of azaleas, rhododendrons, evergreen, and southern foliage plants. Use the following mixture:

**1 oz. of hydrated lime,
1 oz. iron sulphate, and
1 tbsp. of Shampoo
per gallon of water.**

For an extra "kicker," add 2 oz. of Liquid Iron to the mixture.

or by removing the suckers which often appear around the base of established bushes. Cuttings, which may be made in summer of firm shoots, can be rooted in a compost mixture of sandy loam and peat. Seeds may also be sown in the same soil mix in a greenhouse or coldframe in the spring. The named cultivated varieties will not develop true to type from seeds and should be increased by cuttings.

Rhododendron

Let's get something settled right off—all azaleas are classed as rhododendrons, but all rhododendrons are *not* azaleas. Botanists now include azaleas in the genus *Rhododendron,* but gardeners still regard them as quite distinct from other kinds of rhododendrons, and retain their older names.

Rhododendron

Rhododendrons come in a surprising number of forms and variations. Some grow into trees, while others are small bushes or low, prostrate shrubs. Other rhododendrons are suitable for rock gardens, and some are even epiphytes (nonparasitic plants which grow on other plants, deriving their moisture chiefly from the air).

Rhododendrons also display many different kinds of flowers and foliage. Some produce leaves as long as 24 inches, while others have tiny leaves barely an inch long. Flower shapes range from the tubular to the saucer-like, and still others are nearly flat.

Rhododendrons are plants of enchanting beauty, but like azaleas, the limiting factor in growing them is climate. They thrive best in a moist, temperate climate where the heat of the sun is often tempered by cloudy skies, such as in the Pacific Northwest. They are easy to grow along the seaboards, but they are not recommended for amateur gardeners in the central part of North America. However, there are "mini-climates" in every section of the country, and I have seen rhododendrons doing reasonably well in areas where the textbooks said they would not prosper. If their beauty bedazzles you and you want to try growing them, put them in a sheltered location where they will not be exposed to sweeping winds.

Some garden varieties of rhododendron will thrive in full sun provided they have sufficient moisture; but shade is better, especially if you live in an area where the summer sun is intense.

In the case of the large-leaved kinds, moisture is absolutely necessary. The leaves will burn if exposed to too much light. If possible, naturalize your plants in a woodland. If your home grounds make this impossible, plant them on the north side of a building, or even the northwest or western exposure. A southern location is definitely not satisfactory. Also, remember that exposure to strong light in winter is even more harmful than in summer, for it is then that serious scorching of the leaves occurs.

Rhododendrons are shallow-rooted, so the surface of the ground should not be cultivated once they are planted because digging among the roots will harm them. Mulch well to keep down weeds, using leaves, peat moss, pine needles, or even sawdust.

In many areas, some winter protection is desirable. Do not use tight-fitting barrels or boxes—the plants do not need warmth but require shade and good air circulation.

Water them well—that means at least once a week, especially in the late summer and fall in regions where rainfall is not abundant at those times.

Fertilizing is not necessary as long as the plants maintain good growth, but as they grow older and use up the nutrients of the soil, it is a good idea to

COFFEE BREAK TIME...

With all of the entertaining being done around the holidays, and all of the coffee being served, have you ever wondered what to do with all of those leftover coffee grounds? Well, if you're really interested in having an outstanding garden next year, think twice before throwing them out because they are a valuable organic soil conditioner.

Coffee grounds added to your flower beds, and in and around your shrubs and roses result in healthier, more vigorous plants that have more abundant flowers. Azaleas, rhododendrons, and all spring-flowering shrubs also benefit from fall and winter applications of coffee grounds.

add some well-decayed manure or one of the fertilizers recommended for acid-soil plants.

Prune only as necessary after flowering to maintain plants of well-balanced growth. Remove all old flower heads promptly before seeds form.

To really give rhododendrons a hand, apply an anti-transpirant like WeatherProof™ in both the spring and fall. It will eliminate a lot of the weather damage problems, while helping them to grow their very best.

ROBUST RHODODENDRONS

Rhododendrons must have an abundance of organic matter in their soil. They dislike lime, and will not thrive in soil where it is present in any quantity. If necessary, have a soil test made to determine the soil acidity before you plant. If lime is present, dig out the soil, and replace it with soil that is acidic or neutral. The addition of rotted compost or well-decayed manure will help, along with a healthy dose of acidic peat moss.

Rose Acacia
(Robinia Hispiday)

Rose acacia is the "old country" name for the locust, or moss locust, a shrub of the eastern United States that produces numerous suckers. It is a low, shrubby locust with small rose-colored flowers that appear in spring. The flowers are scentless.

Rose acacia forms wide drifts, due to the suckering roots. It is interesting to note that this plant, which grows from 4 to 6 feet tall, has come to rely on suckering as a means of reproduction and has almost stopped producing seed pods.

This shrub is very useful in large, naturalistic plantings and where soil is very poor. It is pretty enough for a border in the home landscape, but impractical because of the difficulty of keeping it in bounds.

Rose Acacia

Smoke Tree
(Cotinus)

When I was young, I greatly admired a gorgeous smoke tree growing in a friend's garden. I decided I must own one for myself. An unscrupulous nurseryperson sold me *C. americanus*, and the amount of smoke produced by this species is exceedingly small. I would instead recommend the European smoke tree, which will grow into a large bush 12 feet tall with wedge-shaped, bluish-green leaves. Beginning in June and on through the summer, the bush is enveloped in a mist of silky, mauve-purple clusters of flowers and fruit. These feathery plumes give the smokelike effect for which the tree is named. Once you behold a mature tree in its full glory, you will not rest until you have one of your very own.

SMOKE TREES AT-A-GLANCE

✓Enveloped in flowers

✓Striking autumn foliage

✓Easily grown

✓Sunny, well-drained location

But this wealth of dainty blossoms is not all that the smoke tree has to offer, for in autumn the foliage takes on striking tints of yellow, orange, and golden red. Add to this the fact that these trees are easily grown in any good garden soil, even succeeding in land that is dry and rocky. As you may have guessed, they prefer a sunny, well-drained location.

Propagate smoke trees by taking softwood cuttings.

Snowball

To my way of thinking, the fragrant snowball *(Viburnum x carlcephalum)* is the most attractive member of the snowball family. To enjoy it most, plant it near your doorway or outdoor living area where its fragrance and outstanding beauty will be prominently displayed. Each May, this lovely shrub bursts into gorgeous blooms, covering itself from top to bottom with sachet-sweet balls of delicate pink, which gradually turn a waxy white. The dense heads measure 2 to 3 inches across. They are so spicily fragrant that you can smell them from several feet away. This shrub also produces bluish-black berries in early summer. In the fall, the leaves turn a lovely wine-red color. They will grow 3 to 20 feet tall and need a sunny location.

Spicebush
(Lindera Benzoin)

The spicebush is a large, aromatic, native shrub of the eastern United States, where it grows in moist soil, sometimes attaining heights of 12 feet or more.

The small, yellow flowers, borne in April, are bunched on the naked branches in great profusion, lighting up the hillsides in a shimmer of yellow-green. The leaves, bright green, oval, and slightly pointed, are about 4 inches long and gradually appear as the blossoms fall. There is a good display in autumn of scarlet berries, about half an inch in diameter, but they do not remain on the bush for very long before falling.

Spicebush has greater value in the larger landscape than in the smaller home grounds where, in my opinion, it takes up too much room for the rather brief decorative effect it achieves.

If you like the spicy odor, have sufficient room and wish to grow it, spicebush presents few problems. It should be transplanted with a ball of earth, but will flourish in any good garden soil. Give it a sunny or slightly shaded location. You may plant it successfully in either fall or spring.

GIVE YOURSELF A BREAK

Are you tired of looking at your neighbors' garbage cans? Or are you afraid that old north wind is going to huff and puff and blow your house down? In either case, a flowering shrub fence is just what you need. You could use evergreens, but they look the same all year long. Flowering shrubs change from season to season, offering blossoms, autumn color, and often fruit or berries.

You can prune flowering fences, but I prefer the natural look myself. Deutzia, euonymus, forsythia, privet, pomegranate, lilac, spiraea, snowball, and cranberry are some of the best choices for an untrimmed hedge. If you choose shrubs of approximately the same height, you can plant several different shrubs in the same hedge, and they need not all bloom at the same time.

319

Spiraea

The spiraeas are a large family, well known, loved, and respected. The name itself refers to the very flexible, graceful branches which at one time were twisted into garlands. This free-flowering shrub is found wild in many parts of the world, including North America, Asia, and Europe.

Bridal wreath *(S. prunifolia)*, a Korean native, is widely grown in American gardens, and is one of the most attractive spring-blooming kinds. The double-flowered variety is named 'Plena.' In both, the pure white flowers grow in numerous clusters along stems of the previous year's growth.

S. vanhouttei is a hybrid type which is very vigorous, growing about 6 feet high with long, arching branches that bear clusters of white flowers in June. It is excellent for an informal hedge. *S. henryi* also bears great clusters of exceedingly dainty white flowers, and grows to be 6 to 9 feet tall. *S. douglasii*, native to the Pacific coast, is another beauty that grows to an average of 8 feet, and bears flowers of a deep rose-red color. Both blossom in late spring. *S. x billiardii*, another hybrid, grows 5 to 6 feet high and bears abundant bright pink flowers in July and August.

You may plant spiraeas in either fall or spring, grouping them in the open or in semi-shaded locations.

Pruning methods for spiraeas differ according to species. 'Plena' has a rather untidy manner of growth, being rather loose and floppy in appearance. This should be corrected by severe pruning following the flowering season.

Spiraeas which flower from buds should be pruned just after flowering by thinning out only the older shoots. Those that flower on the ends of the current year's wood should be cut to within a few buds of the base of the flowering shoots in spring.

All spiraeas are easily increased by inserting cuttings, 4 to 5 inches long, in a coldframe in early summer. They will even root readily outdoors if placed in good soil in a shady location and kept moist.

SPIRAEAS

MAKE

EXCELLENT

HEDGES

Spiraea

Stewartia

Stewartia is a beautiful shrub which may reach the noble height of 50 feet when grown as a tree. Most, however, are grown as shrubs, and are pruned back to 10 feet or less. While generally considered a bit large for the shrub border, stewartia is very desirable as an individual specimen.

Mountain stewartia *(S. ovata)* bears handsome cup-shaped, white flowers from June through August. These are often 3 inches across and are crowned with golden anthers. Its foliage is very colorful in autumn, changing to golden orange and finally to scarlet. Showy stewartia *(S. ovata grandiflora)*, preferred by many, has dramatically beautiful purple stamens. This variety, however, cannot rival the brilliant autumn color of mountain stewartia, for it assumes a rather drab, purplish look as fall approaches.

Stewartia

Stewartias are well worth growing, but remember, they must have considerable space, should be pruned in early fall, and need a sheltered spot and moist, well-drained soil. They are easily propagated by layering a few of the lowest branches in late summer. Cuttings are slow to take root, but seeds may be sown in a slightly heated greenhouse in spring.

Tamarisk
(Tamarix)

Tamarisk is a slender, delicately beautiful tree or shrub whose special attraction is its tiny, ethereal pink flowers. In most kinds, these occur on the upper part of the stems, creating a very showy effect. The leaves are very tiny, and in most species a grayish-green.

SUPER GROWING SECRETS

Sprinkle 1/2 cup of Epsom salts per 3" of stem radius around <u>mature</u> flowering shrubs at the weep line in both spring and late fall. Epsom salts deepen the color, thicken the petals, and increase root structure, all of which benefit the plants greatly.

Sprinkle out here at the weep line (the tip of the farthest branch).

They are borne on very slender branchlets, many of which fall in autumn with the leaves.

Tamarisk, while they will thrive in inland gardens, are best suited for coastal areas, where they are very resistant to salt air. They are useful for hedges, either informal or clipped, and will thrive in either light or heavy soil and will even grow in sea sand. Though best suited for mild climates, they may be grown in colder areas. Even if the top foliage may freeze back during the winter, the roots seldom do, and new shoots will spring up. They should be grown in full sun.

PRUNE
WEIGELAS
AFTER
THEY HAVE
FLOWERED

Tamarisk may be increased by cuttings, generally made 9 to 12 inches long, which should be inserted in a cold-frame in summer or fall.

PEST PATROL

Flowering shrubs are deceptively tough. Most of them are willing and able to defend themselves against the most insistent insect and the most disastrous disease. But if you're the gardener I hope you are, you'll give your shrubs a hand in their battle. The best way to help them is to keep them healthy. Keep the area around them free of debris which could harbor insects or diseases, and prune out any infected or insect-damaged branches.

Remember that birds are truly your shrubs' fine, feathered friends, so make them feel welcome in your yard. They'll thank you by gobbling up thousands of insects, and filling your life with song.

Weigela

Weigelas are well-formed shrubs, growing 4 to 5 feet tall, which will thrive just about anywhere. They are deciduous and of erect growth, and are valued for their handsome flowers borne in great profusion in late spring. The blossoms may be white, pink, deep rose, or crimson, with many variations in between. Some are pink with yellow in their throats. The individual blossoms are rather small, but they are borne in such abundance that they more than make up for their size. Weigelas are moderately hardy but may be killed back. If your winters are very severe, plant weigelas in a protected area or give them some type of protection.

Weigelas like full sun but will grow in partial shade, though they will not bloom as abundantly. A good garden soil, neither too wet nor excessively dry, will accommodate them very well. Occasionally some compost or well-decayed stable manure may be dug into the soil. If you have clay soil, lighten it with sand and organic matter.

Weigela

Since weigelas produce their blossoms on the shoots of the previous year, pruning should not be done until after the flowers have faded. Cut out any crowded older branches and remove any weak or badly placed stems. Weigelas make vigorous growth, so pruning is very necessary from time to time to admit light and air and to give the bush a more attractive shape.

Weigelas are easily increased by making 4- to 6-inch cuttings of half-ripe wood and inserting them in a coldframe in late summer.

Witch Hazel
(Hamamelis)

I've always found the witch hazel to be truly fascinating. This shrub or small tree may grow up to be 20 feet tall. The bark and leaves are used to make a soothing lotion. It grows in the woods of the eastern United States and Canada, and left to its own sweet will, its jointed curving branches will twist and point in all directions. The forked twigs have been used for divining rods, adding further to the plant's mystique. In fact, the name "witch hazel" refers to this use.

SUPER SOIL SECRET

The foundation area around a new house usually has very poor soil because the contractor scrapes off all of the topsoil before beginning to build. So, before planting shrubs there, dig a hole a minimum of three feet deep, remove all of the old soil, and replace it with rich compost and manure mixture. This will guarantee planting success!

Unlike most of the shrubs we have discussed that bear their flowers in spring before the leaves appear, witch hazel does just the opposite. After the leaves die, in October or November, the witch hazel puts forth its blossoms. And what a sight they are to see, for they grow in dainty, feathery clusters. The fruits do not ripen until the next year. Then, in what seems to be a final burst of mischief, the seeds shoot from their small, woody capsules in spring a distance of up to several feet!

The most decorative witch hazel is the Chinese *(H. mollis)*. It forms a spreading bush or small tree which may eventually grow 18 to 20 feet tall. The leaves are larger than those of other types, being 3 to 5 inches long and 2 to 3 inches wide. It bears very fragrant, golden yellow flowers, which look a lot like primroses.

Witch Hazel

Plant your witch hazel in well-drained, loamy soil, mixing in some compost and peat. Choose a sheltered location with a southern exposure. If you want a truly dramatic display, plant it where it will show up best—against a dark background. The flowers are not injured by light frosts, and the wood is seldom damaged by cold.

Propagate by taking softwood cuttings in spring, potting them up in a professional planting mix.

TONIC SUMMARY

PLANTING

Perennials And Annuals

If you are using seed, let it soak overnight in a solution of weak tea water, air dry, and then plant. For more power from your flowers, mix all of the following ingredients in a bucket full of dry peat moss, then put into the rows to be planted: **4 cups of bone meal, 2 cups of gypsum, 2 cups of Epsom salts, 1 cup of wood ashes, 1 cup of lime, 1 tbsp. of baking powder, and 4 tbsp. of medicated baby powder.**

Bulbs

Pack your bulbs an organic lunch when planting: **add 10 lbs. of dry manure or compost, 5 lbs. of bone meal, and 2 lbs. of Epsom salts** per 100 sq. ft. (10' x 10') of soil. Then overspray the area with an All Purpose Plant Food or my **All Season Green-Up Tonic: 1 can of beer, 1 cup of ammonia, 1/2 cup of liquid Lawn Food, 1/2 cup of Shampoo, and 1/2 cup of corn syrup** applied with a 20 gallon hose-end sprayer.

Flowering Trees And Shrubs

As a general rule, when planting trees and shrubs, sprinkle the following tonic into and on the sides of the planting hole (the bigger the hole, the more you mix): **1 cup of Epsom salts, 3 cups of bone meal and 1/2 tsp. of medicated baby powder.** After planting, mulch well with shredded bark.

PLANTING

TONICS WILL

GET THEM

OFF TO

A GREAT

START

Roses

After planting these lovely ladies, water them well, and follow up with a dose of my **Start-Up Meal: 1 tbsp. of liquid dish soap, 1 tbsp. of hydrogen peroxide, 1 tsp. of whiskey, and 1 tsp. of Vitamin B-1 Plant Starter in ¹/₂ gallon of warm tea water.**

FEEDING

Perennials And Annuals

You should add dry garden food to your flower beds at a third of the recommended rate in the fall and again in the spring, before you spade the soil. Then alternate feeding your flowers these 2 tonics every time you feed:

Tonic #1
¹/₂ cup of liquid Rose & Flower Food, ¹/₄ cup of liquid dish soap, and 1 cup of beer in 1 gallon of warm water.

Tonic #2
1 tbsp. of liquid fish fertilizer, 1 tbsp. of bourbon, and 2 tbsp. of instant tea in 2 gallons of warm water.

Bulbs

You already know to fertilize when planting, but bulbs need food as well when they're in active growth. So when the first shoots appear in spring, feed your bulbs with an all-around fertilizer (10-10-10 or the like). This feeding will rebuild the bulbs for next year's flowering.

Roses

Roses must be fed on a regular basis (every 3 weeks) because they work so hard producing the heavy stems and foliage to support the abundant flowers. Alternate their diet, beginning with my **Start-Up Meal.** Next, use liquid Rose & Flower Food mixed in a weak solution of instant tea water, adding 1 tbsp. of liquid dish soap per gallon of water.

The third mixture consists of the following: **$1/2$ tbsp. of fish fertilizer, 2 tbsp. of instant tea, 1 tsp. of (dissolved) baking powder, 1 tsp. of iron, and 1 tbsp. of dry red wine in 1 gallon of warm water.** Each rose bush then gets a quart of the this mixture.

Trees

In early spring, with a tree auger that fits an electric drill, drill holes in 3 circles under your trees. The first is out at the weep line, 8' - 10" deep, 18" - 24" apart. The next circle is on the inside 24", and the third is 24" to the outside. Break tree spikes in half, and drop them down the holes. Sprinkle $1/2$ lb. of Epsom salts over the top of the holes for a mature tree, and water in with this tonic: **1 can of beer, 2 tbsp. of instant tea, 2 tbsp. of liquid dish soap, and 1 tbsp. of fish fertilizer in 2 gallons of warm water.**

Shrubs

Since most shrubs are not meant to grow more than 10' to 12' high, a well-balanced garden food (5-10-5) should be applied in early spring.

For older or sickly shrubs, add 1 tbsp. of fish fertilizer to this tonic: **$1/4$ lb. Epsom salts, 4 tbsp. of instant tea, 2 tbsp. of bourbon or $1/2$ can of beer, and 1 tbsp. of liquid dish soap in 2 gallons of warm water.**

ALTERNATING

FOODS

PRODUCES

STRONGER

PLANTS

INSECT AND DISEASE CONTROL

If you want to make bugs wish they'd never visited your yarden, apply this tonic every 2 weeks with your 20 gallon hose-end sprayer, filling the balance of the sprayer jar with warm water:

All Season Clean-Up Tonic

**1 cup of Shampoo,
1 cup of antiseptic mouthwash, and
1 cup of chewing tobacco juice**

Chewing tobacco juice is made by placing 3 fingers of chewing tobacco into the toe of an old nylon stocking, and soaking it in a gallon of hot water until the mixture is dark brown. It smells like the dickens, but who cares—it really works!

THE USDA PLANT
HARDINESS ZONE MAP

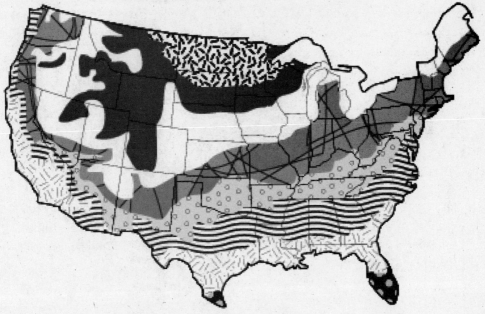

Average Minimum Temperatures For Each Zone

	Zone 3	-40° to -30°
	Zone 4	-30° to -20°
	Zone 5	-20° to -10°
	Zone 6	-10° to 0°
	Zone 7	0° to 10°
	Zone 8	10° to 20°
	Zone 9	20° to 30°
	Zone 10	30° to 40°

Index

A

B

G

❀

Q

R

🌼

T

Y

Z

About the Author

JERRY BAKER is America's foremost authority on lawn, garden, and plant care. He has authored over forty books, including the bestsellers *Plants Are Like People* and *The Impatient Gardener*. Jerry's nationally syndicated radio show, "On the Garden Line," is the most successful gardening program in history. And Jerry publishes *On the Garden Line*®, *America's Gardening Newsletter*™, which is jam-packed full of good old-fashioned advice and home remedies that'll cure what ails your yard and garden!

Look for these wonderful books by Jerry Baker!

THE IMPATIENT GARDENER

---

*How to grow green grass,
gorgeous flowers, and great vegetables—
without a green thumb!*

Jerry Baker, America's master gardener, understands all your hopes and dreams and fears about your garden. And in the pages of this practical, inspiring handbook, he gives you, the impatient gardener, the shortcuts, home remedies, and time-tested tips you need to have a healthy lawn, thriving trees and shrubs, gorgeous flowers, and fabulous vegetables. Now you can have the best-looking garden around—without spending a lot of time or money—even if you're a beginner!

Available in bookstores everywhere.
Published by Ballantine Books
The Ballantine Publishing Group
www.randomhouse.com/BB/

JERRY BAKER'S LAWN BOOK

How to grow a beautiful lawn—
without working yourself into the ground

Let Jerry Baker do the dirty work while you enjoy the green, green grass of home! For he puts his expert reputation on the line—and on your lawn—to give you the kind of yard you've always dreamed of. Here is a complete, step-by-step guide that will save you time, money, and effort and give you a thicker, healthier lawn!

Available in bookstores everywhere.
Published by Ballantine Books
The Ballantine Publishing Group
www.randomhouse.com/BB/